# A Post Keynesian Perspective on 21st Century Economic Problems

# A Post Keynesian Perspective on 21st Century Economic Problems

*Edited by*

Paul Davidson

*Holly Chair of Excellence in Political Economy,*
*The University of Tennessee, Knoxville, USA*

**Edward Elgar**
Cheltenham, UK • Northampton, MA, USA

Published by
Edward Elgar Publishing Limited
Glensanda House
Montpellier Parade
Cheltenham
Glos GL50 1UA
UK

Edward Elgar Publishing, Inc.
136 West Street
Suite 202
Northampton
Massachusetts 01060
USA

A catalogue record for this book
is available from the British Library

**Library of Congress Cataloguing in Publication Data**

A post Keynesian perspective on twenty-first century economic problems / edited by Paul Davidson.
International Post Keynesian Workshop (6th : 2000 : Knoxville, Tenn.)
p. cm.
Includes index.
1. Keynesian economics–Congresses. 2. Economic history–Congresses. I. Title: Post Keynesian perspective on 21st century economic problems. II. Davidson, Paul, 1930- III. Title.
HB99.7 .I579 2000
330.9′05–dc21                                                                              2001050139

ISBN 1 84064 616 0

Printed and bound in Great Britain by MPG Books Ltd, Bodmin, Cornwall

# Contents

# List of figures

# List of Tables

# List of contributors

**Paul Davidson**, Holly Chair of Excellence in Political Economy, University of Tennessee, Knoxville, TN, USA
**Luiz Carlos Bresser-Pereira**, former minister in the Cardoso and Swarney administrations, Brazil
**Alfredo Saad-Filho**, SOAS, University of London, UK
**Lecio Morais**, Advisor, Brazilian Parliament
**Fernando Ferrari-Filho**, Federal University of Rio Grande do Sul and CNPq, Brazil
**Robert A. Blecker**, American University, Washington, DC, USA
**Juan Carlos Moreno Brid**, Harvard University, Cambridge, MA, USA
**Penelope Hawkins**, Feasibility Ltd, South Africa
**William Darity, Jr**, University of North Carolina, NC, USA
**Basil Moore**, Wesleyan University, CT, USA
**Marc-André Pigeon**, Jerome Levy Institute, NY, USA
**L. Randall Wray**, University of Missouri, Kansas City, MO, USA
**Mathew Forstater**, University of Missouri, Kansas City, MO, USA
**Jesus Felipe**, Georgia Institute of Technology, Atlanta, GA, USA
**Hubert Hieke**, Franklin College, Switzerland

# Preface

The Sixth International Post Keynesian Workshop was held in Knoxville, Tennessee from 22 to 28 June 2000. It was attended by 86 participants from 20 countries with the United States participants representing 27 universities, government agencies and think tanks. Except for Antarctica, all continents were represented – North America (Canada, the United States, Mexico), South America (Brazil), Europe (United Kingdom, France, Sweden, Portugal, Spain, Italy, Germany, Switzerland, Denmark), Asia (Japan, Indonesia), Africa (South Africa) and Australasia (Australia, New Zealand).

For six days these participants attended 21 sessions in which 67 papers were presented, discussed and debated. The participants were housed at the same (Hilton) hotel in Knoxville, and had all meals at the same restaurants together so that discussions were extended during the coffee breaks, breakfast, lunch, happy hour, dinner and even after dinner.

The workshop was extremely rewarding for all as it offered insight from participants from all corners of the globe. Although most of the participants came from academic institutions, there were also business people, government policy-makers, and economists from other institutions.

Of the 67 papers presented at the workshop, 12 interesting and provocative ones were selected for publication in this volume.

The first three papers discuss the development problem that Brazil has faced for the last two decades. Although Brazil is, by some measures, the seventh largest economy in the world, it has not been able to live up to its potential in recent decades. Luiz Carlos Bresser-Pereira discusses the problem of incompetence among policy-makers and their desire to build the confidence of international financial markets to help develop the economy of Brazil. As a former minister in the Sarney and Cardoso administrations of Brazil, as well as a renowned academic, Bresser-Pereira provides not only personal experience but also analytical skills to the discussion of why Latin American countries failed to extricate themselves from their international debt crises in the 1980s and instead ended up in a fiscal crisis.

Alfredo Saad-Filho and Lecio Morais attribute the fiscal crisis of the state in Brazil and the inability of Brazilian industry to meet its potential to a group of elite members of Brazilian society who accepted the neomonetarist views of the 'Washington consensus'.

Fernando Ferrari provides a critique of the proposed monetary union in Mercosur – the South American union of Argentina, Brazil, Paraguay and Uruguay.

Robert Blecker presents an excellent paper on globalization and the desire of most developing nations to achieve an export-led growth strategy. As opposed to mainstream neoclassical economics, which argues that long-run growth rates are always determined by the growth of supply-side factors such as labor force growth and efficiency improvements, Blecker looks at demand constraints on growth in an open economy system. Blecker demonstrates that balance of payments-constrainted growth (BPCG) models can imply a fallacy of composition by incorporating an adding-up constraint on many countries all having the same targeted export markets. Blecker's analysis emphasizes relative price effects – effects that are typically ignored in BPCG models. He provides an empirical analysis relevant to 15 countries and the European Union. Blecker demonstrates that optimistic scenarios for export-led growth in the next decade are unlikely. Instead, for political as well as economic reasons, the constraints on export-led growth are not likely to be relaxed in the near future. Blecker then suggests that developing countries should pursue more internally-oriented or regionally-focused development.

Juan Carlos Moreno Brid tests several versions of the BPCG models for the Mexican economy for the period 1966–99. He demonstrates that the balance of payments was the binding constraint on Mexico's long-term economic growth, while the terms of trade played no significant role in Mexico's economic growth rate during this period.

Penelope Hawkins explores how the liquidity preference of banks explains the differential financial provision among borrowers. The model Hawkins develops explains the possibility of an unsatisfied fringe of borrowers and how the size of that fringe varies with changes in bank liquidity preferences.

William Darity, Jr reports on research that he and his associates have been doing on the relationship inter-group disparity and levels of economic development. They utilize data from 13 countries, namely Australia, Belize, Brazil, Canada, India, Israel, Japan, Malaysia, New Zealand, South Africa, Trinidad, Tobago and the United States. Race, caste or ethnicity serve as the basis of group division and differences in economic outcomes. Darity's studies indicate that inter-group disparities are a global phenomenon. These disparities seem impervious to high rates of economic growth, lower levels of general inequality in the system, and improved social status of women. They are supported by labor market discrimination. The persistence of these disparities is inconsistent with neoclassical analysis, and measures to remedy them, such as affirmative action, afford greatest benefit to the most well-placed members of the subaltern group and are most strongly opposed by the less competitive members of the dominant group.

Basil Moore develops his thesis that lower interest rates stimulate both saving and investment using national income and product account concepts as well as flow-of-funds data. In his provocative paper Moore argues that both the loanable funds and the liquidity preference theories of the rate of interest and the Keynesian multiplier theory of income determination are fallacious.

Marc-André Pigeon and L. Randall Wray present a challenging analysis of the 'new economy'. They present an empirical analysis to demonstrate that recent US growth rates in the Clinton years have not been extraordinary. Output growth has not been significantly constrained by supply-side problems with the quality or quantity of factor inputs. Economic growth even during the past few years has been demand rather than supply-constrained. They suggest that US government surpluses in the last few years should lead us to expect a major recession in the near future.

In a similar vein, Mathew Forstater emphasizes that policy-makers must consider not only structural and technological change in developing full employment policies, but must pay significantly more attention to the problem of a lack of effective demand.

Jesus Felipe analyzes the relationship between unemployment and profitability in Spain since 1980. Spain's unemployment rate is at least twice that of the rest of the European Union and almost four times the rate in the United States. In the 1970s, on the other hand, Spain's unemployment rate was not significantly different from that of most other European countries. What accounts for the difference in the last two decades? That is the question that Felipe seeks to answer.

Hubert Hieke notes that Germans have argued for a reduction in the value-added tax for labor-intensive services in order to stimulate employment in Germany by increasing internal demand for the output of labor-intensive activities. Hieke provides empirical evidence to demonstrate that such a VAT tax reduction will not increase employment in these sectors.

These papers provide a challenging set of arguments and suggest the many problems facing decision-makers in their attempt at 'policy-making in the New Global Economy'.

Paul Davidson
*Knoxville, Tennessee*
*September 2000*

# 1. Latin America's quasi-stagnation

## Luiz Carlos Bresser–Pereira*

Behind Latin America's 20-year-old quasi-stagnation are not only interest groups of all kinds, but also serious mistakes in macroeconomic policy-making and institutional reform design. The central argument I will develop here is simple. Latin American countries became involved in the 1980s in a debt crisis and, more broadly, in a fiscal crisis of the state. Why did they not overcome the crisis? Why did they not regain the economic stability that had been lost in the crisis? Why were reforms not as effective as one would expect? Economists and social scientists have a general explanation for this: interest groups created obstacles to adequate policy-making. I have no argument with that, but believe, and will argue in this chapter, that there is a second and more important reason: that policy-makers are often incompetent, out of ignorance, fear or arrogance. Often policy-makers did the wrong thing out of conviction, not because of political pressure. Their decisions were the outcome of bad judgement. This was not relevant in the past, when macroeconomic policy and institutional reform strategy did not actually exist. Today they do exist, and often involve strategic, highly important decisions, given the consequences that may arise. Why do we assume that these decisions are always right? Or that right and wrong decisions compensate for each other, so that they may be ignored?

The last 20 years has been a time of near-stagnation for Brazil and, more broadly, for Latin America. If the 1980s have been called 'the lost decade', the 1990s may be seen as 'the wasted decade'. In absolute terms, income per capita barely grew in this period. If one compares it with the previous 30 years, the results are shocking. In the former period one could say that Brazil was catching up with the developed countries and that Latin America as a whole put in an unsatisfactory but still reasonable performance. Since 1980, however, Latin America has stagnated while the developed countries have continued to grow, although at a reduced pace. Per capita income between 1950 and 1979 grew at 3.3 percent per annum in the OECD countries, 2.3 percent in Latin America and 3.9 percent in Brazil. Between 1980 and 1998, the rate of growth in the developed countries went down to just 2.5 percent, but plummeted in Latin America to 0.5 percent and in Brazil to 0.7 percent (Table 1.1).

*1*

*Table 1.1    Rates of per capita GDP growth compared*

| Average | OECD | Latin America | Brazil |
|---------|------|---------------|--------|
| 1950–59 | 3.1 | 2.2 | 3.7 |
| 1960–69 | 4.2 | 2.5 | 2.9 |
| 1970–79 | 2.7 | 2.2 | 5.1 |
| 1950–79 | 3.3 | 2.3 | 3.9 |
| 1980–89 | 2.3 | −0.3 | 1.0 |
| 1990–98 | 3.0 | 1.4 | 0.4 |
| 1980–98 | 2.5 | 0.5 | 0.7 |

*Note:*  'OECD' comprises Australia, Austria, Belgium, Canada, Denmark, Finland, France, Germany, Italy, Japan, Korea, Netherlands, New Zealand, Norway, Spain, Sweden, Switzerland, the United Kingdom and the United States.

*Source:*   ECLAC, OECD.

The question, then, is why this happened. Why were Latin American countries and particularly Brazil – which I know better – unable to develop their economies in the last 20 years? What went wrong? Are the causes to be found in the markets, or rather in the governments (administrations) and their managing elites? Are the causes essentially domestic, or is there a significant international component involved?

In this paper I will not describe or analyze the macroeconomic instability that prevailed in the Latin American countries. This terrible vicious circle is well known: budget deficits and high public debt leading to fiscal crisis of the state and high inflation; price stabilization causing overvalued currencies, fostering still higher debt; deficits, debt and overvaluation depressing public and private savings, and leading to higher interest rates. All this led to reduced capital accumulation rates and to stagnation or an almost permanent recession. Since I assume that macroeconomic stability is a necessary (although not sufficient) condition for growth, my more general question will be why Latin American countries were unable to achieve it.

In this paper I offer answers to these questions. I will say that a major new historical fact led Latin American countries to near-insolvency, making macroeconomic policy-making and institutional reform design more strategic and more difficult. Politicians and the economists advising them were not able to cope with this added complexity. On several occasions they were incompetent and made serious mistakes, which aggravated the problem they wanted to solve. In section 1, I ask what economic growth depends on. To think just in terms of a production function is not enough.

Capital accumulation and technical progress were sufficient to explain economic growth when long-run macroeconomic stability could be assumed. Now, however, it cannot be. Macroeconomic instability can turn chronic and last for years, particularly when debt is involved. In section 2, I assume that there is today a reasonable consensus on the essential nature of the crisis: that it was a crisis of the developmentalist state.[1] In section 3, I examine the conventional answers to my basic question as given by the right and the left. According to the neoliberal wisdom, the explanation lies in the capacity of local political elites to reform and guarantee property rights. According to the old left, globalization and neoliberal reforms are to be blamed. But we know that the crisis occurred before the reforms. A new historical fact is required. Thus in section 4 I look for a new historical fact that could have prevented macroeconomic stability and caused stagnation. The 1970s foreign debt will be singled out as making macroeconomic policy-making more strategic and more complex in Latin America. In section 5 I review incompetent reform designs, which made their approval in parliament more problematic, and inept macroeconomic policies, particularly the decision to use foreign savings to stimulate growth, and policies to control inertial inflation. In section 6 I underline the wrong decisions leading to exchange rate overvaluation. In the seventh section I discuss the reasons behind these mistakes. In the conclusion I suggest that the incompetence hypothesis cannot be explained in rational or in historical terms. Although these two methods may offer subsidiary explanations for the problem, one should assume that incompetent policy-making is an independent explanatory factor which should be taken on its own.

Governments face serious institutional problems that require well-designed institutional reforms, and must make strategic and day-to-day macroeconomic policy decisions. My hypothesis is that, although interest group analysis may explain why decisions were not timely and correct, failures were more of a personal than of an institutional character. Given the existing pressure groups and ideologies, growth in Latin America would have been possible with the existing institutions if policy decisions had been correct and competent. Institutional reforms to foster growth would have been approved more easily if they had been properly designed. In other words, according to what we could call 'the incompetence hypothesis', the inability to overcome the crisis and resume growth lay mostly in the incompetence of local elites and international advisors to face the new challenges originating from the fundamental changes in international markets, particularly from the debt crisis and the increase in capital flows.

## GROWTH AND MACROECONOMIC STABILITY

Growth assumes macroeconomic stability. When an economist is asked what economic growth depends on, the standard answer will be capital accumulation and technical progress. This I would call the 'classical school' answer, and the best simple answer available. If we say that economic development depends essentially on entrepreneurial innovation, we add a Schumpeterian perspective. If we stress the role of externalities, we may be referring to the structuralist economists' balanced growth theory of the 1940s or to the unbalanced growth theory of the 1950s which, in the last 15 years, the new endogenous theory of growth was able to formalize. Refer to the crucial role of human capital, and we have the more significant Chicago contribution to the theory of growth. Say that institutions are essential, and we will be repeating what classical and structuralist political economists said long ago, but with a new rational choice appeal.

I will not go over the enormous and fascinating literature on the subject. Growth theory assumed macroeconomic stability. Why? Maybe because part of this literature was written before Keynes' invention of macroeconomics. Maybe because, when a larger part of the contemporary literature on economic growth was elaborated (in the post-World War II golden years), macroeconomic stability seemed to have been achieved. Now that this illusion is long over, and keeping to the basics, we may summarize by saying that economic growth or an increase in general productivity depends essentially on capital accumulation, technical progress and macroeconomic stability. Capital accumulation, in turn, depends on the one hand on domestic savings, and on the other on favorable profit prospects for businessmen. Technical progress depends on the level of education, supply of entrepreneurial capacity, commitment of business enterprises to research and development (R&D) and rate of capital accumulation (since new investments tend to embody new technology). Macroeconomic stability depends on, or rather may be defined by considering, macroeconomic fundamentals: a balanced budget, a manageable level of indebtedness and having prices right, particularly a 'realistic' exchange rate and an interest rate consistent with international rates.

There is no rule of thumb to define what is a manageable level of indebtedness. We know, however, that when a country has a high foreign debt, it is supposed to realize extra savings just to pay interest on it. Extra savings means either higher profit rates, if the private sector is the indebted one, or extra taxes, if the state is mainly responsible for the foreign debt. In both cases, it means lower wages and reduced consumption, which can only be achieved if the country has a relatively undervalued currency. Thus, a 'realistic' exchange rate for indebted developing countries is a relatively devalued currency, as I will demonstrate later. If we include the domestic debt in our simple model, and if the state is the one particularly indebted internally, extra taxes may be necessary even if the foreign debt is mostly private. In any case, the cost has to be paid in terms of lower wages received by workers and the new middle class. One can always ask that the extra burden be directed to profits, but the limits to such a policy are set by a simple fact: if the expected profit rate is not high enough and secure enough, capitalists will not invest.

More generally, economic growth depends on adequate institutions that can create incentives to save and to invest in physical and human capital, and on competent reform design and policy-making, which is not automatically assured when institutions are fitted.

## THE BASIC DIAGNOSIS

Assuming these general propositions, let me go back to my basic question: why have Latin American countries displayed such poor growth rates in the last 20 years, or, more specifically, why has macroeconomic instability been a constant throughout this period? Answers involve, on one side, a diagnosis of the historical circumstances that led so many countries, first to the crisis, and second, to an inability to overcome it. About the historical circumstances that gave rise to the crisis there is a reasonable consensus that it was essentially a crisis of the state. The developed countries have faced crises of the welfare state since 1973, when the first oil price shock signalled that the state had grown out of control, had become increasingly a victim of rent-seeking activity, and was immersed in growing internal problems, while government intervention distorted market allocation. The requisite fiscal adjustment and market-oriented reforms were then initiated. The Latin American crisis came later, in the 1980s, since economic growth was artificially protracted by the foreign debt adventure. But it came stronger, since the distortions of a developmentalist state were more severe than those of a welfare state.[2]

When at last, at the beginning of the 1980s, the debt crisis broke and the Latin American countries had no alternative but to adjust and reform, the task they faced was formidable. If in 1973 market distortions caused by generalized rent seeking and the imbalance in public finances in Latin America were already more severe than the corresponding distortions in the developed countries, what to say seven years later? Besides permitting the deepening of the existing distortions, the borrowing policy had led to outrageously high foreign debt.[3]

Thus, Latin American macroeconomic instability is associated with the excessive and distorted growth of the developmentalist state, and with the acquisition of a high foreign debt. The import substitution strategy that had been effective in promoting industrialization between the 1930s and 1950s was exhausted by the early 1960s. The economic crisis of the 1960s was a clear indication that the time for change had arrived; that the infant industry argument did not hold any more. But in the same way as fiscal adjustment would be protracted after the 1973 shock, so was the change to an export-oriented strategy in the 1960s. Foreign loans made both delays feasible, but had distressing consequences.

I believe that today there is a reasonable consensus for this basic diagnosis of the crisis. The neoliberal right will have difficulty accepting that, for a period, the developmentalist state was successful, since it is in conflict with historical reasoning. The old left will insist that the reason for macroeconomic instability was not the unavoidable distortions that evolve out of excessive protection of local industry and immoderate growth in state expenditures, but some conspiracy connecting local business and multinationals. But most will accept that the state, which, between the 1930s and 1960s, was active in promoting development and welfare, had since the 1980s turned into a problem, requiring fiscal adjustment and reform. Public savings, which had been positive and were contributing to overall savings, turned negative. The budget deficit that previously financed investment now chiefly financed consumption. State-owned enterprises, which had a major role in establishing an industrial infrastructure for the national economy, were now highly indebted. The state bureaucrats who, for a time, were committed to national projects in which their role was clear, were now lost in their own crisis – a crisis that led many of them to resort to rent seeking if not outright corruption.

## THE CONVENTIONAL WISDOM(S)

After 1982, when the debt crisis broke, macroeconomic instability emerged as the central economic problem. Latin American countries had no alternative but to adjust and reform. Pressed by creditor countries and by circumstances, they did just that, but they did not achieve macroeconomic stability. What went wrong? Was it that fiscal adjustment and reforms were not effectively undertaken, or that they were, but nevertheless did not perform? About this there is deep controversy. The right and the left have their own conventional wisdom.

The conservative conventional wisdom is clear. Latin America failed to undertake the reforms that are required in a global world. 'Reform' became a kind of *passe partout*, a miracle word that would solve all problems. Thus if growth did not resume, the explanation must be that reforms did not unfold. Never mind that fiscal adjustment was implemented severely in many countries, that trade liberalization and privatization are now definitive facts in Latin America, that administrative reforms are under way in some countries, that labor markets were made somewhat more flexible. Reforms were 'just on paper' or were 'not enough', or new ones are required.

According to the new conservative view, what is needed is 'economic freedom'. The think tank Economic Freedom of the World publishes an index ranking countries accordingly.[4] This curious index, in which China is freer than Brazil and Peru ranked higher than Denmark, is, notwithstanding, taken seriously by *The Economist*, since it expresses in correct terminology the right's truth. The magazine's editor, Bill Emmott (1999: 28), for instance, asks in a special survey why the poorer countries haven't caught up in the 20th century. He dismisses answers like lack of skills, lack of capital or lack of entrepreneurship, to conclude with a platitude: that what is lacking is economic freedom and the due protection of property rights, since 'the freer the economy, the higher the growth and the richer the country'. Reforms will lead to this freedom, will reduce the size of the state and deregulate the economy, allowing the market to do its work. If growth did not evolve, it was because reforms were not carried out or were incomplete.

The market-oriented reforms required in Latin America have been undertaken: fiscal adjustment, trade reform, privatization, social security reform and administrative reform. To say that these reforms were not undertaken is simply false. To say that they are incomplete is always true, but it does not explain macro instability. This is a short-run problem, which has to be solved mostly with short-term policies, while institutional reforms have mostly medium-term outcomes. Even economic reforms involving short-term results, such as trade liberalization, do not automatically entail stability and growth. Recently Rodrik (1999), after extensive cross-country regression analysis, concluded that trade reform was not related in a significant way to growth in the 1980s and 1990s; the significant variables were capital accumulation and macroeconomic stability.[5] The only policy directly related to macro stability is fiscal adjustment, but that, although it may partially depend on fiscal reform, is not itself a reform.

But, continues mainstream conventional wisdom, reforms were not carried out, or were insufficient, because they were, and are, opposed by interest groups and populist politicians in Latin America.

Latin American politicians do indeed engage in populist practices more easily than those in developed countries. This is also part of a developing country by definition. But how can we explain that, with the same politicians, Latin America was able to achieve reasonable macroeconomic stability and high rates of per capita GDP growth in the previous 30 years? One cannot explain new events with old facts. Besides, it is reasonable to say that political behavior in Latin America has improved in the last 20 years. Democracy has become the dominant political form throughout the region. The Latin American democracies cannot be compared with the ones existing in the developed countries, but they are at least democracies. This means they have better institutions and better politicians.

Thus, the conservative or mainstream conventional wisdom about what went wrong in Latin America is not convincing. Unable to reason in historical terms, it tries to explain a new problem – economic stagnation – with old facts: 'lack of economic freedom', 'populist politicians', 'incomplete reforms'. This despite the record of improvement: property rights are now better protected than before, politicians are more modern and democratic, and extensive reforms, although necessarily incomplete, have been accomplished.

The conventional wisdom of the old left goes in the opposite direction but has similar flaws. If globalization is a grace for the right, as it means that markets are becoming dominant all over the world, to the old left it is a curse for the same, but oppositely valued, reason. In the last quarter-century market coordination has advanced while state intervention first came to a halt and then was (moderately) reduced; the left believes this is to blame for stagnation. The curious thing is that it shares with the right the belief that globalization inevitably leads to a reduction in state autonomy. It does not seem to realize that the devious ideological aspect of globalization is precisely that: to say that the state has definitively lost autonomy, and that there is nothing to do about it but to accept and adjust to this new reality.

Together with globalization, continues the old left, came the neoliberal reforms that further reduced state autonomy, leaving developing economies at the mercy of market irrationality. Thus whereas, for the right, it is the lack of reforms that is to be censured, for the old left, it is the excess of reforms and their distorted character that explain Latin America's economic problems. That in some countries reforms were misguided there can be no doubt. Consider, for instance, the case of privatization in Argentina. But one cannot generalize the argument. Actually the old left's wisdom does not make sense for the simple reason that the crisis that led to stagnation has its roots in the 1970s, when neither globalization nor reforms had come of age. Globalization in real (rather than ideological) terms, viewed as the worldwide reorganization of production led by multinational corporations and as the emergence of world financial markets, was a historical fact on its way, but not yet dominant. Reforms came in the 1980s as an answer to the crisis, and thus cannot be its cause.

The right's difficulty of thinking in historical terms is easy to understand. Its present intellectual religion is neoclassical economics and rational choice reasoning, which are notable scientific realizations but are, by definition, ahistorical, of an essentially logical–deductive character. But it is harder to understand why the left is equally unable to think in historical terms, when this is strictly required. After all, we are looking for the causes of a new historical event, namely economic stagnation in Latin America. Historical reasoning is not a monopoly of the left, but it is good to remember that its major thinker, Marx, thought always in historical terms. It was the historical method that permitted him to draw such a profound analysis of capitalism.

Thus both right and left shun history. Not because the historical method is a risky way of reasoning, prone to ideological distortion, but because it involves identifying and coping with change. This is always painful to the right and the left. It requires real thinking, not just the application of stereotypes. It is fashionable to speak of the increasing pace of technological and social change, but when interests and ideologies are involved, it is much easier to stick with an immutable conventional wisdom of a sort.

## THE NEW HISTORICAL FACT

Difficult and risky as it may be, there is no alternative but to think in historical terms when we have a historical problem to solve. What was the new historical fact that kept macroeconomic instability unresolved, that turned it into an almost chronic phenomenon? I have already accepted the basic diagnosis for why the problem came about in the early 1980s – it was a crisis of the developmentalist state caused by excessive and distorted growth. But when a crisis emerges and its causes are identified, it is reasonable to expect that it will subsequently be overcome. Why did this not happen?

The failure to take correct strategic policy decisions and adopt well-designed reforms is my main explanation. Reforms are institutional changes; policy decisions are the day-to-day management of the economy. Reforms involve medium-term outcomes; policy decisions may also have medium- and long-term consequences, but usually produce results immediately. The economists in charge of policy decisions in Latin American countries, both domestic and foreign (the latter usually IMF or World Bank advisors) failed grossly in stabilizing Latin American economies. Stabilization strategies, specifically price stabilization strategies, took too long to achieve results  or cost too much in loss of income. Some cost too much because hyperinflation developed, as in Argentina. In other cases, they cost too much because they involved extremely severe cuts in demand

and particularly in wages, as was the case in Chile. And in other cases, such as Brazil, high costs were related to the time they took to succeed: starting from 1979, when the crisis began, 12 stabilization attempts – some hetero-dox, most orthodox – failed before the heterodox Real Plan was able to stabilize inflation.

But the same argument that I used earlier to reject the conventional wisdom that populist politicians were to blame for the failure to stabilize applies to my argument as well. The same economists – although certainly less well prepared theoretically – were in Latin America in the previous 30 years, when macroeconomic stability and economic growth prevailed. Thus, before surveying wrong strategic decisions, I still need a new historical fact that changed the picture and caused poor decision-making.

I offer two new historical facts for discussion. One is specific to Latin America: the debt crisis and consequent fiscal crisis of the state. The other – the fact that macroeconomic policy-making is relatively new – will give a more universal character to the analysis.

**The Debt Crisis**

The debt crisis was effectively a new historical fact, as we may see in Table 1.2: the increase in debt outstanding of Latin America as a whole and Brazil in particular from 1970 to 1980 was immense. This new fact, in this case, is supposed to have two qualities. First, it must have imposed a severe blow on the Latin American economies. I will not offer further evidence for this because it is well known that high indebtedness represented a disaster for Latin America. And second, this new fact, producing such a grave and enduring crisis, should have made economic policy decisions more strategic and more complex. In other words, it is supposed to have produced what on another occasion I have called 'abnormal times', that is, an atypical situation in which distortions of all sorts assume an overwhelming character, requiring exceptionally proficient decisions. If, in these circumstances,

*Table 1.2    Outstanding Brazilian and Latin American foreign debt ( US$ million)*

| Year Ending | Latin America | Brazil |
|-------------|---------------|--------|
| 1970 | 27,633 | 5,020 |
| 1980 | 187,255 | 57,981 |
| 1990 | 379,669 | 94,340 |
| 1998 | 558,919 | 157,553 |

*Source:*    World Bank, *Global Development Finance.*

policy decisions are not made at the right time and in the right direction, the country may stagnate for many years.

The debt acquired by the Latin American countries in the 1970s and early 1980s, before the 1982 breakdown, fits these two requirements. We had foreign indebtedness before, in the 19th century and in the 1920s, but never to such an extent. What is more important, since the 1930s' crisis, when several developing countries had to restructure their debts, private loans to Latin America were closed, except loans to finance trade. The relatively high rates of growth achieved between 1930 and 1969, and particularly between 1960 and 1969, were thus secured without making use of long-term debt. Quasi-stagnation only appeared after Latin American countries became indebted.

In the 1950s and 1960s Latin American economists and politicians longed to obtain long-term loans, believing that in this way they would speed up growth. When, in the 1970s, they were given this power, given the excess liquidity prevailing in the international financial markets, the Latin American countries became indebted and a predictable, but not predicted, disaster ensued. Very few things are more dangerous to any organization, be it a business organization or a national economy, than to suddenly have access to a large amount of money. The probability that this money will be spent poorly is enormous. There are not enough good investment projects to be financed, nor enough competent management to lead the projects. In the 1970s the Latin American foreign debt grew so quickly and became so large, while the international banks took so much time to stop it (for a while), that when this eventually happened, in 1982, most Latin American countries were insolvent. They were left with a huge debt overhang which had to be served out of current national income.

This is old and well-known history. A history of a problem that the Brady Plan, from 1990 on, did not solve but simply got under control, by allowing for restructuring and limited discounting. Here, the important thing is to understand the long-run consequences. On the other hand, since I am assuming that the Latin American countries can only rely on themselves, it is essential to know how the debt affected growth and policy-making in Latin America. That it affected long-term growth negatively is not in dispute. The problem is that, additionally, it made policy-making, already a difficult and hazardous task, even more complex. If this is true for advanced economies, where macroeconomic problems seldom assume a dramatic character, what is there to say of the developing countries, which faced practical insolvency due to the debt? A country enjoys macroeconomic stability when inflation rates are similar to those prevailing in the advanced countries, and interest rates just a little above. Foreign (and domestic) large debts made macroeconomic stabilization in the Latin

American countries much more difficult to achieve, demanding more competent economists and politicians than the ones at the region's disposal.[6]

### The 'New' Macroeconomics

Macroeconomic policy is a 50-year-old phenomenon. Before Keynes and the rise of macroeconomics – before central banks became established and relatively independent – one could hardly speak of an overarching macroeconomic policy. Governments adopted forms of economic policy and strove for fiscal and trade account balance, but theory was so poor, and macro data so faulty, that governments were far from having a real macroeconomic policy. Thus, it was understandable that economists, historians and social scientists in general, when trying to understand the economic performance of nations, looked only for interests, not for mistakes. Bad or good decisions would arise systematically out of interest groups or unsystematically out of decisions. Often historians would speak of a 'good' or a 'bad' government, but nevertheless, right and wrong government decisions were supposed to be so evenly distributed that they could mostly be ignored.

This is no longer the case now that macroeconomic policy, and, more recently, institutional reform strategy, has turned into a usual and essential government process. This is a new historical fact. Economic policy has become strategic and may now be held responsible for a substantial part of a government's success or failure. Thus policy decisions (right and wrong), as well as interests, have to be taken into consideration by social scientists, if they want to understand what is going on.

I am not saying that there are no good economists in Latin America, nor that there is a systematic explanation for macro instability. Latin America today probably has better-prepared politicians and economists than it did in the past. Latin American countries are more democratic, and politicians have learned to live with democracy. Since the late 1960s economists have started to study for PhDs abroad, particularly in the more prestigious American universities, giving them more sophisticated economic techniques to work with. But this does not mean that they have a greater – or lesser – ability to make correct and courageous decisions. There is here a trade-off between technical capacity and a deeper knowledge of the economic and political reality in each country. I will not discuss this subject here.[7] Rather, I want to emphasize that the debt crisis and, more generally, the crisis of the Latin American states made economic policy-making more challenging that it was before. More broadly, the emergence of macroeconomic policy and institutional reform strategy made decisions in this area more significant and more subject to error. Good institutions such as those existing in advanced countries will limit the costs involved in perhaps mistaken decisions, but nevertheless, policy decisions now need to be more relevant and strategic than they were in the past.

## INCOMPETENT STRATEGIC DECISIONS

What were the mistakes that were made? Has policy-making really been as misguided and unsuitable as I am suggesting? In order to respond to these questions, I will review some basic macroeconomic policy decisions and some decisions on the design of institutional reforms over the last 20 years, asking if they succeeded or not. The criterion for success is different in each case. Success in institutional design is achieved when the reform is approved by congress and, later on, when it is implemented and produces the expected outcomes. I will refer here only to reform approval. Success in macro policy-making is achieved when the economy first stabilizes and then grows. In the case of reforms, we have a political success criterion; in the case of macro policy decisions, we have a technical one.

Many institutional reforms were approved and implemented in Latin America. When a reform does not pass congress, the usual explanation is that voters did not support it or that opposing interest groups were too strong. Both are true, but an entirely different kind of answer must also be considered, an answer that I believe is particularly important. Many reforms are not approved by parliament because the reform design was not competent. Usually proficient design is taken for granted. It should not be. One should not underestimate politicians acting in parliaments. A poorly designed reform is much more difficult to pass than a well-designed one. The reform design has to be simple, its objectives clear, its benefits well defined, its costs sized. All this must be part of the reform design, so that it can be easily understood and gain the support of the public.

There is a growing literature on what is called 'deliberative' democracy, a polity that 'is governed by the public deliberation of its members'. There are advocates of deliberative democracy, such as Cohen (1989: 67), whose definition I just used, or Bohman (1998), who refers to 'the coming age of deliberative democracy'. There are also critics, such as Przeworski (1998), according to whom deliberation easily gets transformed into indoctrination since, in the process, power agents make use of money and privileged information to persuade others. I will not discuss this matter here. Przeworski is correct when he says that the distortions in the deliberation process are usually great. Good laws do not necessarily derive from the public deliberation of citizens. I will only say that public debate, or what Habermas calls 'communicative action', is essential to democracy.

The democratic regime is always deliberative in the sense that citizens' votes in elections and politicians' votes in parliaments are the outcome of individual deliberation preceded by public debate. If a reform is really important, a national debate is necessary for securing support. It is almost impossible to debate at the national level a reform that is poorly designed.

In Brazil the social security reform submitted to congress in 1995 was an example of a poorly designed reform. This reform was extremely necessary, particularly the reform of the civil servants' pension system, since the privileges and consequent costs were huge. According to the Brazilian constitution, civil servants are entitled to a full pension corresponding to the last salary before retirement, which they usually secure at an early age. In contrast, the private workers' pensions system grants few if any privileges. Reform of it was required, but to a lesser extent. Thus, the right thing to do in political terms would have been to present two separate constitutional amendments. Instead, only one amendment was submitted, permitting a few powerful public officials to hide behind the mass of private workers who, although not being deprived of significant entitlements, felt threatened. This threat was felt still more strongly because the reform had additional design flaws. It was complex and obscure. A lot was left to be regulated by ordinary law. Even though Brazilians admit that they have an excessively detailed constitution, they contradictorily require that their rights be defined clearly in the constitution. The consequence was that, notwithstanding the efforts of the federal government in this matter, only a fraction of what was contemplated was approved.

In the case of the second major reform that the Brazilian government committed to in the 1994 elections – tax reform – the design problem has been still more serious. Up to now the finance ministry has not been able to arrive at its own proposal. There is a consensus that the reform is needed but, fearing a reduction in the tax burden, the government has not been able, internally, to arrive at a conclusion.[8]

An interesting research project would be to survey other institutional reforms in Latin America to check to what extent they failed – when they did – because of flawed design. I will now turn to macroeconomic policies, highlighting three areas: foreign debt policy, price stabilization policy and exchange rate policy. I will not bring up decisions on the interest rate, because these are a part of day-to-day monetary policy depending on decisions in the above areas.

Latin American countries made a great mistake in becoming highly indebted in the 1970s – a mistake that I suggested was the historical new fact that made macroeconomic policy-making considerably more difficult than it had been. Yet one could argue that this is an old question. Indeed it is. But what is there to say about so many Latin American countries engaging, in the 1990s, in new debts? The 'growth-cum-debt' strategy, the fantasy that it is possible to stir growth with foreign savings, is back in Latin America.

It is a serious mistake to rely on debt to stimulate growth. This might be reasonable if the countries were not already highly indebted, and if limits were strictly defined. I do not forget basic economic theory, which says that it is valid to borrow when the rate of interest is lower than the expected rate of profit. Yet this kind of microeconomic reasoning is misleading in macro terms. It is impossible to guarantee that borrowing will be directed to new investments. The moment a country opens its financial markets to foreign borrowing, be it short or medium term, it loses control of how the resources will be used.

There is a general condemnation of short-term borrowing given the high volatility of capital flows. Medium-term debt is certainly less harmful than short-term indebtedness. But both are bad. In the 1997–98 emerging markets financial crisis, the countries that were not highly indebted – and that were not tending to acquire more debt given their current account deficits – were not molested. A debt is always a burden for future generations. If the borrowed resources are used well, this burden can be justified. But the chances that this will happen are small when huge amounts of money are suddenly offered to a country. It represents a permanent threat of foreign insolvency. And, while foreign resources are entering the country, the exchange rate will tend do go down, that is, the local currency will be valorized. In the next section I discuss how bad this can be for an indebted country.

In relation to inflation one could argue that it too is an 'old problem', since most Latin American countries have already been able to control their inflation. But at what cost? Take the case of Chile. Pinochet and his foreign advisors were indeed able to control inflation and stabilize their foreign accounts in the 1970s. Chile was the first Latin American country to achieve macroeconomic stability. That is why one cannot speak of economic stagnation in the last 20 years when we refer to Chile. But in the 1970s and early 1980s serious mistakes were made, the costs involved being huge. The country remained stagnant in income-per-head terms from 1973 to the late 1980s. Only after Buchi became finance minister and adopted competent policies did Chile resume growth.

Brazil faced a different problem. Inflation, besides revealing the fiscal crisis of the state and the external imbalance of the economy, assumed an inertial (formally and informally indexed) character. In order to stabilize the economy, fiscal adjustment was essential and trade liberalization would help – has indeed helped – but these two actions were not enough. It was also necessary to neutralize inertia. Most Brazilian economists in government and their local and foreign advisors, particularly from the IMF and the World Bank, knew little or nothing about inertial inflation. It was understandable that they ignored inertia for some time. Most of the ideas related to it were developed principally in Latin America, but also in Israel, between 1980 and 1984. That the first stabilization plans after 1979, when high (more than 100 percent per year) inflation started, did not take into account the new theory one can understand without referring to the incompetence hypothesis. But when we remember that it was only in 1994 that Brazil was able to neutralize inertia and control inflation, and that between 1979 and 1994 12 stabilization plans failed, there is no alternative but to say that incompetence was involved. Only one or two of these plans failed for lack of political support; most – orthodox plans in the large majority – failed for sheer ignorance of economic theory, or for ignorance combined with fear or arrogance.[9]

In Argentina the costs involved in controlling inflation were still higher. Inflation again had an inertial character, although not so clearly as in Brazil. The Austral (1985) plan had a good design but failed for lack of political support for fiscal adjustment – the same reasons that led the Cruzado Plan in Brazil (1986) and the Bresser Plan (1987) to fail. In these cases, mainstream thinking was confirmed. But, differently from Brazil, Argentina did not have time to try many other stabilization plans. Given the fragility of the economy at that time – 1989 – high inflation soon turned into hyperinflation. For two years Argentina lived through episodes of hyperinflation that further disorganized its economy. It was only in 1991, when a currency board was put to work, that price stability was achieved.

The Cavallo Plan was successful. As a matter of fact, it was the only alternative left for Argentina, whose economy was caught by two torments: dollarization and hyperinflation. But the plan had an essential flaw: it started from an overvalued peso, which Roberto Frenkel denounced the day after the plan was started. In accepting a currency overvaluation in order to unequivocally assure price stability, Argentina was reproducing the same mistake Mexico was making at that same moment – a mistake Brazil would also make after the Real Plan. For a few years the Cavallo Plan worked. It even produced two years of high GDP growth, as the economy respired after so many years of disorder, but in 1994 it was clear that the convertibility could not go ahead. Argentina was heading toward exchange rate crisis and default. The Real Plan, overvaluing the Brazilian currency, gave an extra life to Argentinian currency board, as Argentina was able to compensate for its large trade deficits with the rest of the world with a sizeable surplus with Brazil. But in the medium term a currency board makes no sense for a large economy like Argentina's. With the January 1999 devaluation of the Real, which is now in a floating exchange rate regime,

Argentina will have no alternative but to devalue and float its own currency, too.

## THE EXCHANGE RATE

The late Mário Henrique Simonsen used to say that inflation cripples but the exchange rate kills. There is no worse mistake for a developing and highly indebted country than to have an overvalued currency. Nevertheless, Latin American countries again and again make this mistake. Why is over-valuation such a big blunder? And why is it a recurrent phenomenon?

The exchange rate is the most important price in an economy. For a highly indebted economy it is even more important, since it will increase a debt that is already too high. It is often assumed that an equilibrium exchange rate is one that balances the trade account. It is not. If the country can count on some direct investment, it will be consistent with a reasonable current account deficit – a deficit smaller than the inflow of direct invest-ment so that, besides paying interest, the country may gradually pay off the principal. Thus one might say that a highly indebted country, as are most in Latin America, should have an 'undervalued' currency – an exchange rate that produces a trade account surplus. When in doubt the debtor country should opt always to have its currency undervalued. As a trade-off, creditor countries should have 'overvalued' currencies, that is, a deficit in the trade and current accounts, so that debtor countries can pay off the principal bit by bit.

Financial people in creditor countries do not like to hear that debtor countries should start paying off the principal. What will they do then with their capital surpluses? The same is true of politicians and policy-makers in developing countries. Why should they have to pay a debt that was acquired previously? Why should they reduce the rate of growth – or, more plainly, the level of consumption – to fix a problem that others created? That is why, probably, we don't often hear this kind of argument. Instead of the phrase, 'when in doubt, have an overvalued currency', there is a much more popular maxim among both debtors and creditors: 'a debt is not to be paid, it is to be rolled over'.

Economists in the international commercial banks and in the IMF and World Bank prefer to speak of the dangers of domestic debt than to speak about the foreign debt. But the fact is that when a country goes bankrupt, it is always because, after an irresponsible lending–borrowing venture, the international creditors suddenly suspend credit. And since a country, in contrast to a firm, cannot go completely bankrupt and close, since the pop-ulation and the territory are always there, the country is always 'open for business'. The subsequent 'business' of a country that has incurred foreign insolvency will not just be an increase in risk premiums, but years and years of economic stagnation.

Before that happens, the inflow of foreign money will keep the local currency overvalued, inflation will go down and wages will go up. Governments, using the easy credit, will increase state expenditures – or cut them less than they should. The classical populist cycle will be reproduced. Its harm will depend on the degree of over-evaluation of the currency and the relative size of the domestic budget deficit.[10] Soon the loans that were thought to be financing investment projects showing a rate of return superior to the rate of interest being paid (despite the large risk premiums paid) are financing consumption. Debt is accumulating and a crisis is just a question of time.

In the 1970s currencies were overvalued in anticipation of higher rates of growth coming from debt-financed investments. The outcomes are well known. In the 1990s a new reason for overvaluation popped up: to guarantee the just-achieved price stabilization. Thus in Mexico, Argentina and finally Brazil, currency overvaluation was the immediate outcome of price stabilization – an outcome which many took, rather, as a tool. Control of inflation would come out of an 'exchange rate anchor'. In Argentina in 1991, the exchange rate was in fact the anchor. But in Mexico in 1987, the price and wage freeze that partially neutralized inertia, and the social agreement achieved with workers were crucial. In Brazil, the URV (*Unidade Real de Valor*, or real value unity), which fully neutralized inertia, was the significant variable in achieving price stabilization.

Once stabilization has been achieved, and after a period of time – a few months, a year maybe – it would be reasonable to expect the exchange rate to reach an equilibrium. But this did not happen. Why? Because, almost without noticing it, Latin American countries were soon back in the 1970s. Debt is once again a tool for growth. The international financial community's discourse to a country that has just stabilized prices is clear: 'Behave well, control the budget and make the reforms, and we will finance your growth'. For the developing countries' elites this is a wonderful discourse. The fact, to repeat Barbosa Lima's phrase, that 'capital is made at home' – that countries cannot rely on foreign savings to develop their economies, that usually countries finance more than 95 percent of their capital accumulation out of their own savings – was soon forgotten.[11] We are back to the twin evils of increasing debt and exchange rate overvaluation.

When a country has an overvalued economy and the financial community is aware of the fact, besides costs related to increased consumption and increased indebtedness, there is another terrible cost: potential growth loss. Financial markets immediately add an 'exchange rate risk' to the interest rate to be paid by the country – an exchange rate risk that adds to the existing 'country risk'. The interest rate skyrockets. On the supply side of loanable funds, loans will only continue to be rolled over if the interest rates include these premiums. On the demand side, the local authorities are constrained to maintain the high interest rate for another reason: they must keep aggregate demand – and thus, imports – under control, in order to avoid increasing current account deficits and further international loss of credibility. High interest rates mean lower investment rates, and potential growth loss.

What do economists in government and their advisors say about all that? To answer this question look, for instance, at what happened to Brazil between the second semester of 1994 and the Russian crisis in September 1998. Almost all economists said that productivity increase would solve the problem; or that fiscal adjustment would do the job. Economic theory is a realm open to debate, but assertions like that simply show economic ignorance. The proponents of the productivity increase argument forgot that other countries also increase their productivity, and that one has no control over that. The fiscal adjustment proponents forgot that fiscal adjustment might lead only to devaluation if it is so drastic that it provokes deflation. With deflation the prices of non-tradable goods, particularly wages, are reduced in relation to those of tradable goods, thus accomplishing real devaluation. This is not a rational form of devaluing. Besides the unavoidable reduction in wages, it produces widespread unemployment.[12] It was only after the Russian crisis, around three years after the real should have been devalued, that most economists realized that devaluation was required.[13] A few months later, in January 1999, the decision was taken, but the huge costs in terms of potential growth loss and increased indebtedness had already been incurred, and could not be recovered.

## REASONS

These policy mistakes, that is, unsuitable policies or reform designs, were adopted due to poor judgement or incompetence. Similar policies may have been adopted for rational motives, in response to self-interest or the demands of pressure groups. I am not dismissing the relevance of interests. I am saying that there is not just one reason (interests) but two reasons (interests and incompetence) behind a wrong policy decision, a decision that produces detrimental outcomes. In both cases we have mistaken policies, but if the cause is interest group pressure or populism, one cannot say they were the fruit of mistakes. In the second case, however, the mistake, the bad judgement, is the relevant variable. In many cases the two causes may come together. But my contention is that, in relation to the damaging policies just surveyed, the main reason why they were adopted was incompetence. In some cases the policies were severe, imposing sacrifices on the population and elites. Thus, they were not the result either of populism or pressure group action. They were the consequence of ignorance, fear, arrogance or a mixture of all these. As Whitehead (1997: 11) observes, over the past 20 years governments in Latin America have confronted extremely complex economic dilemmas, while 'one of the features of both apolitical *técnicos* and the more politically empowered technocrats or technobureaucrats is that they tend to apply with great authority and self confidence, ideas they have derived at second-hand and without drawing on strong local tradition of theoretical elaboration and debate'.

They involved ignorance of the complexities of economic theory or unqualified application of abstract economic theory to Latin American economic problems. In saying that, I am not returning to the old argument that economic theory does not apply to developing countries. It does, as it applies to the developed countries. But it applies provided, in one case as in the other, that the theory is not applied automatically, is not transformed into a series of clichés, but is proficiently defined and implemented. Alec Cairncross, a distinguished economist who spent a large part of his life in and out of government, emphasizes the gap between theory and practice – a gap that, I would add, makes mistakes unavoidable. In his words: 'Specialists in economic theory do not reach the same conclusions on controversial issue . . . [A] wide gap necessarily exists between the ideas embodied in economic theory and the matters to which policy has to give attention' (Cairncross 1996: 256).

Besides ignorance, fear and arrogance, there is a second argument to explain these policy mistakes or incompetence: 'confidence building'. This is an area between self-interest and incompetence. Latin American elites are subordinate elites. They do not limit themselves to seeing the United States and, more broadly, the developed countries, as richer and more powerful nations, whose political institutions and scientific and technological development should be imitated. No, they see the elites in the developed countries both as the source of truth and as natural leaders to be followed. This subordinate internationalism ideology, already called 'colonial inferiority complex' and *entreguismo*, is as detrimental to a country as old-time nationalism. With the industrialization of Latin America and the emergence of new local elites after the 1930s, some predicted that this ideological subservience would recede. Indeed, for some time it was possible to see signals of a new mood in Latin American governments and elites. But when the countries became highly indebted, and their economies came to depend more on financial market credit, subordinate internationalism was back in place.

Now, however, it had a 'good' economic theory argument behind it. As international financial markets and mainstream economic theory assert, economic policy must be endowed with 'credibility'. There is an extensive literature on this subject. In strict macroeconomic terms an administration has credibility when it decides that it will follow a given policy, and then follows it. But in the political realm, credibility is identified with credit and confidence. Thus, a policy will have 'credibility' if international economic authorities, in Washington, and international financial markets believe that it is consistent and adequate. In this case, the country viewed as being committed to stability is able to build confidence and obtain access to credit.

The indebted developing countries need 'credibility' and credit, so they faithfully and uncritically follow Washington's and New York's recommendations, whether specific or vague, reasonable or mistaken. They are followed as if ultimate macroeconomic truth was crystallized in Washington (the official view) and New York (the financial market view). I may be engaging in some caricaturist simplification, but this is not far from reality. The confidence-building game is the new form of international subordination in Latin America and, more generally, in the developing countries. It is a source of serious economic policy mistakes.

One could say that there is no alternative for the developing country, that the World Bank and IMF have no choice but to define lock-in strategies that, when followed, will show creditors that a particular country will honor its obligations. I am not discussing the developed countries' and their agencies' alternatives. I am not criticizing the World Bank's or the IMF's 'incompetence'. On average, they are quite competent agencies, but as bureaucratic agencies, they are not well prepared to face abnormal times. However, this is not my subject. I am speaking about the alternatives facing developing countries' governments. They may either adopt a critical, although sympathetic, approach to foreign advice, or just engage in confidence building. They may follow the policies they believe correct, negotiating and compromising when this is necessary, or they may just assume that what the creditor expects them to do is correct. When they choose the last alternative, as Latin American countries have done again and again, they will be prone to serious problems.

Philippe Faucher observed that countries will engage or not in the confidence-building game depending on their relative strength or weakness in a negotiation. Somehow economic agents can impose their views and decide on the warranties that they wish to extract in transactions with other agents. Any owner of a property will do a credit check and/or ask for a warranty before signing a rental contract. This is a real constraint, a code of conduct imposed upon economic agents.[14] I agree with Faucher. The relative strength of the negotiators is a decisive factor. Sometimes, in their negotiations with the IMF and the World Bank, governments are supposed to compromise. But how much? How far? I have nothing against serious and critical confidence-building efforts, nor even against compromises. What I am singling out as a major source of incompetent macroeconomic policies is the uncritical adoption of developed countries' recommendations.

When a country does what it believes should be done, and not what it is expected to do, it may, for a time, lose confidence. But if the assessment of its policy-makers is correct, good outcomes will soon spring up. Financiers, politicians and bureaucrats in New York and Washington are pragmatic: they only care about results. In the 1930s, while Argentina paid off all its foreign debt, Brazil did not pay, engaged in extensive negotiations, and more than once did not honor its commitments. Nevertheless, given its superior economic performance, it was not treated differently from Argentina by creditors.[15]

Salinas' Mexico was the first Latin American country to consistently follow this strategy. In August 1989, it irresponsibly signed the term sheet of a debt agreement with commercial banks, just six months after the Brady Plan was announced. The debt reduction was insignificant but, as it was then argued, it 'built confidence' and reduced interest rates paid by Mexico. From then on up to the December 1994 crash, the Salinas administration was fully engaged in confidence building, often at the expense of the national interest and/or of the macroeconomic fundamentals. The rushed debt agreement was clearly against the Mexican national interest. The fixed exchange rate policy was opposed to macro fundamentals. While financial markets did not realize the increasing overvaluation, their confidence in the Mexican economy increased with the 'strength' of the peso. Since then, in other Latin American countries, this confidence-building practice has been repeated again and again.

In saying that, I am not saying that it is bad to build confidence in international markets. Nor am I saying that their vision is always wrong, much less that the national interests of developing and developed countries are always in conflict. I believe just the opposite. Foreign analysts' appraisal of the macroeconomic problems in Latin America is usually proper. On the other hand, developed and developing countries increasingly have mutual interests. But sometimes national interests are in conflict, and often economists and financial people in Washington and New York are plainly wrong on strategic issues, as we have just seen.

Latin American elites – particularly politicians and economists – are supposed to think with their own heads, since they have responsibility for what happens in their countries. In each Latin American country local thinking capacity is already available. There is no reason to trust foreign analysts, who know little about each economy and are not really committed to the countries they review or advise.[16] To build confidence is convenient if not necessary. But Latin American governments should do that in their own terms, instead of just asking the rich countries what they should do. This is not just an absurd form of national subordination, it is also a mistaken generalization about what economists in the developed countries think. Their views are in fact much more varied and complex than financial markets and confidence builders assume.[17]

## A METHODOLOGICAL CONCLUSION

One could argue that this is not a 'well-behaved' explanation: to emphasize incompetence and relate it to ignorance, fear and arrogance. Instead, taking it for granted that mistaken decisions were made, would it not be adequate to fall back on conventional rational choice analysis? Rather than saying that people are incompetent, would it not be more reasonable to ask about the incentives and punishments leading to the wrong decisions? More broadly, according to the traditional way of thinking of all social science, would it not be more acceptable to say that pressure from interest groups and social classes, or popular demand, led to ill-advised decisions? No doubt I could have adopted this alternative. It is a safe one. But I would not be adding anything to the understanding of what happened in Latin America.

First, it should be remembered that there are good and bad governments and so there are right and wrong decisions. Good governments are those whose politicians and officials take decisions that are mostly right, as good states are those that rely on institutions to help government leaders make more secure investment decisions in the private and in the public sector. The history of a country is usually the story of how good governments have pushed the country ahead and how bad governments have held it back. When we study history we are able to say that one country, in a given period, achieved peace and prosperity because it was well governed, while another failed for lack of good government.

We know very well that often inflation was not controlled because this or that interest group would suffer from macroeconomic stability, or the hard policies required to achieve it. But when there is high inflation and almost everybody is suffering, this type of reasoning loses a large part of its explicative power. Strong political support emerges for harsh policies to fight inflation. If, in these circumstances, policy-makers are not able to control inflation, interests cease to explain what is taking place, and we have no alternative but to look for incompetence.

I have said in this paper that the strategy of using foreign savings to achieve growth was of mutual interest to both creditors and debtors, that in the short term an overvalued currency is wonderful for everybody. So, one may say that there are rational reasons behind mistaken policy decisions. But should I then conclude that the policy-makers who made the wrong decisions were not incompetent but dishonest, protecting their own interests or those of their constituencies rather than the public interest? In some cases I would accept that this is true. But if we go over it more carefully, this view, in spite of its academic prestige, is more shocking than my incompetence hypothesis. And probably endowed with less explanatory power.

My hypothesis is particularly useful in understanding the quasi-stagnation Latin America underwent in the last 20 years if the wrong policy decisions and the mistaken reform designs do not involve a vote in congress, as most do not, or, if they do involve a parliamentary decision, if the required majority is not too big.[18] Most of the wrong macroeconomic policy decisions and all of the faulty reform designs I have referred to in this paper did not depend on a vote in parliament. In many cases, previous popular support was not necessary and interest groups were divided or just not involved. If the decisions were wrong or inept, the only explanation is incompetence.

But, the questioning could go on, why, in several crucial stands, were policy-makers incompetent and misled? Because the new problems, the high debt overhang in particular, were too difficult for them to tackle. Because, being ideologically subordinate, they gave up their own judgement and resorted to confidence building. Because good institutions were not present to facilitate their job – institutions that in Latin America have never been fitted. Because making the right decisions requires courage not only to assume the consequences – this is a rational choice problem – but also to think for oneself, and the humility to learn from one's errors. In government, among officials, fear and arrogance are pervasive emotions. These are tentative responses, since to explain why people are incompetent or competent is almost as difficult as to ask why they are usually selfish but sometimes generous.

Critiques coming from an alternative methodological perspective could question whether it would not be more reasonable to explain the crisis using historical or structural arguments – the crisis of the state, the debt crisis, globalization. I have done that. The method is powerful in explaining why the crisis erupted, but limited in informing us as to why governments were not able, for so many years, to overcome it.

But, one can still ask, am I not ignoring the learning process? No, I am not. Economists in Latin America or advising Latin American countries finally learned to control inertial inflation. They also know today better than they knew before the costs of an overvalued currency sustained only through high interest rates. Maybe sometime they will learn the dangers involved in the growth-cum-debt strategy. The problem with macroeconomic policy, however, is that new problems are emerging, requiring new solutions. The problems may be less dramatic than those confronted by Latin American countries in the last 20 years. That is the case in the advanced countries, where macroeconomic stability has prevailed for many years. But this does not mean that the policy-makers of developed countries are exempt from mistakes. Their mistakes are probably less serious, less evident, but they are there.

In synthesis, the failure to stabilize and resume economic growth following the debt crisis in Latin America has been attributed to incompetent macro policy-making, and to a confidence-building strategy that subordinated policy to international official institutions and the financial community. The crisis came out as a crisis of the state – the Latin American developmentalist state. Reforms and short-term macroeconomic policies were not able to restore stability and growth, less because they were not implemented or were excessive than because they were flawed. Their failure was due not so much to interest group pressure – although this was relevant – but because they were marked by serious policy mistakes, incompetence and bad judgement. Incompetence and mistakes in Latin America were magnified or made more frequent due to two new historical facts. One is specific to Latin America: the foreign debt acquired in the 1970s and the consequent relative international insolvency, which made policy-making more difficult to design and implement. The other has a broader reach: the fact that macroeconomic policy is a historically recent, 50-year-old phenomenon. Before that policy decisions could be viewed as relatively irrelevant, with mistakes compensating for right decisions, and none having much impact on the economy. Not any more: with the growth of the state in this century and the emergence of macroeconomic policy and, more recently, institutional reform strategy, decisions cannot be ignored. Good and bad governments matter.

## NOTES

\*    This paper was written while I was visiting fellow at Nuffield College and the Centre for Brazilian Studies, Oxford University. I am indebted to Laurence Whitehead, John E. Roemer, Philippe Faucher, Robert Delorme, Robert Devlin, Antoni Estevadeordal, Rodrigo Bresser-Pereira and, particularly, Adam Przeworski for comments and suggestions.

1.   I have defined Latin America's and Brazil's crisis as a crisis of the state – as a fiscal crisis, a crisis of the mode of state intervention and a crisis of the bureaucratic form in which it was managed – in many works. Here I will refer only to Bresser-Pereira (1993).

2. In others papers I have defined the 20th century as the 'social–bureaucratic state', which assumed three basic forms: the 'welfare state' among the developed countries, particularly the European ones; the 'developmentalist state' in the developing countries, particularly the Latin American ones; and the 'communist state' or the 'Soviet-type state'.

3. Ten years later, in 1990, the Brady Plan did not solve the debt crisis; it simply permitted the restructuring of debt. In doing so, it gave room for a new wave of international lending and led to the concept of 'emerging markets'.

4. See Gwartney and Lawnson (1999) and www.freetheworld.com. The organization uses 53 institutions around the world to arrive at its Economic Freedom Network Index. In Brazil, where a practically unknown institution is in place, the 1997 freedom index, which can vary from 0 to 10, was 5.5, out of 119 countries surveyed.

5. According to Rodrik (1999: 1): 'The claims made by the boosters of international economic integration are frequently inflated or downright false . . . The evidence from the experience of the last two decades is quite clear: the countries that have grown most rapidly since the mid-1970s are those that invested a high share of GDP and maintained macroeconomic stability'.

6. Domestic public debt in Brazil, for instance, which was around 2 percent of GDP from the 1940s to the 1960s, rose to around 6 percent of GDP in the 1970s, 15 percent in the 1980s and 30 percent in the 1990s. Often in the later periods the domestic debt increased with foreign debt: given the inflow of foreign currency, the local government would buy it, in principle in order to sterilize it and so control the money supply, but in fact as an easy form of financing the budget deficit.

7. It should, however, be said that in the case of Brazil, where local PhD programs in economics and political science are well established, I favor short-term (one-year) stages in foreign universities over complete PhD programs.

8. On this subject, see Melo (1998) and Bresser-Pereira (2001).

9. I described these 12 cases in Bresser-Pereira (1996).

10. On the populist cycle see the classical papers of Canitrot (1975) and Sachs (1989). I edited a book on the subject in Brazil.

11. According, for instance, to Martin Feldstein (1995), the author of a study on how investments were financed in the OECD countries, the correlation between gross savings and gross investments in the period 1970–72 is almost perfect: if a country saves little, it will invest little. In this study Japan appears at the top of the list: it saves 34 percent and invests domestically 32 percent of GDP; the United States, at the bottom, saves 18 percent and invests 19 percent of GDP. The other countries are dutifully distributed between the two extremes, maintaining the close correlation between savings and investment.

12. In this period my official responsibilities made it impossible for me to expose my views in public. But even so I was able to present these arguments in a short paper that made no explicit reference to Brazil (Bresser-Pereira 1997).

13. The ideal moment to devalue the Real was October 1995. At that moment the economy was already fully de-indexed, and, responding to the Mexican crisis, a tight monetary and a severe fiscal policy had brought down demand.

14. Remarks made by Faucher in an e-mail commenting on a draft version of this paper.

15. See Abreu (2000).

16. Writing on Russia, Fareed Zakaria (1999), for instance, asserts that although Russia bears most of the blame for its crisis, 'advice given by thousands of advisers with billions of dollars and accompanying aid, has proved incomplete, ineffective or counterproductive, depending on whose analysis you accept'. Although the Russian case is extreme, in Latin America the role of advisors was not essentially different.

17. Paul Krugman, for instance, belongs to the American elite, but cannot be mixed up with the ideas confidence builders in Latin America take for granted. Writing about the 1997–98 emerging countries' financial crisis, Krugman (1998) gave to his article the title 'confidence game'. It is precisely the same thing that I have been calling 'confidence building' for some years. He first criticizes the economic policies offered by multilateral organizations and financial institutions – policies that contradict good and simple eco-

nomic theory. And then he concludes: 'During the past four years, seven countries – Mexico, Argentina, Thailand, South Korea, Indonesia, Malaysia, and Hong Kong – have experienced severe economic recessions, worse than anything the United States has seen since the '30s, essentially because playing the confidence game forced them into macroeconomic policies that exacerbated slumps instead of relieving them. It now looks extremely likely that Brazil will be forced down the same route and that much of the rest of Latin America will follow. This is a truly dismal, even tragic, record'.

18. An excessively large required majority is, for instance, that required in Brazil to reform the constitution: three-fifths.

# REFERENCES

Abreu, Marcelo de Paiva (2000), 'Foreign Debt Policies in South America, 1929–1945', *Brazilian Journal of Political Economy*, 20(2), April, 63–75.

Bohman, James (1998) 'The coming of age of deliberative democracy', *The Journal of Political Philosophy*, 6(4), December, 400–425.

Bresser-Pereira, Luiz Carlos (1993) 'Economic reforms and economic growth: efficiency and politics in Latin America,' in Luiz Carlos Bresser–Pereira, José Maria Maravall and Adam Przeworski (eds), *Economic Reforms in New Democracies*, Cambridge: Cambridge University Press, 15–76.

Bresser-Pereira, Luiz Carlos (1996), *Economic Crisis and State Reform in Brazil*, Boulder, CO: Lynne Rienner Publishers.

Bresser-Pereira, Luiz Carlos (1997), 'As três formas de desvalorização cambial', *Revista de Economia Política*, 17(1), January, 143–6.

Bresser-Pereira, Luiz Carlos (2001), 'Reflections on changing institutions in a democratic state', in Ben Ross Schneider and Blanca Heredia (eds), *Reinventing Leviathan*, Miami: North-South Center Press.

Cairncross, Alec (1996), *Economic Ideas and Economic Policy*, London: Routledge.

Canitrot, Adolfo (1975), 'La experiencia populista de redistribución de Ingresso', Buenos Aires: *Desarrollo Económico*, 15, October, 331–351.

Cohen, Joshua (1989), 'Deliberation and democratic legitimacy', in James Bohman and William Rehg (eds), *Essays on Reason and Politics: Deliberative Democracy*, Cambridge, MA: MIT Press (paper originally published in 1989).

Emmot, Bill (1999), 'Freedom's journey – a survey of the 20th century', *The Economist*, 11 September.

Feldstein, Martin (1995), 'Global capital flows: too little, not too much', *The Economist*, 30 June.

Gwartney, James and Robert Lawnson (1999), *Economic Freedom of the World 1998/1999 – Interim Report*, Washington: Free the World and the Fraser Institute.

Krugman, Paul (1998), 'The confidence game', *New Republic*, September.

Melo, Marcus André (2001), 'When institutions matter: the politics of administrative, social security, and tax reform in Brazil', Recife: Universidade Federal de Pernambuco. Also published in Ben Ross Schneider and Blanca Heredia (eds), *Reinventing Leviathan*, Miami, North-South Center Press.

Przeworski, Adam (1998), 'Deliberation and ideological domination', in Jon Elster (ed.), *Deliberative Democracy*, Cambridge: Cambridge University Press.

Rodrik, Dani (1999), *The New Global Economy and Developing Countries: Making Openness Work*, Washington: Overseas Development Council, and Baltimore, MD: Johns Hopkins University Press.

Sachs, Jeffrey D. (1989), 'Social conflict and populist policies in Latin America', in R. Brunetta and C. Dell-Arringa (eds), *Labor Relations and Economic Performance*, London: Macmillan Press.
Whitehead, Laurence (1997), 'Economics in Mexico: the power of ideas, and the ideas of power', Oxford: Nuffield College, Oxford University, copy.
Zakaria, Fareed (1999), 'The effort to fix Russia was botched', *Herald Tribune*, 21 September.

# 2. Neomonetarist dreams and realities: a review of the Brazilian experience

**Alfredo Saad-Filho and Lecio Morais***

This chapter reviews the performance and changing structure of the Brazilian economy during the 1990s. This was a remarkable decade, partly because of the economy's dismal growth rates,[1] and partly because of the changes in the system of accumulation.[2] The most important change was the abandonment of import-substituting industrialization for a new system of accumulation, based on the microeconomic integration of Brazilian industry and finance into transnational capital. There were two main reasons for this change. First, in the late 1980s most analysts argued that Brazilian import-substituting industrialization faced three insuperable problems: the fiscal crisis of the state; the perceived inefficiency of the manufacturing, service and financial sectors; and the continuing difficulty of creating a dynamic national system of innovation. As a result, economic growth rates tended to decline, and inflation to accelerate, until the accumulation process was largely blocked after the 1982 international debt crisis.[3]

Second, in the early 1990s a new consensus gradually emerged across the Brazilian elite. It was argued that the neomonetarist economic policies associated with the Washington Consensus and the predominance of finance over industrial interests provided the best, or even the only, prospect of long-term economic growth. This strategic shift was validated by strong pressure from the Washington institutions and foreign and Brazilian transnational capital, and by the seemingly outstanding economic performance of Argentina, Mexico, South Korea and other countries.

This policy shift was contingent upon substantial inflows of foreign goods, services and finance. In the early 1990s, this was achieved relatively easily because of the exceptional liquidity and low interest rates prevailing in the international financial markets. In spite of significant successes, among them the elimination of high inflation, rapid manufacturing productivity growth and (by certain criteria) large fiscal surpluses, the neomonetarist experiment has, so far, failed to deliver rapid and sustained growth, and it has destabilized the productive system and the balance of payments.

The liberalization of the trade and capital accounts implies that the new system of accumulation is highly vulnerable to fluctuations in international liquidity and in the cost of foreign finance. This vulnerability is the main reason for the increase in the average real (overnight) interest rate in Brazil from 12 percent per annum between June 1990 and December 1991 (when the degree of liberalization was small) to 23 percent between January 1992 and May 1994 (before the real stabilization plan), and 24 per cent between July 1994 and December 1998 (during the real plan). High interest rates are among the most important causes of the dismal performance of the economy, and of the central government's fiscal disequilibrium.[4] In sum, international financial turbulence has shown that the neomonetarist policies have increased the vulnerability of the Brazilian economy to fluctuations in the international liquidity and cost of foreign finance, making the costs of transition to the new system of accumulation much higher than had been anticipated. This was demonstrated dramatically by the impact of the financial crises in Mexico, East Asia and Russia, which culminated, in Brazil, in the currency crisis of January 1999.

This chapter reviews the nature, impact and costs of neomonetarism in Brazil in its seven sections. The first reviews theoretically the underpinnings of neomonetarism and the limitations of this economic policy. The second analyzes the neomonetarist policy shift in Brazil in the early 1990s. The third argues that neomonetarism increased the external vulnerability of the Brazilian economy, and that external events played an important role in the growing fragility of this system of accumulation. The fourth explains the changes in the mode of competition, in the wake of the neomonetarist experience. The fifth analyzes the fiscal, financial and monetary impact of neomonetarism. The sixth reviews the causes and consequences of the currency crisis of January 1999. Finally, the seventh critically analyzes the policies being implemented after the currency devaluation. The conclusion summarizes the most important issues discussed in this chapter.

## GLOBAL NEOMONETARISM

Arestis and Sawyer (1998) have identified the essential features of the neomonetarist economic policies. They have much in common with those policies inspired by the Washington Consensus, and they can be analyzed at two distinct levels. At the microeconomic level, neomonetarism presumes that in a decentralized and deregulated economy free competition leads unproblematically to full employment equilibrium (the implications of second-best analysis are invariably ignored). It naturally follows, first, that the (financial) markets, rather than the state, should address such economic problems as the pattern of international specialization, industrial competitivity, employment generation and, more generally, the sources of long-term welfare gains for the majority. Second, 'vertical' (that is, sector-specific) industrial policies should be avoided, because they systematically shift the relative prices and the allocation of resources in ways which may not be agreeable to the (financial) markets.[5]

At the macroeconomic level, neomonetarism is pragmatically based upon the purported advance of 'globalization', which is usually defined superficially and imprecisely as if it were an uncomplicated, relentless and unavoidable process (for a critique, see Radice 1998, 1999 and Rodrik 1998). It is argued that globalization increases the liquidity of transnational productive and financial capital, and their responsiveness to country-specific policies. This allegedly implies that countries can easily attract large foreign capital inflows, which supplement domestic saving and investment, and bring in new technologies and market access. However, countries can also face unsustainable capital outflows, depending on government policies. Obviously, the capital inflows will be larger, faster and more sustained the closer these policies are to the neomonetarist Identikit, including fiscal balance, trade and capital account liberalization, the deregulation of product and factor markets, and privatization.[6]

The most important neomonetarist policy tool is the interest rate. The 'correct' interest rate allegedly can help to achieve sustainable levels of investment and consumption, balance of payments equilibrium and low inflation simultaneously and, therefore, high growth rates in the long run (Arestis and Sawyer 1998). These policies imply that domestic interest rates are generally higher than they would be under an alternative regime, in which similar objectives may be pursued through a wider range of policy tools. However, relatively high interest rates tend to reduce the levels of employment, investment, output and income relative to what they would be otherwise, in the short and in the long run. More specifically, long-term unemployment tends to increase because capacity tends to become fully utilized, and the balance of payments constraint becomes binding, before unemployment declines substantially. It is usually expected that foreign savings may counteract the depressive impact of high interest rates; however, this presumption remains to be substantiated.[7]

In spite of these limitations, neomonetarist policy reforms *can be sufficient* to deliver short-term macroeconomic stability and growth because they are part of the conventional wisdom of our age and, therefore, they are credible by definition (Arestis and Glickman, forthcoming). Moreover, if international liquidity is high and international interest rates are low, as was the case in the early 1990s, trade and capital account liberalization seem to abolish the balance of payments constraint. They can attract capital inflows sufficient to finance a large trade deficit, which allows consumption, investment and growth rates to increase rapidly, in a virtuous circle that can last several years.

## THE POLICY SHIFT

The attraction of real and financial resources from the rest of the world was one of the most important objectives of the neomonetarist reforms in Brazil. In 1988 the domestic financial system was reformed and, from 1989, international capital flows were liberalized substantially (Studart 1999b). In the early 1990s the exchange rate regime became increasingly flexible (Banco Central do Brasil 1993), while import restrictions were gradually lifted. From late 1991, successive governments adopted strongly contractionary monetary policies in order to control demand and inflation, generate exportable surpluses and attract foreign capital. Finally, a thoroughly neomonetarist economic program was implemented from the mid-1990s through the real stabilization plan.

The neomonetarist policy shift was associated with a substantial change in the economic role of the Brazilian state. Sectoral development policies were abandoned, and the state guided the 'liberalization' and 'deregulation' of the economy. Federal agencies such as the National Bank for Economic and Social Development (BNDES), the central bank and the Treasury organized, promoted and financed the privatization of the largest state enterprises, and assisted the Brazilian and transnational firms interested in bidding for them. It was expected that the integration between domestic and foreign capital at the microeconomic level, through partnerships and mergers and acquisitions, and increasing the supply of foreign finance for domestic investment, would have a range of positive implications, especially transfers of foreign savings and technology, higher levels of investment and productivity growth, and greater macroeconomic stability. More generally, they would ensure Brazil's development in harmony with the 'global economy' (see 'Money, credit and finance', below).[8]

These policies were partly successful. In 1992–93, in spite of domestic political instability and high inflation, foreign capital inflows were restored, the availability of imported goods improved the possibilities of consumption, and the economy began to grow more strongly (see Table 2.1).

In order to assess the impact of the neomonetarist policy shift, let us define the real and financial resource transfers and the monetary impact of the foreign sector.

*Real resource transfers* (RT) are equal to the visible and invisible trade balance (net exports of goods and non-factor services). If $RT>0$, the

*Table 2.1   Brazil: Gross Domestic Product, 1990–99*

|      | US$ million | Real Growth Rate (%) |
|------|-------------|----------------------|
| 1990 | 445 918.5   | −4.35                |
| 1991 | 386 184.0   | 0.34                 |
| 1992 | 374 324.0   | −0.82                |
| 1993 | 430 266.0   | 4.92                 |
| 1994 | 561 305.0   | 5.85                 |
| 1995 | 704 142.0   | 4.22                 |
| 1996 | 774 791.0   | 2.76                 |
| 1997 | 807 215.0   | 3.68                 |
| 1998 | 786 956.0   | −0.12                |
| 1999 | 529 165.0   | 0.82                 |

*Sources:*   IBGE and *Bulletin of the Central Bank of Brazil.*

country transfers real resources (iron ore, steel, orange juice, soya beans) to the rest of the world. These transfers are associated with foreign currency inflows. These inflows can be accumulated in the country's foreign reserves, or spent through the transfer of financial resources to the rest of the world (such as debt service payments or profit remittances). Alternatively, if the country is a net importer of goods and services, its residents receive real resource transfers from abroad (machines, crude oil, automobiles, freight and tourism in exotic locations), and RT<0. In this case, balance of payments equilibrium requires the simultaneous transfer of financial resources from the rest of the world (for example, foreign investment or loans) to provide the hard currency required to cover the outflows.

*Financial resource transfers* (FT) include unilateral financial flows (UF) and foreign debt flows (FD). UF includes the net flows of foreign direct and portfolio investment, profit and dividend remittances, payment for other factor services, unilateral transfers, and the errors and omissions in the balance of payments. FD includes new loan disbursements and debt service payments (interest and amortization) by the private sector and the central government.

If the private sector must surrender its hard currency to the central bank, private foreign transactions affect the primary liabilities of the central government (monetary base plus domestic public debt). Foreign currency inflows expand the monetary base or, if sterilized, domestic public debt; alternatively, currency outflows reduce the primary liabilities. However, it is different with central government currency transactions. If the central government borrows money abroad or issues sovereign bonds in order to finance its own foreign liabilities, increase foreign reserves or set market standards (or if it repays debt), the primary liabilities remain unaffected; only the stock of reserves changes. In contrast, if a central government agency borrows abroad in order to finance domestic investment or current expenditures, the currency inflow affects the stock of primary liabilities through an increase in the fiscal deficit (the repayment of the loan reduces the fiscal deficit). In what follows, the *monetary impact of the foreign sector* is determined by the domestic currency value of the foreign transactions of the private sector (defined in footnote 4).

These concepts allow the impact of neomonetarism to be evaluated more precisely (Table 2.2). In 1990–91, Brazil made real resource transfers to the rest of the world worth US$15.7 billion. The corresponding currency inflow was used to finance foreign debt net repayments of US$14.4 billion and unilateral financial outflows of US$1.1 billion. The Brazilian balance of payments changed sharply in the following period. Between the liberalization of the capital account, in 1992, and the first half of 1994 (before the real plan), the transfer of real resources to the rest of the world reached US$27.7 billion. New loans and rescheduling improved the foreign debt flows to US$2.6 billion, while the unilateral financial inflows increased sharply, to US$11.4 billion (especially because of foreign investment inflows of US$15.6 billion). As a result, the balance of payments surplus reached US$41.6 billion, and foreign reserves increased from US$9.4 billion to US$42.9 billion. The monetary impact of the foreign sector was strongly expansionary, at US$41.4 billion.

In spite of these achievements, inflation rates increased slowly but relentlessly (Figure 2.1). Inflation control became essential for the political legitimacy and economic viability of the neomonetarist accumulation strategy.

High inflation was eliminated through the real plan.[9] This plan synthesized monetarist views, in which public deficits cause inflation through monetary expansion, with a neostructuralist approach, which emphasizes the role of indexation in the perpetuation of inflation. In this case, contractionary policies are necessary but insufficient to reduce inflation; de-indexation coordinated by the state is also essential (Saad-Filho and Mollo, forthcoming).

The real plan included three main elements; fiscal reforms, the elimination of indexation and the introduction of a new currency, the real. Stabilization was supplemented by trade liberalization, the overvaluation of the real and a range of other neomonetarist policies (see next section). These policies were initially highly successful. Inflation rates declined rapidly, aggregate demand expanded, and the country seemed to be poised for an extended period of growth based on foreign investment and rising labor productivity.

*Table 2.2   Brazil: Balance of payments, selected variables, 1990–99 ( US$ million )*

| | Real Resource Transfers (a) | Financial Resource Transfers | | | Balance of Payments (e = a + d) | Monetary Impact of the Foreign Sector (f) | Notes |
|---|---|---|---|---|---|---|---|
| | | Foreign Debt Flows (b) | Unilateral Flows (c) | Total (d = b + c) | | | |
| 1990.I–1991.IV | 15 672.7 | −14 388.5 | −1 136.1 | −15 524.6 | 148.1 | −4 873.2* | (1) |
| 1992.I–1994.II | 27 654.5 | 2 566.8 | 11 411.0 | 13 977.8 | 41 632.3 | 41 365.3 | (2) |
| 1994.III–1995.I | −2 310.1 | −3 710.0 | −2 941.7 | −6 651.7 | −8 961.8 | −6 504.9 | (3) |
| 1995.II–1998.II | −39 181.9 | 32 307.7 | 45 513.1 | 77 820.8 | 38 638.9 | 49 110.7 | (4) |
| 1998.III–1999.I | −10 829.5 | −43 517.0 | 7 846.7 | −35 670.3 | −46 499.9 | −45 629.3 | (5) |
| 1999.II–1999.IV | −4 371.6 | −18 109.7 | 19 997.0 | 1 887.3 | −2 484.3 | n.a. | (6) |

*Notes:*
(1) Relatively closed trade and capital accounts.
(2) Relatively closed trade; relatively open capital account.
(3) Mexican crisis; overvalued currency.
(4) Relatively open trade and capital accounts; overvalued currency.
(5) Russian crisis; overvalued currency.
(6) Relatively open trade and capital accounts, currency devaluation.
a   Trade surplus (goods and services).
b   New loans minus interest payments and amortization.
c   Net inflows of foreign direct and portfolio investment, profit and dividend remittances, other factor services, unilateral transfers and errors
     and omissions in the balance of payments.
*   1991.
(f)  see text

*Source:*   Calculated from *Bulletin of the Central Bank of Brazil.*

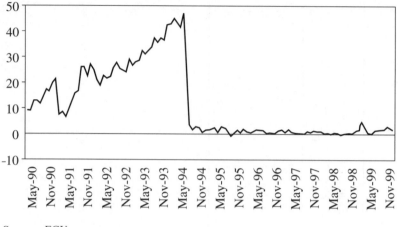

*Source:*   FGV.

*Figure 2.1     Brazil:  Monthly inflation rate, May 1990 – December 1999 (%)*

## INTERNATIONAL TURBULENCE AND BRAZILIAN VULNERABILITY

In spite of these successes, the neomonetarist policy mix was potentially unstable because of five related problems.

First, capital flows to Third World countries are usually more responsive to circumstances in First World financial markets than to recipient country macroeconomic policies (Bird 1996; Calvo et al. 1996). Consequently, trade and capital account liberalization increase the economy's vulnerability to fluctuations in international liquidity and the cost of finance, because the the economy becomes structurally more dependent upon capital flows (see 'Currency crisis', below, Chang 1999 and Palma 1998).

Second, financial and capital account liberalization are destabilizing because they necessarily raise domestic interest rates and increase financial fragility (Brazilian real interest rates increased sharply after the liberalization of the capital account in 1992; see Figure 2.2 and 'Money, credit and finance' below). The financial fragility, and the costs associated with the high interest rates, especially the growing cost of servicing the domestic public debt, can be alleviated, but not entirely eliminated, by improvements in financial supervision and regulation (Arestis and Demetriades 1999; Arestis and Glickman, forthcoming).

Third, foreign capital inflows tend to overvalue the exchange rate. Currency revaluation has often been justified because it stimulates produc-

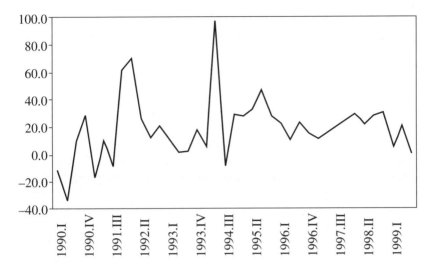

*Note:* Annualized quarterly Selie (overnight) rates, deflated by the IGP-DI.

*Source:* Central Bank of Brazil.

*Figure 2.2    Brazil: Real interest rates, 1990–99 (%)*

tivity growth, stabilizes the country's foreign reserves and reduces the monetary impact of the foreign sector without restrictions on capital flows. However, currency overvaluation increases the need for high interest rates, partly to sterilize the capital inflows and partly to finance the trade deficit, which has a cumulative impact on the government deficit and the financial fragility of the private sector (see below).

Fourth, high interest rates stimulate the accumulation of foreign debt and create scope for arbitrage through foreign borrowing for investment in domestic financial assets, especially government securities (see 'Money, credit and finance' below).

Fifth, the stabilization program included a policy mix based on capital account liberalization, sterilized intervention and exchange rate overvaluation. However, it is well known that these policies prevent the interest rate differential from narrowing, and stimulate short-term capital flows with the negative consequences outlined above (Calvo et al. 1996; Palma 1998).

Let us now review the implementation of these policies in Brazil, in the aftermath of the real plan. It was shown above that the liberalization of the capital account attracted large unilateral financial flows to Brazil, leading to the rapid accumulation of foreign currency reserves. In the first half of 1994, high international liquidity and high domestic interest rates contributed to a sharp increase in foreign capital inflows, leading to financial transfers to Brazil worth US$11.8 billion. These currency inflows and the government's implicit support for the revaluation of the real were largely responsible for the appreciation of the currency. On a trade-weighted basis, the Brazilian currency rose 16 percent in the second half of 1994 and, between July and October, the dollar fell from R$1 to only R$0.82.[10]

By mid-1994, it seemed that these capital inflows were sufficient to finance the country's foreign commitments, even without real resource transfers to the rest of the world. Moreover, trade liberalization had become politically very important, for three main reasons. First, it would reduce the market power of the oligopolies and the labor unions and increase the supply of consumer and investment goods, which should increase economic efficiency and help to reduce inflation. Second, it would force domestic industry to invest in new technologies, leading to growth and more employment opportunities. Third, it would reduce the trade surplus and, therefore, the monetary impact of the foreign sector, which would help to curb the growth of the domestic public debt and reduce the government's interest payments. In sum, as long as domestic policies were 'credible', cheap foreign savings would finance rapid and sustained capital accumulation.

Partly in the belief that foreign capital inflows provided a shortcut in the road to development, and partly out of conviction that the financial markets should play a more prominent role in resource allocation, the government abandoned its gradualist strategy in the second half of 1994. Most export incentives were eliminated, imports were liberalized further, and the authorities condoned the overvaluation of the real, in order to eliminate Brazil's trade surplus:

> [T]he logic of the exchange rate policy is to reduce exports, increase imports and the current account deficit and, therefore, make the country import capital again. This capital and the domestic savings accumulated by the private sector will finance economic growth (Pedro Malan, Minister of Finance, *Gazeta Mercantil*, 24 October 1994).

These policies were highly successful. The real resource transfers to the rest of the world shifted rapidly, from US$8.3 billion (that is, a trade surplus) in the first three quarters of 1994, to minus US$9.1 billion (that is a trade deficit) in the next three quarters. Unfortunately for the Brazilian government, international liquidity dried up in mid-1994. Between May and December, the US Federal Reserve raised the discount rate six times, from 3 percent to 4.75 percent. These interest rate changes helped to shift the international capital flows back into developed country financial markets. This made it difficult for the so-called 'emerging' economies to finance their growing current account deficits. Toward the end of the year, the foreign reserves of several countries were declining rapidly. The crisis hit Mexico particularly hard, in the last days of 1994. Brazil was also severely affected, and the country lost reserves worth US$9.7 billion between the third quarter of 1994 and the first quarter of 1995. (For an overview of the impact of the crisis, see Table 2.2, row 3). Similar capital flow reversals also occurred after the Asian crisis, in 1997, and the Russian crisis, in 1998 (see below). After each of these crises, the international financial markets would temporarily shun the 'emerging' economies. These recurrent shifts in international capital flows badly destabilized the neomonetarist accumulation strategy in Brazil.

In spite of the crisis (and, to a certain extent, because of market volatility), the Brazilian government decided to support the overvalued currency through higher interest rates, which should reduce the capital outflows and lower import demand,[11] and the further privatization of state-owned enterprises, often with incentives for foreign bids in order to attract investment. The exchange rate regime finally shifted in March 1995, when sliding bands were introduced, initially with the dollar at R$0.86–0.90. The government intended to devalue the real by half a percentage point in excess of domestic inflation every month, in order to increase export competitiveness and reduce the current account deficit incrementally. In addition, restrictions were imposed on consumer goods imports, while export incentives were partly restored:

At the beginning of the year [1995] the *policy of maintaining trade balance deficits was reevaluated*, in light of the uncertainty in foreign financial markets. Consequently, the government sought to define a strategy aimed at balancing trade flows. Initially, special attention was given to the export sector, so as to increase revenues through added foreign sales. Later on, steps were taken to regulate imports in sectors less detrimental to the process of price stabilization and industrial modernization. However, on several occasions, the priority accorded [to] the fight against inflation made it necessary to facilitate imports in order to offset supply deficiencies on the domestic market (Banco Central do Brasil 1995: 103, our emphasis, original in English).

These measures improved the trade balance, but they did not eliminate the real resource transfers to Brazil. Even more seriously, the government was unable to devise a viable strategy to finance the balance of payments in the long term, especially if international liquidity fluctuated sharply. In spite of the underlying vulnerability of Brazil's balance of payments, the restoration of international liquidity in 1995 seemed to support the government's claims. The financial resource transfers reached US$25 billion in the last three quarters of 1995, and Brazil's international reserves climbed by US$18.1 billion to US$51.8 billion (see Table 2.2, rows 3 and 4). The high domestic interest rates increased the opportunities for speculative gain in the open market, especially in the light of the industrial slowdown. Eventually, these high interest rates destabilized central government finances and the balance sheets of the banking system and the local governments, leading to a severe fiscal and financial crisis (see 'Money, credit and finance', below).

## THE NEW MODE OF COMPETITION

The neomonetarist policies introduced a new mode of competition into the economy, based on the microeconomic integration of production and finance into transnational value chains. It was expected that intense competition would lead to partnerships and mergers and acquisitions or to the collapse of presumably inefficient firms, thus raising average productivity across the economy.[12]

Neomonetarism had a mixed impact on the Brazilian manufacturing base, in spite of the high levels of investment. First, the share of imported manufactured goods increased sharply (Table 2.3). Second, the participation of foreign firms in the mergers and acquisitions in Brazil, and foreign purchases of minority stakes in domestic companies, increased significantly. (For an illustration, see Table 2.4 and Gonçalves 1999a: 138–42.)

*Table 2.3    Brazilian manufacturing industry, import coefficients, 1993 and 1996 (%)*

| Sector | 1993 | 1996 |
|---|---|---|
| 1.  Standardized capital goods and electronic goods | 29 | 65–75 |
| 2.  Chemical inputs, fertilizers, resins | 20–26 | 33–42 |
| 3.  Auto parts, natural textiles, capital goods made to order, rubber | 8–15 | 20–25 |
| 4.  Pharmaceuticals, tractors, electric and electronic consumer goods, glass, chemical goods | 7–11 | 13–16 |
| 5.  Synthetic textiles, petrochemical inputs, cars, food, paper and cardboard | 3–6 | 9–12 |
| 6.  Beverages, shoes, plastics, dairy products, semi-processed foods | 0.7–3 | 4–8 |
| 7.  Non-tradable goods | 0.5–2.5 | 1–4 |

*Source:*    Coutinho, Baltar & Camargo (1999: 70).

*Table 2.4    Brazil: Foreign participation in mergers and acquisitions and purchases of minority stakes in domestic companies, 1990–99*

|      | Number of Operations | Foreign Participation | %    |
| ---- | -------------------- | --------------------- | ---- |
| 1990 | 186                  | 56                    | 30.1 |
| 1991 | 184                  | 47                    | 25.5 |
| 1992 | 252                  | 83                    | 32.9 |
| 1993 | 260                  | 89                    | 34.2 |
| 1994 | 249                  | 100                   | 40.2 |
| 1995 | 322                  | 132                   | 41.0 |
| 1996 | 394                  | 188                   | 47.7 |
| 1997 | 458                  | 251                   | 54.8 |
| 1998 | 480                  | 321                   | 66.9 |
| 1999 | 491                  | 341                   | 69.5 |

*Source:*    PriceWaterhouse Coopers, Folha de S. Paulo, 21 January 2000: 2–1.

The sectors most affected by this wave of transnational integration were those manufacturing electric and electronic goods, telecommunications equipment, car parts and processed foods. In these and in other sectors, large domestic firms were absorbed by transnational conglomerates, for example, Metal Leve, Lacta, Cofap, Freios Varga, Arno, Refripar, Renner, Agroceres and the banks Nacional, Garantia, Bamerindus, Real and Banespa.

Growing foreign participation contributed to the search for efficiency gains, especially in the manufacturing industry. The new mode of competition influenced this process at several levels. First, it led to a shift in management techniques toward 'modern' methods and the downsizing of the workforce. Second, manufacturing unemployment increased sharply because of the introduction of new labor-saving technologies. Third, firms tended to shift their output mix toward simpler products with less value-added locally, in order to reap efficiency gains. As a result, manufacturing productivity increased, on average, by 7.6 percent annually between 1990 and 1997 (Feijó and Carvalho 1998).

The spatial impact of this process was uneven, with traditional manufacturing areas losing out, especially the São Paulo metropolitan area, while greenfield sites in the south and northeast of the country tended to gain. In 1995, 180,000 manufacturing jobs were lost in Greater São Paulo (Lacerda 1996: 19). In the country as a whole, one million (net) manufacturing jobs were lost between 1989 and 1997, reducing manufacturing employment by

30 percent (Bonelli 1999: 89). Finally, the open unemployment rate in Brazil increased from 3.9 percent in December 1990 to 8.6 percent in June 1998, according to the government's statistical service, IBGE.[13] Coutinho, Baltar and Camargo (1999: 66, 73) rightly conclude that:

> [the] avoidance of industrial development policies by the State . . . strongly contributed to the increasing exposure of domestic industry to imports, especially in high value added sectors and those with high technological content . . . [T]he explosion of imports rapidly 'hollowed out' the productive chains, and led to a large reduction in intra-industry demand . . . which sharply reduced the economy's capacity to create jobs . . . [T]he frantic attempts to cut costs have led to successive rounds of innovation and rationalisation in the productive process, that generated strong tensions in the labour market . . . [This is partly due to the] entry of new competitors and the redefinition of strategic alliances [that] have destabilized the oligopolistic structures inherited from previous decades . . . The 'modernisation' of [these] oligopolistic structures has ruptured the existing supply chains, led to the entry of new [foreign] suppliers, reduced the degree of verticalisation and increased the import coefficients . . . [The] higher coefficient of imported inputs and components (and, therefore, the substantially lower value creation in the country), means that the success of efforts to stimulate domestic demand for intermediate goods and employment will tend . . . to be very modest.

The investment projects currently being implemented by domestic and foreign companies generally reproduce these features, and they tend to have low export propensity:

> [The] large majority of [domestic] investment projects was driven by the strong growth of the domestic market [in 1994–95], and they had a very small export component. With respect to foreign investment, it has been shown that the Brazilian market is also the main target of current foreign direct investment projects (Coutinho, Baltar and Camargo 1999: 72; see also Laplane and Sarti 1999: 237, 263).[14]

## MONEY, CREDIT AND FINANCE

The neomonetarist policies pursued by the Brazilian government had a strong fiscal and financial impact, at three levels.

First, high interest rates, the revenue transfers from local to central government associated with the real plan, and the faltering tax revenues due to the economic stagnation following the Mexican crisis, had a strong impact on local government finances, with implications for the central government. Between the Mexican crisis and the end of 1996, local government domestic debt increased from US$28.6 billion to US$48.1 billion, even though their primary deficit was only US$5.2 billion. The impending devaluation of the capital represented by local government bills persuaded the central government to swap its own securities for these bills. This asset swap reached US$84 billion by September 1999.

Second, the financial sector was badly weakened by the real plan, especially because of the elimination of annual inflation transfers equivalent to 2.5 percent of GDP (Cysne 1994). In addition to this, several small and medium-sized institutions suffered severe problems in 1995, partly because of the lack of international liquidity, and partly because of the rising share of non-performing loans due to the contractionary policies implemented that year. The threat of a severe financial crisis was avoided through extensive central bank intervention, at a cost of approximately US$20 billion, and the restructuring of the domestic banking system.[15] Between 1995 and 1997, the central bank took control, and closed or forced the sale of 72 of the 271 Brazilian banks which existed in July 1994 (Barros and Almeida Jr 1997). Their assets were sold to other institutions, especially foreign banks. Consequently, the Brazilian financial system became substantially more concentrated and internationalized.[16]

Third, the monetary impact of the foreign sector reached US$35.2 billion between the second quarter of 1995 and the end of 1996 (minus US$5.7 billion in 1997). In that period, the monetary base increased by US$4.2 billion (US$11.2 billion in 1997), showing that the domestic public debt absorbed, to a large extent, the monetary impact of the foreign sector, especially in 1995–96. The expansionary effect of the monetary impact of the foreign sector was largely due to the rapid growth of Brazil's foreign debt, which, in turn, responded to the search for cheaper sources of industrial finance abroad and interest rate arbitrage. These pressures were the main factors responsible for the doubling of the foreign debt between 1991 and 1998, when it reached US$243.2 billion.

As a result the domestic public debt started growing strongly in mid-1995 (Carvalho 1999; Morais 1998; Rosar 1999). Throughout the 1990s, the central government attempted to control the growth of the domestic public debt mainly through expenditure cuts, and fiscal surpluses were achieved in every year except 1991 (Table 2.5). In spite of these fiscal surpluses, the debt increased by US$39.4 billion in 1995, US$58.5 billion in 1996, US$59 billion in 1997 and US$40.9 billion in 1998.

The neomonetarist policy of permanently high interest rates subsidized the accumulation of financial capital at the expense of industrial capital and employment creation. This was part of the long-term shift of the allocative, coordinating and industrial policy responsibilities of the federal government to the financial system, which started in the mid-1960s and developed unevenly across the following decades (Studart 1995). However,

*Table 2.5   Brazil: Fiscal balance and domestic public debt (DPD), 1991–98 (US$ million)*

|      | DPD      | % GDP | Fiscal Balance | % GDP | Financial Expenditures |
|------|----------|-------|----------------|-------|------------------------|
| 1991 | 16368.2  | 4.2   | −3596.0        | −0.9  | 19791.2                |
| 1992 | 49169.5  | 13.1  | 4305.8         | 1.2   | 76314.7                |
| 1993 | 63160.5  | 14.7  | 3362.6         | 0.8   | 130244.9               |
| 1994 | 73106.1  | 13.0  | 9504.0         | 1.7   | 123050.1               |
| 1995 | 112536.9 | 15.7  | 4899.3         | 0.7   | 36165.1                |
| 1996 | 170995.6 | 22.1  | 2594.8         | 0.3   | 37564.0                |
| 1997 | 229975.6 | 28.6  | 16849.9        | 2.1   | 44264.9                |
| 1998 | 270921.6 | 34.9  | 10734.1        | 1.4   | 70996.3                |

*Note:*   The fiscal balance is the cash balance of the Treasury and social security system, excluding financial revenues and expenditures. The financial expenditures include the cost of the domestic public debt and the costs of the contractual domestic and external debt of the central government.

*Sources:*   Calculated from *Bulletin of the Central Bank of Brazil* and from unpublished data from the Office of the National Treasury (details available from the authors on request).

Brazilian financial markets are mostly shallow and fragile, and they have been unable to carry out these tasks without government assistance.

The limitations imposed on the neomonetarist accumulation strategy by the Mexican crisis had three important macroeconomic effects. First, the rapid growth of the domestic public debt increased the central government's financial expenditures, especially interest payments (Table 2.5). The drainage of productive and money capital and wages by the tax system in order to service the domestic debt is a reflex of the financial priority of the neomonetarist economic policies. These policies tend to concentrate income (Bulmer-Thomas 1994; Cepal 1999; Kane and Morisett 1993), and they reduce the country's long-term growth prospects (Saad-Filho, Morais and Coelho 1999).

Second, the conflict between monetary and fiscal policies became increasingly severe. Permanently contractionary monetary policies tended to relax the fiscal policy stance, because they increased the costs of the domestic public debt and, at a further remove, the stock of debt. In order to induce the financial markets to hold the growing stock of securities, the Treasury and the central bank issued dollar-indexed bills. They also sanctioned an increase in the liquidity and a reduction in the maturity structure of these securities (Table 2.6). The growing financial expenditures of the

*Table 2.6   Brazil: Indexation and maturity of central government securities, 1991–99*

| | Indexation of Securities (%) | | | | | | Average Maturity (months) |
|---|---|---|---|---|---|---|---|
| | Index-linked Securities | | | | Fixed Interest Securities | Total | |
| | Daily rate[a] | Exchange Rate | Prices[b] | Other[c] | | | |
| 1991.IV | 67.20 | 11.47 | 5.27 | – | 16.06 | 100.00 | n.a. |
| 1992.IV | 9.00 | 3.00 | 23.60 | 9.60 | 54.80 | 100.00 | n.a. |
| 1993.IV | 3.80 | 17.26 | 42.05 | 10.47 | 26.42 | 100.00 | n.a. |
| 1994.I | 2.50 | 22.83 | 27.82 | 13.88 | 32.97 | 100.00 | n.a. |
| 1994.II | 50.30 | 9.24 | 28.03 | 12.42 | 0.00 | 100.00 | n.a. |
| 1994.III | 27.50 | 6.09 | 22.31 | 13.69 | 30.42 | 100.00 | n.a. |
| 1994.IV | 16.00 | 8.30 | 12.53 | 22.96 | 40.20 | 100.00 | n.a. |
| 1995.I | 24.44 | 9.23 | 11.99 | 17.58 | 36.75 | 100.00 | n.a. |
| 1995.II | 24.38 | 9.24 | 11.55 | 27.79 | 27.03 | 100.00 | n.a. |
| 1995.III | 40.61 | 5.93 | 8.80 | 12.17 | 32.48 | 100.00 | n.a. |
| 1995.IV | 37.77 | 5.29 | 5.26 | 8.98 | 42.70 | 100.00 | n.a. |
| 1996.I | 26.08 | 7.94 | 2.92 | 11.79 | 51.27 | 100.00 | n.a. |
| 1996.II | 18.86 | 8.04 | 2.34 | 10.80 | 59.94 | 100.00 | n.a. |
| 1996.III | 17.86 | 7.85 | 1.95 | 9.97 | 62.37 | 100.00 | n.a. |
| 1996.IV | 18.61 | 9.38 | 1.75 | 9.26 | 61.00 | 100.00 | n.a. |
| 1997.I | 19.13 | 12.47 | 1.54 | 8.88 | 57.98 | 100.00 | n.a. |
| 1997.II | 19.39 | 9.28 | 2.33 | 8.95 | 60.05 | 100.00 | n.a. |
| 1997.III | 18.82 | 9.72 | 0.97 | 12.11 | 58.38 | 100.00 | 5.82 |
| 1997.IV | 34.78 | 15.36 | 0.34 | 8.61 | 40.91 | 100.00 | 6.48 |
| 1998.I | 27.78 | 15.13 | 0.32 | 6.10 | 50.68 | 100.00 | 4.69 |
| 1998.II | 42.73 | 16.49 | 0.41 | 5.23 | 35.13 | 100.00 | 4.49 |
| 1998.III | 65.70 | 21.38 | 0.61 | 5.27 | 7.05 | 100.00 | 3.84 |
| 1998.IV | 69.05 | 21.00 | 0.36 | 6.07 | 3.51 | 100.00 | 3.73 |
| 1999.I | 68.19 | 25.48 | 0.23 | 4.88 | 1.22 | 100.00 | 4.53 |
| 1999.II | 64.01 | 23.98 | 0.22 | 3.65 | 8.14 | 100.00 | 3.38 |
| 1999.III | 59.50 | 26.28 | 0.28 | 3.16 | 10.78 | 100.00 | 3.31 |

*Notes:*
a   Overnight (Selic).
b   Price indices: IGP-DI and IGP-M.
c   TR, TBF, TJLP.

*Sources:   Bulletin of the Central Bank of Brazil* and central bank press releases.

central government and the increasing liquidity of the domestic public debt induced the government to engage in frequent rounds of fiscal and monetary policy contraction, in a vicious circle that gradually increased its own financial fragility. The solution to this conflict requires a constant increase in the fiscal surplus (which is politically impossible), privatizations (which are limited by the availability of assets) or, more realistically, lower interest rates (which is limited by the balance of payments constraint, see the following two sections).

Third, the discrepancy between domestic and international interest rates was one of the main reasons why the central government's primary liabilities increased much more rapidly than the foreign reserves. The stock of reserves increased by 120.1 percent between 1994 and mid-1998, from US$32.2 billion to US$70.9 billion. In the same period, the primary liabilities increased by 317.2 percent, from US$69.8 billion to US$291.2 billion. The decline in the foreign reserve cover, from 46.1 percent to only 24.2 percent of the primary liabilities, increased the vulnerability of the real to capital outflows, in spite of the growth in reserves (Garcia 1995; Nogueira Batista 1996). In short, interest rate rises can temporarily stem capital outflows, but they tend to increase the economy's long-term vulnerability to speculative attack. The rapid growth of the domestic public debt was one of the most important consequences of the government's neomonetarist economic strategy. This was a symptom of the inefficacy of conventional fiscal and monetary policies, and it increased the financial fragility of the state and the external vulnerability of the economy.

## CURRENCY CRISIS

The external vulnerability of the Brazilian economy made the real a natural target for speculative attack, especially after the Asian crisis. The Brazilian government was well aware of market perceptions and did its best to postpone the (largely unavoidable) *dénouement*. Its strategy focused on offering investors and currency speculators hedge opportunities through the sale of forward exchange-rate contracts and index-linked securities and, when necessary, exceptionally high interest rates. In other words, the government nationalized the exchange rate risk. Between December 1997 and December 1998, the stock of dollar-linked securities increased from US$35.4 billion (15.4 percent of the domestic public debt) to US$56.9 billion (21 percent). In addition to this, the central bank, operating through Banco do Brasil, sold US$15–20 billion in futures contracts.

The authorities failed to appreciate that their commitment to exchange rate stability and the increasingly generous terms being offered to speculators were counterproductive. After the Russian crisis, the impression that Brazil's exchange rate was unsustainable gained credence. In the light of this perception, the government's exchange rate policy became a Ponzi scheme, which could be aborted only through the collapse of the real. Brazil's international reserves declined from US$70.9 billion in June 1998 to only US$33.8 billion nine months later (see Table 2.2, row 5). This was mainly due to short-term capital outflows and the difficulty of refinancing the foreign debt. (The net foreign debt outflow reached US$43.5 billion in this period.) In these three quarters, the balance of payments deficit reached US$46.5 billion, in spite of domestic interest rates of nearly 50 percent (inflation rates were close to zero throughout this period). In addition to these difficulties, the domestic public debt also developed Ponzi features, in the sense that the maturity of government securities declined sharply, and their cost increased, largely because of financial market perceptions of the risk of central government financial meltdown.

Later in 1998, the Brazilian government negotiated with the IMF and the G7 a financial support scheme involving US$41.3 billion over three years. This agreement includes the conventional policy measures advocated by the Washington Consensus, especially high primary fiscal surpluses (around three percent of GDP since 1999), and the implicit commitment to liberalize the exchange rate and reduce the current account deficit. The central bank was also barred from operating in currency futures. This agreement was very important for the international financial community, because it would signal to the markets that developing country governments would be supported when following the 'correct' economic policies (that is, those currently favored by the US Treasury Department). Domestically, the agreement should prevent the devaluation of the (foreign and domestic) capital invested in Brazil, while preserving its freedom to leave the country.

Toward the end of 1998, the central government's portfolio imbalance was already extremely serious. In spite of a fiscal surplus of US$10.7 billion, the domestic public debt increased by US$41 billion during this year, reaching US$270.9 billion in December (34.9 percent of GDP). The average maturity of federal securities had declined to only 3.3 months, and the country's international reserves had declined by US$40 billion in six months. The sharp decline in foreign reserves, in spite of the interest rate increase to the politically feasible limit of 49.8 percent, demonstrated the failure of neomonetarism both as an accumulation strategy and as a crisis management policy.

In the early days of January 1999, the central bank widened the exchange rate bands of the real, effectively devaluing the currency by 8 percent, from

R$1.21 to R$1.32 per dollar. The currency immediately collapsed, forcing the government to float the real. By the end of January the exchange rate reached R$1.98 per dollar (the real fell 40 percent in 17 days).

The devaluation of the real was very different from the currency crises elsewhere in the 1990s. These crises took most investors by surprise and led to substantial capital losses. In contrast, the collapse of the real was widely anticipated, and it brought substantial financial gains. The currency devaluation increased the net public sector debt by R$43.6 billion between December 1998 and June 1999 (mainly because of its impact on the dollar-linked federal securities; see *Bulletin of the Central Bank of Brazil*, Table IV.13, December 1999). In addition to this, the central bank lost around R$7.8 billion in the futures market, raising the direct cost of the devaluation for the central government to 5.6 percent of GDP. In contrast, several financial institutions reported profits *in January* that were nearly twice as high as their previous *annual* profit.[17] The currency crisis showed that Brazil has a travesty of the welfare state which protects financial capital efficiently, mainly at the expense of wage earners and productive capital.[18]

In March 1999 the central bank introduced a policy of managed fluctuation of the real with inflation targets, in agreement with the IMF (the inflation targets for the first two years, 8 percent in 1999, and 6 percent in 2000, with bilateral margins of two percent, were reached, but in 2001 inflation may exceed the 4 percent target). The fluctuation of the real should help to consolidate the competitive advantage gained through devaluation and increase the scope for interest rate cuts, which are essential in order to stabilize domestic public debt and restore the conditions for stable capital accumulation.

The new exchange rate policy offered investors the opportunity to make a new speculative attack, this time against the dollar. At the end of February 1999 the real was clearly undervalued at R$2.06 per dollar. Interest rates were still around 40 percent, in spite of the imminent disbursement of US$4 billion by the IMF. Moreover, the central bank extended the tax relief on capital gains for foreign investors and reduced the minimum period for investment in Brazil. In March, there was a net capital inflow of US$2.7 billion, mainly for investment in government securities and the stock market. This inflow led to an appreciation of the exchange rate to R$1.72 per dollar, bringing capital gains of up to 20 percent in one month to the speculators.

The success of these speculative maneuvers, first 'for' the real (in 1994–95), then 'against' it (in 1998), then 'for' once again (in 1999), demonstrates the rationale of neomonetarist policies in Brazil. The monetary authority is fundamentally committed to the short-term interests of private financial institutions. Substantial capital losses will be bailed out allegedly in order to avoid systemic risks, while long-term gains are guaranteed by the financial subsidy implicit in the formulation and implementation of monetary policy.

## UNCERTAIN STEPS

The currency devaluation pointed to a slow but sustained recovery based on (foreign) investment and exports. The government, the IMF and their acolytes in Brazil and abroad have hailed these modest achievements as if they were significant triumphs in the face of overwhelming adversity. This praise is not entirely warranted, and not understandable except in the light of the gloomy forecasts made by the IMF, the Brazilian government and most analysts immediately after the devaluation (including ourselves, see Saad-Filho, Morais and Coelho 1999: 14). It was widely believed that Brazilian GDP would contract by 3–5 percent in 1999 and total (open and disguised) unemployment would increase toward 25 percent of the labor force. However, Brazilian GDP actually grew by 0.8 percent in 1999 and 4.5 percent in 2000, while unemployment has stabilized (however, performance has deteriorated considerably in 2001).

Brazil's performance has been very different from that of other crisis-hit countries. This difference can be explained at two levels. First, the Brazilian economy is relatively large, and the influence of the foreign sector is, correspondingly, small (trade flows were equivalent to 17 percent of GDP only in 1998), which reduces the potential impact of a given devaluation relative to more open economies. In addition to this, the Brazilian economy is well integrated and diversified, including developed industrial centers (mostly in São Paulo state), highly productive agribusiness areas (including large swathes of the states of São Paulo and Mato Grosso do Sul, and patches across the south, center and northeast), and relatively poorer areas which provide raw and processed inputs, labor power, markets and financial transfers for the developed centers (especially the northeast, but also parts of Minas Gerais and the south). This network of productive and financial relations is very resilient and, historically, it was developed through a highly dynamic long-term growth process.[19] Its remarkable stability in spite of the poor economic performance of the last two decades has helped to cushion the Brazilian economy against the depressive tendencies associated with the neomonetarist reforms and the currency crisis.

Second, it was shown above that the currency crisis was a cost to the government but a source of considerable gains to the financial sector and, indirectly, to productive capital engaged in currency speculation. The protection of private financial assets and, in many cases, the exceptional profitability of financial investment, provided funds which may have helped to deflect the crisis tendencies unleashed by the devaluation of the real. Moreover, in contrast to the international debt crisis of 1982, the international capital flows to Brazil were not substantially reduced by the devaluation (see Table 2.2, row 6). This helped to support the real at a level of between R$1.70 and R$1.90 per dollar until the third quarter of 2000. (These inflows were, obviously, largely dependent on the stability of the US economy, which could not be taken for granted. In spite of this, most highly volatile financial capital had already left Brazil by early 1999, and small international interest rate changes did not have a strong effect on the stability of the real or the Brazilian balance of payments.)

It is unlikely that the policy of inflation targets had any significant influence on these events. Domestic interest rates were gradually cut since the devaluation, to a minimum of 15.25 percent in early 2001, but this was possible largely because of the favorable international environment and the balance of payments stability. When these conditions ceased to apply, the real began to decline rapidly toward R$2.50–3.00 per dollar, even though domestic interest rates had risen to 19 percent by mid-2001. The Brazilian recovery after the devaluation was limited by the renewed bout of instability in the world economy and the difficulties in Argentina. More generally, the government's achievements since the devaluation of the real could be assessed only when instability threatened the world economy. In the absence of significant challenges, the range of potentially successful policies is too broad to allow discrimination between them.

## CONCLUSION

The Brazilian economy grew very little but changed substantially in the 1990s. The average annual rate of growth of GDP was the lowest in the 20th century, at only 1.7 percent, while total unemployment increased from 8 to 17 percent of the labor force. Manufacturing employment fell by one-third, and productive capacity declined in several important sectors, especially the capital goods industry. Industrial restructuring reduced the economy's employment-generating capacity, and Brazil became more heavily dependent on imports and foreign finance. Consequently, the balance of payments constraint became more severe. The 1990s were, in many ways, worse than the so-called 'lost decade' of the 1980s, largely because of the neomonetarist policy shift implemented with increasing consistency and determination across the decade. This policy shift presumed that high interest rates and trade and capital account liberalization would induce a substantial transfer of real and financial resources to Brazil, and guarantee high growth rates over long periods.

However, experience in Brazil and elsewhere has shown that market reforms provide an inconsistent blueprint for a development strategy. They rely on variables that countries like Brazil influence only marginally, especially the availability and cost of foreign finance. They have shifted the engine of growth toward externally financed consumption and investment in non-traded goods, reducing domestic savings, worsening the balance of payments, and triggering fiscal and currency crises. Consequently, economic stagnation has become more deeply entrenched. Rising unemployment and the deterioration of the distribution of income have neutralized the initial gains made under the real plan (Gonçalves 1999 and Neri and Considera 1996). In sum, the poor macroeconomic performance of the Brazilian economy in the 1990s was due to both internal and external causes. However, growth is increasingly limited by the attempt to impose an accumulation strategy that, until now, has been stable only exceptionally.

## NOTES

\*    We are grateful to Philip Arestis, Maria Amarante Baracho, Nelson Barbosa Filho, Luiz Carlos Bresser-Pereira, Gary Dymski, Ben Fine, Costas Lapavitsas, Julio López Gallardo, Maria de Lourdes Mollo, Tom Palley, Bruno Saraiva, Malcom Sawyer, Marcio Valença and Howard Walker for their helpful comments and suggestions. Special thanks are due to Paul and Louise Davidson. This research project was partly funded by the Nuffield Foundation (SGS/LB/203), and this paper draws upon Saad-Filho and Morais (2000).

1    In 1981–89, the so-called 'lost decade', Brazilian annual average GDP growth was 2.2 percent. In the 1990s, annual average GDP growth was only 1.7 percent.

2    The system of accumulation is determined by the economic structures and institutional arrangements that typify the process of capital accumulation in a specific region, in a certain period of time (Fine and Rustomjee 1996).

3    For a critical review of this period, see Bresser-Pereira (1996), Castro and Souza (1985), Fiori (1992) and Studart (1995).

4    The central government includes the federal government (Treasury), the social security system and the Central Bank of Brazil. The state and municipal governments, state enterprises and federal trusts (except social security) are included in the private sector, because they enjoy financial autonomy and cannot monetize their own debts.

5    For extensive analyses of industrial policies in newly industrializing economies, see Auty (1991), Chang (1994) and Nembhard (1996).

6    These views are severely criticized by Grabel (2000), Kregel (1996) and Palley (2000).

7    For a detailed analysis, see Bird (1996) and Calvo et al. (1993, 1996).

8    '[The] main function of this new flow of [foreign direct] investment [FDI] was to replace consumption as the inducing and supporting mechanism of economic growth and, therefore, to establish a new, stable and lasting, pattern of economic development. In the medium and long term, the FDI flows would allow the displacement of the foreign constraint to growth' (Laplane and Sarti 1999: 198–9); see also Coutinho et al. (1999).

9    Governo do Brasil (1993); see Dornbusch (1997), Nogueira Batista (1996), Saad-Filho and Maldonado Filho (1998), Saad-Filho and Mollo (forthcoming), Saad-Filho, Morais and Coelho (1999) and Sachs and Zini (1996).

10    For estimates of the overvaluation of the real, see Bacha (1997: 201), Dornbusch (1997: 375), Fishlow (1997), Kilsztajn (1996) and Nogueira Batista (1996: 34).

11    These contractionary monetary policies led to a sharp increase in interest rates on per-
      sonal loans to 237 percent in May, while rates on short-term commercial loans reached
      176 percent (Nogueira Batista 1996: 48; see also Dornbusch 1997: 375).
12    'One of the most important aspects of the on-going transformation [of Brazilian
      industry] is related to the deepening of foreign integration in the productive sector which
      is reflected, above all, in the large and increasing flow of foreign direct investment'
      (Laplane and Sarti 1999: 197).
13    The methodology used by IBGE tends to underestimate the level of unemployment.
      According to the union-sponsored research institute, DIEESE, total (open and dis-
      guised) unemployment in São Paulo exceeded 20 percent between April and July 1999,
      and declined afterwards toward 16 percent by late 2000. For an overview of the erosion
      of the formal labor markets under the new system of accumulation, see Pochmann
      (1999).
14    For a detailed analysis of the changes in productivity, structure of employment, labor
      'flexibility' and unemployment growth under the real plan, see CNI/Cepal (1997), Paes
      de Barros et al. (1998) and Ramos and Almeida Reis (1998). For a long-term analysis,
      see Bonelli and Gonçalves (1998) and Urani (1998).
15    See Bacha (1997: 190) and Nogueira Batista (1996: 56).
16    See Gonçalves (1999a: 106, 134), Cardim de Carvalho (1999) and Studart (1999a,
      1999b).
17    Annual bank profit rates in Brazil are usually around 11 percent. In January 1999, several
      banks' profit rates reached 200 to 400 percent. Total bank profits in 1998 were R$1.8
      billion; in the month of January 1999, these profits reached R$3.3 billion (Aloysio
      Biondi, *Folha de S. Paulo*, 6 March 1999, p. 2).
18    George Soros famously declared that the devaluation of the real had a very small impact
      on the international financial system because it had been widely anticipated, and that
      Brazil offered protection mechanisms unavailable to investors elsewhere.
19    For an overview, see Amado (1997), Baer (1995), Studart (1995) and Tavares (1978).

# REFERENCES

Amado, A. (1997), *Disparate Regional Development in Brazil: A Monetary Production Approach*, Aldershot: Ashgate.

Arestis, P. and P. Demetriades (1999), 'Financial liberalization: the experience of developing countries', *Eastern Economic Journal*, 25(4): 441–57.

Arestis, P. and M. Glickman (forthcoming), 'Financial crisis in South East Asia: dispelling illusion the Minskyan way', *Cambridge Journal of Economics*.

Arestis, P. and M. Sawyer (1998), 'New Labour, New Monetarism', *Soundings*, Summer. Reprinted in *European Labour Forum*, 20, Winter, 1998–99.

Auty, R.M. (1991), *Economic Development and Industrial Policy: Korea, Brazil, Mexico, India and China*, London: Mansell.

Bacha, Edmar (1997), 'Plano Real: Uma Segunda Avaliação', in IPEA/CEPAL (eds), *O Plano Real e Outras Experiências Internacionais de Estabilização*. Brasília: IPEA, pp. 177–204.

Baer, Werner (1995), *The Brazilian Economy: Growth and Development*, 4th ed. Westport, CO: Lynne Rienner.

Banco Central do Brasil (1993). *O Regime Cambial Brasileiro: Evolução Recente e Perspectivas*. Brasília: Banco Central.

Banco Central do Brasil (1995). *Relatório Anual*. Brasília: Banco Central.

Barros, J.R.M. and M. Almeida, Jr (1997), 'Análise do ajuste do sistema financeiro no Brasil', *Política Comparada*, 1(2).

Bird, G. (1996), 'How important is sound domestic macroeconomics in attracting capital inflows to developing countries?', *Journal of International Development*, 11: 1–26.

Bonelli, Regis (1999), 'A reestruturação industrial Brasileira nos anos 90: reação empresarial e mercado de trabalho', in OIT (ed.), *Abertura e Ajuste do Mercado de Trabalho no Brasil*, São Paulo: Editora 34, pp. 87–115.

Bonelli, R. and R.R. Gonçalves (1998), 'Para onde vai a estrutura industrial Brasileira?', in IPEA (ed.). *A Economia Brasileira em Perspectiva*, Brasília: IPEA, pp. 617–64.

Bresser-Pereira, Luíz C. (1996), *Economic Crisis and State Reform in Brazil*, London: Lynne Rienner.

Bulmer-Thomas, Victor (ed.). (1994), *The New Economic Model in Latin America and Its Impact on Income Distribution and Poverty*, London: Macmillan.

Calvo, G., L. Leiderman and C. Reinhart (1993), 'Capital inflows and exchange rate appreciation in Latin America: the role of external factors, *IMF Staff Papers*, 40(1): 108–51.

Calvo, G., L. Leiderman and C. Reinhart (1996), 'Inflows of capital to developing countries in the 1990s', *Journal of Economic Perspectives,* 10(2): 123–39.

Cardim de Carvalho, Fernando J. (1999), 'Sistema bancário e competitividade: efeitos da penetração do capital estrangeiro no setor bancário Brasileiro', in C.A.N. Costa and C.A. Arruda (eds), *Em Busca do Futuro: A Competitividade no Brasil*, Rio de Janeiro: Campus.

Carvalho, Carlos E. (1999), *As finanças públicas no plano real*, Unpublished manuscript, Brasília.

Castro, Antonio B. and Francisco E.P. Souza (1985), *A Economia Brasileira em Marcha Forçada*, Rio de Janeiro: Paz e Terra.

CEPAL (UN Economic Commission for Latin America) (1999), *Panorama Social da América Latina, 1998*, New York: United Nations.

Chang, Ha-Joon (1994), *The Political Economy of Industrial Policy*, London: Macmillan.

Chang, Ha-Joon (1999), *Industrial policy and East Asia: the miracle, the crisis, and the future*, Unpublished manuscript, Cambridge.

CNI/CEPAL (National Confederation of Industry/UN Economic Commission for Latin America) (1997), *Investimentos na Indústria Brasileira 1995–1999 – Características e Determinantes*, Rio de Janeiro: CNI/CEPAL.

Coutinho, L., P. Baltar and F. Camargo (1999), 'Desemprenho industrial e do emprego sob a política de estabilização,' in OIT (ed.). *Abertura e Ajuste do Mercado de Trabalho no Brasil*, São Paulo: Editora 34, pp. 61–86.

Cysne, Rubens P. (1994), 'Imposto inflacionário e transferências inflacionárias no Brasil', *Revista de Economia Política*, 14(3).

Dornbusch, Rudiger (1997), 'Brazil's incomplete stabilization and reform', *Brookings Papers on Economic Activity*, 1: 367–94.

Feijó, C.A. and P.G.M. Carvalho (1998), *Structural changes in the Brazilian economy: an analysis of the evolution of industrial productivity in the 1990s*, Unpublished manuscript, Rio de Janeiro.

Fine, Ben and Zavareh Rustomjee (1996), *The Political Economy of South Africa: From Minerals-Energy Complex to Industrialisation*, London: Hurst & Co.

Fiori, José Luís (1992), 'The political economy of the developmentalist state in Brazil', *CEPAL Review*, 47, August: 173–86.

Fishlow, Albert (1997), 'Is the Real Plan for Real?' in S.K. Purcell and R. Roett (eds), *Brazil under Cardoso*, Boulder, CO: Lynne Rienner Publishers, pp. 43–62.

Garcia, Márcio G.P. (1995), 'Política monetária e cambial: algumas lições do período 1991–1994', *Estudos Econômicos*, 25(3): 329–53.

Gonçalves, Reinaldo (1999a), *Globalização e Desnacionalização*, Rio de Janeiro: Paz e Terra.

Gonçalves, Reinaldo (1999b), 'Distribuição de riqueza e renda: alternativa para a crise Brasileira', in Ivo Lesbaupin (ed.), *O Desmonte da Nação: Balanço do Governo FHC*, Petrópolis: Vozes, pp. 45–74.

Governo do Brasil (1993), *Exposição de Motivos n° 393 do Ministro da Fazenda*. Brasília: Congresso Nacional.

Grabel, Ilene (2000), 'The political economy of "policy credibility": the new-classical macroeconomics and the remaking of emerging economies', *Cambridge Journal of Economics*, 24: 1–19.

Kane, Cheikh and Jacques Morisett (1993), 'Who would vote for inflation in Brazil? An integrated framework approach to inflation and income distribution', *World Bank Policy Research Working Paper 1183*, September.

Kilsztajn, Samuel (1996), 'Ancoragem cambial e estabilização', in R.R. Sawaya (ed.), *O Plano Real e a Política Econômica*, São Paulo: Educ, pp. 31–42.

Kregel, Jan (1996), 'Some risks and implications of financial globalisation for national policy autonomy', *UNCTAD Review*.

Lacerda, Antonio C. (1996), 'Os paradoxos da política econômica do real', in R.R. Sawaya (ed.), *O Plano Real e a Política Econômica*, São Paulo: Educ, pp. 13–30.

Laplane, M.F. and F. Sarti (1999), 'O investimento direto estrangeiro no Brasil nos anos 90: determinantes e estratégias', in D. Chudnovsky (ed.), *Investimentos Externos no Mercosul*, Campinas: Papirus, pp. 197–300.

Morais, Lecio (1998), 'A crise Brasileira, a dívida e o déficit públicos: para que superávit Fiscal?', Princípios, Agosto.

Nembhard, Jessica G. (1996), *Capital Control, Financial Regulation, and Industrial Policy in South Korea and Brazil*, Westport, CO: Praeger.

Neri, Marcelo and Claudio Considera (1996), 'Crescimento, desigualdade e pobreza: o impacto da estabilização', in IPEA (ed.), *A Economia Brasileira em Perspectiva*, Brasília: IPEA, pp. 49–82.

Nogueira Batista Paulo, Jr (1996), 'Plano real: estabilização monetária e desequilíbrio externo', *Cadernos Temáticos*, 2, Sindicato dos Engenheiros do Rio de Janeiro, pp. 1–64.

Paes de Barros, R., J.M. Camargo and R. Mendonça (1998), 'A estrutura do desemprego no Brasil', in IPEA (ed.), *A Economia Brasileira em Perspectiva*, Brasília: IPEA, pp. 533–74.

Palley, Thomas I. (2000), *Escaping the 'Policy Credibility' Trap: International Financial Markets and Socially Responsive Macroeconomic Policy*, Unpublished manuscript, Washington, DC.

Palma, Gabriel (1998), 'Three and a Half Cycles of "Mania, Panic and [Asymmetric] Crash": East Asia and Latin America Compared', *Cambridge Journal of Economics*, 22(6): 789–808.

Pochmann, Marcio (1999), *O Trabalho sob Fogo Cruzado: Exclusão, Desemprego e Precarização no Final do Século*, São Paulo: Contexto.

Radice, Hugo (1998), '"Globalization" and National Differences', *Competition & Change*, 3: 263–91.

Radice, Hugo (1999), 'Taking globalisation seriously', *Socialist Register*, 1–28.

Ramos, L. and J.G. Almeida Reis (1998), 'Emprego no Brasil nos anos 90', in IPEA (ed.), *A Economia Brasileira em Perspectiva*, Brasília: IPEA, pp. 501–32.

Rodrik, Dani (1998), 'Globalisation, social conflict and economic growth', *The World Economy*, 21(1): 143–58.

Rosar, Orlando Oscar (1999), *Considerações Sobre a Evolução da Dívida Pública Brasileira nas Últimas Três Décadas*, Anais do IV Encontro Nacional de Economia Política, Porto Alegre.

Saad-Filho, A. and E. Maldonado-Filho (1998), Inflation, growth and economic policy in Brazil', *Indicadores Econômicos*, 21, September, pp. 87–103.

Saad-Filho, A. and M.L.R. Mollo (forthcoming), 'Inflation and stabilization in Brazil: a political economy analysis', *Review of Radical Political Economics*.

Saad-Filho, A. and L. Morais (2000), 'The costs of neomonetarism: the Brazilian economy in the 1990s', *International Papers in Political Economy*, December, pp. 1–39.

Saad-Filho, A., L. Morais and W. Coelho (1999), 'Financial liberalization, currency instability and crisis in Brazil: another plan bites the dust', *Capital & Class*, 68, Summer: 9–14.

Sachs, J. and A. Zini Jr (1996), 'Brazilian inflation and the *Plano Real*', *The World Economy*, 13–37.

Studart, Rogério (1995), *Investment Finance in Economic Development*, London: Routledge.

Studart, Rogério (1999a), *Estrutura e Operação dos Sistemas Financeiros no Mercosul: Perspectivas a Partir das Reformas Institucionais dos Anos 1990 e para a Integração Financeira das Economias do Bloco*, Relatório CEPAL/IPEA/IE-UFRJ, Rio de Janeiro.

Studart, Rogério (1999b), Financial Opening and Deregulation of Brazil's Financial Systems in the 1990s: Possible Effects on its Pattern of Development Financing, Unpublished manuscript, Rio de Janeiro.

Tavares, Maria da Conceição (1978), *Da Substituição de Importações ao Capitalismo Financeiro*, Rio de Janeiro: Zahar.

Urani, André (1998), 'Ajuste macroeconômico e flexibilidade do mercado de trabalho no Brasil: 1981/95', in IPEA (ed.), *A Economia Brasileira em Perspectiva*, Brasília: IPEA, pp. 57–112.

# 3. A critique of the proposal for monetary union in MERCOSUR

**Fernando Ferrari-Filho**

## INTRODUCTION

In 1999, the presidents of the countries of the Common Market of the South, MERCOSUR – Argentina, Brazil, Paraguay and Uruguay – mentioned that the final step of an integration process in this region could be the adoption of a single currency among these countries.[1] Based on the theory of optimum currency areas and on the experience of the European Monetary Union, the proposal of a currency union among the MERCOSUR countries aims to (1) create a new framework for economic management to change the style of fiscal policies among governments of MERCOSUR and modify the financial and monetary system of the member countries, as well as (2) prevent new currency crises in the region.

In general, the analysis of optimum currency areas shows that fixed exchange rates are more appropriate for countries that are completely integrated. In this context, a country's decision to join a currency area is determined by the weight of the advantages and disadvantages of having (or not having) fiscal and monetary policies centralized to promote economic integration and cooperation policy.

Post Keynesian critique of the theory of optimum currency areas focuses on the ability of member countries to manage fiscal and monetary policies. Thus, for example, countries joining a monetary union lose their ability to implement economic policies to stimulate effective demand and solve unemployment problems.

We begin by presenting the main idea related to the theory of optimum currency areas. We show how inconsistent the proposal of creating a currency union among the countries of MERCOSUR is, as the final step in an integration process for this region. Moreover, we argue that, despite the fact that one of the objectives of the proposal is to promote regional prosperity, only the reform of the international monetary system, in the light of post Keynesian ideas,[2] can reconcile full employment with payments balance in a global world.

The chapter proceeds as follows. The first section briefly presents a survey of the literature on optimum currency areas. Based on the original work of Mundell (1961) and the contributions of McKinnon (1963) and Kenen (1969), this section explores the arguments for and against countries adopting a single currency. The second section, on the assumption that the proposal of creating a monetary union in MERCOSUR is inevitable, discusses the preconditions, convergence criteria and economic consequences of integrating and coordinating a monetary union in MERCOSUR. The third section, after presenting different views about the problems and solutions of global financial crises, explores post Keynesian scenario for an international monetary arrangement that aims to prevent international currency crises and promote full employment and economic growth in a global economy. This is followed by a concluding section.

## THE THEORY OF OPTIMUM CURRENCY AREAS: A BRIEF REVIEW

At the beginning of the 1960s, the debate on optimal exchange rate arrangements concentrated on the choice between fixed and flexible exchange rates. At this time, Mundell (1961) formulated a new conceptual framework for analysing optimal exchange arrangements whereby optimum currency areas were seen as an international monetary arrangement. Arguing that 'periodic balance-of-payment crises will remain an integral feature of the international economic system as long as fixed exchange rates and rigid wage and price levels prevent the terms of trade from fulfilling a natural role in the adjustment process' (Mundel 1961: 657), he rejected the idea that flexible exchange rates were an efficient system for stabilizing the economy – that is, maintaining, at the same time, external balance and full employment. He concentrated on defining the structural characteristics in favor of an optimal exchange rate system in which two (or more) countries could fix the exchange rate between their currencies, as a condition for maintaining the stability of relative prices and promoting economic integration. Thus, the theory of optimum currency areas emerged.

Starting from the assumption that the main goal of economic policy is to maintain external balance and full employment, Mundell's analysis argues that the degree of factor mobility – capital and/or labor – is an important issue in determining the optimal choice of exchange rate regime. In this context, Mundell concludes that the limits of an optimum currency area are found by analyzing the trade-off between factor mobility and the size of the area. According to him, '[t]he fault [would not lie] with the type of currency area, but with the domain of the currency area. The optimum currency area is *not* the world' (Mundell 1961: 659, emphasis added). On the contrary, in his words, '[t]he optimum currency area is the region' (p. 660).

Since then, the idea of creating a single currency for two or more countries, with identical characteristics, has been part of the international academic debate. McKinnon (1963) and Kenen (1969), for instance, made important extensions to Mundell's theory.

McKinnon emphasized the relevance of the size and openness of an economy – that is to say, the relation between the tradable and non-tradable goods production of a country – in determining the efficiency of the exchange rate system. According to him, the greater the size and openness of an economy, the greater the internal wage and price-level change in response to an exchange rate change. Based on this premise, McKinnon concluded that the greater the size and openness of an economy, the more efficient would be a fixed exchange rate to restore the external balance and maintain internal stability. In his own words, 'if we move across the spectrum from closed to open economies, flexible exchange rates become both less effective as a control device for external balance and more damaging to internal price-level stability' (McKinnon 1963: 719).

Kenen (1969), arguing in favor of a fixed exchange rate regime, emphasized Mundell's idea of the degree of geographic factor mobility as an important condition in the optimal choice of exchange arrangements. According to him, the optimal arrangement would depend on the degree of inter-industry factor mobility. Kenen argued that the greater the diversity of an economy's production, the less persistent would be the unemployment or inflationary costs to the economy.

To sum up, according to the theory of optimum currency areas, (1) factor mobility, (2) size and openness of an economy, and (3) diversity of production are considered the structural characteristics in the choice of exchange rate arrangements.

Under these circumstances, what are the advantages and disadvantages for a specific country when it decides to join a monetary union, according to the theory of optimum currency areas? Given Mundell's analysis, a country would have the following reasons to join a monetary union: (1) the inflation rate in the monetary union would be significantly lower; (2) the transaction and hedging costs of economic agents related to the risk of exchange rate changes would decrease and/or be eliminated; (3) the purchasing power parity of the country would be stable; (4) the elimination of board taxes would standardize the products of the economy; (5) exchange control barriers to factor mobility would be removed; and (6) regional integration would be stimulated. On the other hand, the main reason why a country might avoid joining the monetary union is that it prefers to operate an independent economic policy to promote economic growth, payments balance and full employment, using the exchange rate as an instrument of economic policy.[3]

To summarize the main idea of this section, the discussion shows that, before deciding whether to enter a monetary union, countries have to analyze the pros and cons of the economic policy consequences. If a country decides to join a currency area, then the relations between this country and its partners should conform with these basic principles: (1) the integration process is dynamic; (2) the factor mobility is high; and (3) the main economic variables – such as the inflation rate, interest rate and fiscal deficit – converge. On the other hand, it is important to emphasize that, under a monetary union, the monetary authorities and/or governments lose their power to operate monetary, fiscal and exchange rate policies. In other words, a country's decision to join a monetary union creates a trade-off: microeconomic gains resulting from coordination policy *vis-à-vis* macroeconomic loss as a consequence of not operating independent monetary and fiscal policies.

## CONDITIONS FOR A MONETARY UNION IN MERCOSUR

This section supposes and supports the idea that the final step of an integration process in MERCOSUR would be the adoption of a single currency among member countries – that is to say, a monetary union will be created in the future. Three questions are addressed in this section. What are the preconditions for creating a monetary union in MERCOSUR? What are the convergence criteria that MERCOSUR countries must have for joining the monetary union? What expectations are held concerning the economic consequences for member countries of a MERCOSUR monetary union?

Before answering these questions, it is important to mention two things. First, according to the Assunción Treaty, which was signed in 1991, MERCOSUR was created to be *only* a Customs Union. Second, it is important to emphasize that the creation of a monetary union in MERCOSUR means that all participating countries would have to accept full financial liberalization, adopt a fixed exchange rate regime, and lose independence over their fiscal and monetary policies. Only in this context could an independent regional central bank be created to complete the harmonization of financial liberalization and print a single currency.

Concerning the first question, the literature related to optimum currency areas, as was shown in the previous section, argues that there are some pre-conditions that countries have to meet before entering a monetary union. These are: (1) the trade and financial integration process among countries must be intensified; (2) factor mobility – labor and capital mobility – must also be intensified; and (3) there must be convergence of macroeconomic magnitudes among the member countries.

Analysis of the preconditions for entry to the MERCOSUR monetary union raises a number of problems. First, the evidence shows that trade and financial integration among the countries of MERCOSUR is incipient. Looking at the intra-regional export figures for Argentina, Brazil, Paraguay and Uruguay, we see that these countries export, on average, less than 2 percent of GDP.[4] Second, labor mobility practically does not exist.[5] Moreover, there is not a significant register of inflows of foreign capital among the member countries of MERCOSUR. As well, the recent financial liberalization in the MERCOSUR area – so important for promoting capital mobility – rather than promoting competition in the national banking system, has intensified concentration in the financial markets.[6] Third, instead of convergence of macroeconomic figures among the member countries of MERCOSUR, the statistical data show that inflation rates, interest rates, economic growth rates, unemployment rates, and so on are moving in different directions.[7]

There are a number of convergence criteria reflecting certain aspects of economic behavior that must be similar among countries to enable them to join a monetary union. Based on the European Monetary Union experience,[8] it is possible to argue that the conditions for entry of any South American country to MERCOSUR must be as follows: (1) countries should not devalue their exchange rate as they have to maintain their exchange rate within the normal margins determined by the regional central bank; (2) the inflation rate in a specific country should not be, for instance, 1.5 percent higher than the average of the best-performing countries; (3) the interest rate should not be, for example, 2 percent higher than the average of the best-performing countries in terms of the inflation rates; (4) no country should have an excessive fiscal deficit – for instance, the budget deficit should not exceed 3 percent of GDP; and (5) the gross national debt of any country should not exceed, for example, 60 percent of GDP.

Once again, in the case of MERCOSUR countries, some problems appear. Consider the criteria that MERCOSUR countries have to accept the same monetary and exchange rate regimes: the evidence shows that Argentina has a currency board system, the monetary regime in Brazil, since the currency devaluation in 1999, is one where a floating exchange rate regime has been adopted, and Paraguay and Uruguay have adopted a crawling peg system as an exchange rate regime. As was shown above, inflation and interest rates in MERCOSUR countries are very different, and it seems practically impossible that they can converge. Looking at fiscal deficits in MERCOSUR countries, the figures show that the average budget deficit in Brazil since 1995 was greater than 3 percent of GDP, while the average budget deficit in Argentina, Paraguay and Uruguay was less than the virtual criterion.[9] Finally, the only virtual criterion for MERCOSUR countries that is converging is the relation between gross national debt and GDP: in Argentina, Brazil, Paraguay and Uruguay this does not exceed 60 percent.[10]

What do economic agents expect from the MERCOSUR monetary union? As was discussed earlier, there can be no doubt that a monetary union could bring some economic advantages to MERCOSUR. The main advantages are that: (1) a common currency facilitates the elimination of border taxes on trade as well as eliminating other transaction costs; (2) currency unification eliminates the foreign exchange risk; (3) a single currency can reduce domestic prices due to competition; and (4) an independent central bank can discipline low inflation through a low interest rate. On the other hand, once countries decide to join the MERCOSUR monetary union, policy-makers will lose the power to use economic policies – basically, monetary and fiscal policies – to promote stability and economic growth. These arguments must be debated closely before the presidents of Argentina, Brazil, Paraguay and Uruguay (and any other country that decides to join the MERCOSUR zone) present a real proposal for currency unification.

## INTERNATIONAL MONETARY REFORM: A POST KEYNESIAN ALTERNATIVE[11]

Since the collapse of the Bretton Woods system in the early 1970s, intense and extensive international mobility of capital and financial liberalization, that is, the globalization process, has substantially altered the dynamic process of international economy. Macroeconomic policies with the specific aim of stimulating effective demand and, as a consequence, increasing the level of employment have been limited.[12] Moreover, in the absence of government macroeconomic policies to limit the movement of capital flows, international speculative capital flows have created serious monetary problems, such as the European monetary crisis of 1992–93, the Mexican peso crisis of 1994–95, the Asian crisis of 1997, the Russian crisis of 1998 and the 1999 Brazilian crisis. These have provoked high rates of unemployment, exchange rate disequilibria, persistent balance of payments imbalances, severe liquidity crises in the banking systems of industrialized countries and so on. To sum up, rather than producing stability and economic growth in the global economy, the globalization process has caused global economic problems such as exchange rate instability, low growth rates and high unemployment rates, and balance of payment imbalances.

In the post Keynesian view, these financial and monetary crises have resulted from unprecedented volatility in financial and foreign-exchange-rate markets, which has increased the liquidity preference of economic agents. Moreover, the recent international experience has demonstrated that current international institutions such as the IMF are unable to monitor and solve these financial crises in today's global economy.

In this context, economists and policy-makers have discussed what should be done to avoid instability in financial and exchange rate markets and, thus, financial crises in the global economy. Even if there were consensus in international academic and policy circles about the necessity of resolving world economic problems, there would still be controversy about how to answer the following question: what can be done to prevent instability in financial and exchange rate markets and, as a consequence, avoid financial crises in the global economy? Eichengreen (1999: Chs 6 and 7) and Taylor (1998), for instance, have differing views about global economic problems and their solutions. The solutions offered vary from more flexible exchange rate regimes to fixed exchange rate regimes; some policy-makers advocate free capital markets while others believe that effective controls on short-term capital flows are necessary; some argue that an international lender of last resort should be created to avoid international financial crises while others believe that this would produce moral hazard and further disruption; some suggest that all countries participating in the global economy could improve the transparency and supervision of the financial system, place prudential taxes on capital inflows and adopt exchange rate flexibility, while others focus on the reform of the international monetary system to improve world economic performance.

The proposals for reform of the international monetary system deserve special attention. Among the several proposals that have been made, at least four have been part of the academic debate: (1) Williamson's (1987, 1992–93) proposal to establish target zones for exchange rates, which aims to limit the flexibility of exchange rates as a way of maintaining internal and external equilibrium; (2) McKinnon's (1988) fixed nominal purchasing-power-parity exchange rate system, which concerns the creation of optimum currency areas based on the main international currencies;[13] (3) the Tobin tax, elaborated originally by Tobin (1978), in which the idea is to introduce a tax on all foreign transactions, especially hot money transactions, as an attempt to establish an international bond insurance agency; and (4) Davidson's (1994) International Money Clearing Union proposal.

It is the last one that this section explores, considering that Keynes's revolutionary analysis provides us with a starting point for designing a new international monetary system that may be able to resolve the current financial crises and at the same time promote full employment and economic growth in the global economy. Thus, bringing back Keynes's ideas and proposals on the international monetary system, post Keynesian theory, in the work of Davidson, forms the basis for an interesting proposal for reform of the international monetary system.[14]

In many of his writings, Keynes discussed and suggested schemes to reform the international monetary system. For example, in *A Tract on Monetary Reform* (1923/1971) he proposed the abandonment of the gold-standard regime; in *A Treatise on Money* (1930/1976) he outlined a proposal for the operation of a Supranational Central Bank to maintain the stability of international price levels; in *The Means to Prosperity* (1933/1972) he proposed an international agreement under fixed, but adjustable, exchange rates; and in his proposal for an International Clearing Union (1944/1980), Keynes developed a scheme based on an international currency, the *bancor*. However, it is Keynes's revolutionary proposal for an International Clearing Union that deserves especial attention.

The main idea here is 'the substitution of an expansionist, in place of a contractionist, pressure on world trade' (Keynes 1944/1980: 176). Thus Keynes suggested a scheme, set out in an international agreement, as follows.

> We need an instrument of international currency having general acceptability between nations . . . We need an orderly and agreed method of determining the relative exchange values of national currency units . . . We need a quantum of international currency, which is *neither determined in an unpredictable* and irrelevant manner . . . *nor subject to large variations depending on the gold reserve policies of individual countries*; but is governed by the actual current requirements of world commerce, and is also capable of deliberate expansion and contraction to offset deflationary and inflationary tendencies in effective demand world. We need a system possessed of an internal stabilising mechanism, by which pressure is exercised on any country whose balance of payments with the rest of the world is departing from equilibrium in *either* position, so as to prevent movements which must create for its neighbours an equal but opposite want of balance (. . .) We need a central institution . . . to aid and support other international institutions (Keynes 1980: 168–9, emphasis added).

Moreover, Keynes, aiming to reduce entrepreneurial uncertainties, proposed (1) an international agreement under a fixed, but alterable, exchange rate, and (2) the control of capital movements.

The proposal is to establish a Currency Union . . . based on international bank money, called (let us say) *bancor*, fixed (but not unalterably) . . . The system contemplated should greatly facilitate the restoration of international credit loan for loan purposes . . . distinguishing . . . between movements of floating funds and genuine new investment for developing the world's resources (Keynes 1944/1980: 179–86).

Davidson (1994) develops a post Keynesian proposal for reforming the international monetary system. After defining a specific taxonomy to explain the economic dynamism of an open, unionized monetary system (UMS) and an open, non-unionized monetary system (NUMS),[15] Davidson attempts to present the rules required to operate an international monetary agreement according to a UMS. This system can, he says, '(1) prevent a lack of global effective demand . . . (2) provide an automatic mechanism for placing a major burden of payments adjustments on the surplus nations, (3) provide each nation with the ability to monitor and, if desired, to control movements of capital, and finally (4) expand the quantity of the liquid asset' (Davidson 1994: 268).

Like Keynes, Davidson argues that the international monetary system must be rooted in a new international currency to regulate international liquidity, a stable exchange rate system to protect exchange rates from speculatory activity, and an agreement currency clause to eliminate a balance of payments disequilibrium in either position. Thus, Davidson's proposal must include provisions such as: (1) an international money clearing unit (IMCU) as a reserve asset for international liquidity; (2) a mechanism to permit IMCUs to be held *only* by the national central banks; (3) a system of fixed, but adjustable, exchange rates between the national currency and the IMCU to help countries solve balance of payments problems; and (4) a 'trigger mechanism' to put more pressure on balance of payments adjustments in creditor than in debtor countries – that is, according to this mechanism a creditor nation would be encouraged to spend its excessive credit in three ways: by buying products of any other country in the international payment system, by investing capital in deficit countries (foreign direct investment projects), and by providing foreign aid to deficit countries (Davidson 1994: 268–72).

The first two provisions are preconditions for preventing people from holding the international asset, the IMCU, as a store of value. As a consequence, IMCUs would be used only for international financial and commercial transactions. In other words, national central banks and governments have the power to control the quantity of liquid assets to expand global effective demand. The third provision is a necessary condition to stabilize the long-term purchasing power of the IMCU. At the same time, it restricts private speculation in the IMCU; that is to say, there is no possibility of the IMCU losing its international purchasing power. Finally, the 'trigger mechanism' is the main instrument to guarantee that 'export–import imbalance . . . [would be] eliminated without unleashing significant recessionary forces' (Davidson 1994: 272).

Thus we realize that the post Keynesian proposal creates conditions to alter the current logic of financial globalization – that is, it can substitute the process of international production for the dynamic of international speculative capital – and, as a consequence, can reduce the entrepreneur's uncertainties, which is necessary to expand global effective demand. As Keynes points out, an international monetary system of this type 'could use its influence and its power to maintain stability of prices and to control the trade cycle' (Keynes 1944/1980: 190–91).

## CONCLUSION

Davidson (1997: 672), considering the possibility of another Great Depression at the end of the 20th century due to the international financial crises in the global economy, stated that 'what is necessary is to build per-manent fireproofing rules and structures that prevent "beauty contest" induced currency fires. *Crisis prevention rather than crises rescues must be the primary long-term objective*'. This quotation expresses the main idea of the previous section: although the international monetary problems we now face are more difficult than those faced in Keynes's period, we can use Keynes's revolutionary analysis of the the international monetary system to help us understand the necessity of creating an international standard currency to promote full employment economic growth as well as maintain long-run price stability.

Following on from this, any attempt to create a regional monetary union is open to a range of objections. We showed earlier, for instance, that there are problems with creating a monetary union in MERCOSUR, in the new millennium: (1) there are macroeconomic inconsistencies between member countries of MERCOSUR; (2) MERCOSUR's factor markets are not suffi-ciently unified to make it an optimum currency area; and (3) countries like Argentina, Brazil, Paraguay and Uruguay cannot tie their economic poli-cies and replace their monies with a single currency because the social costs of doing so would be dramatic. Moreover, the experience of the European Monetary Union provides some validation for the views expressed in this paper. With the introduction of the euro, the member countries of the European Monetary Union lost their policy instruments – specifically, those related to fiscal policy – to stimulate effective demand and, as a result, reduce high unemployment. The European Central Bank does not provide the necessary finance for full employment in the euro zone, and does not provide an anti-speculative mechanism to control movements of capital.[16] Moreover, on current evidence the euro is not challenging the dollar as the world's leading currency. On the contrary, it has devalued against the dollar.

In view of these arguments, rather than proposing a monetary union or a dollarization process, such as a currency board system, for MERCOSUR, based on the theory of optimum currency areas, the presidents of Argentina, Brazil, Paraguay and Uruguay should concentrate their efforts on creating an international arrangement for the global era to reduce the real disruptive outcomes derived from speculative activity in financial markets. This international arrangement could have the following basic elements: (1) an international monetary system with the objective of expanding world effective demand and promoting full employment; (2) an international central bank to regulate the international currency, issued by the same international central bank, and to provide long-term lending; (3) a system of fixed, but adjustable, exchange rates; and (4) some sort of control on capital flows to mitigate instability and fragility in the global economy. This is one of the principal legacies of Keynes's ideas. This is our – post Keynesian – challenge today!

## NOTES

1. More specifically, the former president of Argentina, Carlos Menem, proposed the 'dollarization' of MERCOSUR economies. It is important to comment that his proposal is based on the Argentinian currency board system in which Argentina ties its monetary policy to the dollar under the constitution.
2. As section 3 will show, the post Keynesian proposal to reform the international monetary system is based on four important provisions: an international central bank, with its own currency; a fixed but adjustable exchange rate system; controls over capital movements to avoid speculative attacks on currencies; and overdraft facilities to make balance of payments adjustments possible.
3. Once again, it is necessary to emphasize that, under monetary union, governments are not able to manage independent monetary policy and, as a result, cannot monetize their fiscal deficits. Thus, fiscal and monetary policies are completely tied.
4. In 1999, for instance, the relation between the total f.o.b. exports of Argentina, Brazil, Paraguay and Uruguay to MERCOSUR area and the total GDP of these countries was 1.82 percent (US$15.3 billion over US$841.6 billion). This relation, elaborated by the author, is based on the figures of CEPAL/ECLAC (2001) and MERCOSUL (2001).
5. In practice, it is not difficult to present some reasons why labor mobility is relatively limited within the MERCOSUR area: (1) there are different technical and professional qualifications among workers; (2) wages are not converging – for instance, the minimum wage in Argentina, Paraguay and Uruguay is around US$200, while in Brazil it is around US$80; and (3) labor markets in these countries are regulated.
6. At least in Brazil, the evidence shows that financial liberalization in the 1990s stimulated concentration in the financial and banking system. See, for instance, Paula, Sobreira, and Zonenschain (1999) and Meirelles (1999).

7. For example, between 1995 and 1999, the figures for the inflation rate ($\pi$) and interest rate ($i$), GDP rate ($y$) and unemployment rate ($u$) in Argentina, Brazil, Paraguay and Uruguay show how divergent the economic variables are in these countries. The average rates of these economic variables in member countries of MERCOSUR are as follows: Argentina: 0.17% ($\pi$), 8.38% (i), 2.16% (y) and 15.35% (u); Brazil: 9.05% ($\pi$), 35.88% (i), 2.25% (y) and 6.17% (u); Paraguay: 8.93% ($\pi$), 30.84% (i), 1.91% (y) and 7.31% (u); and Uruguay: 17.02% ($\pi$), 22.72% (i), 2.03% (y) and 11.02% (u). These average rates were estimated by the author, based on CEPAL/ECLAC (2001) and MERCOSUL (2001).
8. It is important to say that we are assuming that MERCOSUR will adopt the same convergence criteria as the European Monetary Union. A special commission created in MERCOSUR, with the specific aim of elaborating the macroeconomic convergence criteria for Argentina, Brazil, Paraguay and Uruguay thought that MERCOSUR could have the same convergence criteria as the European Monetary Union.
9. From 1995 to 1998, the average budget deficit relative to GDP in Argentina, Brazil, Paraguay and Uruguay was, respectively, 1.4%, 4.8%, 1.5% and 1.9%. These figures were produced by the author, based on CEPAL/ECLAC (2001) and Inter-American Development Bank (2001).
10. See, for instance, the figures of CEPAL/ECLAC (2001) and Inter-American Development Bank (2001).
11. This section is based on Alves et al. (1999–2000).
12. Davidson (1999–2000: 201), for instance, shows that after the breakdown of the Bretton Woods system, in 1973, the world real growth rate was practically half of what it was during the period from 1950 to 1973.
13. According to McKinnon (1988: 102), the idea is to create 'an international gold standard without gold'.
14. Davidson's proposal, as we will observe later, is more complete than others in that it presents a set of rules for the stabilization of exchange rates, control of speculative capital flows and elimination of inconsistencies in the balance of payments among countries. By the way, Davidson's critique of the Tobin tax and of Williamson's and McKinnon's proposals can be observed, respectively, in Davidson (1997) and Davidson (1994: Ch. 16).
15. According to Davidson (1994: Ch. 12), in an open, unionized monetary system (UMS), the contracts are expressed in the same monetary system – that is, the exchange rate is fixed – while in an open, non-unionized monetary system (NUMS), the contracts are expressed in different currencies and, as a consequence, the exchange rate is flexible.
16. See, for instance, Arestis (1999).

# REFERENCES

Alves, A., Jr., F. Ferrari, Jr. and L.F.R. Paula (1999–2000), 'The post Keynesian critique of conventional currency crisis models and Davidson's proposal to reform the international monetary system', *Journal of Post Keynesian Economics*, 22(2): 207–25.

Arestis, P. (1999), 'The independent European central bank: Keynesian alternatives', *Archè Interdisciplinar/Universidade Candido Mendes-Ipanema*, 8(23): 145–77.

CEPAL/ECLAC (2001) http://www.cepal.org.

Davidson, P. (1994), *Post Keynesian Macroeconomic Theory*, Aldershot: Edward Elgar.

Davidson, P. (1997), 'Are grains of sand in the wheels of international finance sufficient to do the job when boulders are often required?', *Economic Journal*, 107(442): 671–86.

Davidson, P. (1999–2000), 'Capital movements, Tobin tax, and permanent fire prevention: a response to De Angelis', *Journal of Post Keynesian Economics*, 22(2): 197–206.

Eichengreen, B. (1999), *Toward a New International Finance Architecture: A Practical Post Asia Agenda*, Washington, DC: Institute for International Economics.

Inter-American Development Bank (2001) http://www.iadb.org.

Kenen, P. (1969), 'The theory of optimum currency areas: an eclectic view', in R. Mundell and A. Swoboda (eds), *Monetary Problems of the International Economy*, Chicago, IL: University of Chicago Press, pp. 41–60.

Keynes, J.M. (1923/1971), *A Tract on Monetary Reform*, London: Macmillan (Volume 4 of *The Collected Writings of John Maynard Keynes*).

Keynes, J.M. (1933/1972), *Essays in Persuasion*, London: Macmillan (Volume 9 of *The Collected Writings of John Maynard Keynes*).

Keynes, J.M. (1939/1979), *A Treatise on Money*, New York: AMS Press.

Keynes, J.M. (1944/1980), *Activities 1940–1944: Shaping the Post-war World, the Clearing Union*, London: Macmillan (Volume 25 of *The Collected Writings of John Maynard Keynes*).

McKinnon, R.I. (1963), 'Optimum currency areas', *American Economic Review*, 53(4): 717–25.

McKinnon, R.I. (1988), 'Monetary and exchange rate policies for international finance stability: a proposal', *Journal of Economic Perspectives*, 2(1): 83–100.

Meirelles, A.C. (1999), 'Tamanho é documento na competição bancária, *fórum de Lideres/Gazeta Mercantil*, 1(1): 54–72.

MERCOSUL (2001) http://www.mercosul.org.

Mundell, R. (1961), 'The theory of optimum currency areas', *American Economic Review*, 51(4): 657–65.

Paula, L.F.R., R. Sobreira and C.N. Zonenschain (eds) (1999). *Perspectivas para o Sistema Financeiro Nacional: Regulação do Setor e Participação do Capital Estrangeiro*, Rio de Janeiro: Universidade Candido Mendes-Ipanema.

Taylor, L. (1998), 'Capital market crises: liberalisation, fixed exchange rates and market-driven destabilisation', *Cambridge Journal of Economics*, 22(6): 663–76.

Tobin, J. (1978), 'A proposal for international monetary reform', *Eastern Economic Journal*, 4(3/4): 153–9.

Williamson, J. (1987), 'Exchange rate management: the rate of target zones', *American Economic Review*, 77(2): 200–4.

Williamson, J. (1992–1993), 'On designing on international monetary system', *Journal of Post Keynesian Economics*, 15(2): 181–92.

# 4. The balance of payments-constrained growth model and the limits to export-led growth

**Robert A. Blecker***

## INTRODUCTION

Popular critiques of globalization often claim that the promotion of an export-led growth strategy for large numbers of developing countries rests upon a 'fallacy of composition'. A few countries, such as the original Asian 'Four Tigers' (South Korea, Taiwan, Hong Kong and Singapore), could succeed at export-led growth while they were the only countries adopting this strategy, according to the critique. However, the efforts of other countries to emulate this strategy are bound to foster chronic problems of over-investment and oversupply, resulting in disappointing growth for the developing world as a whole even if some individual countries succeed at the expense of others. For example, Greider (1997) argues that the 'manic logic of global capitalism' will inevitably lead to a global glut of manufactured commodities, as nations that are competing for the same export markets install surplus capacity relative to international demand – a problem that is only exacerbated by the depressed level of wages and the resulting constriction of consumption in the export-oriented developing countries themselves.

Remarkably little attention has been given to this fallacy-of-composition argument in the academic literature on trade and development. Most scholars of trade and growth tend to ignore demand-side constraints on export-led growth altogether, including both neoclassical and structuralist development economists. Of those who explicitly discuss such constraints, most tend to dismiss them as unlikely to be important in practice. Only a handful of previous studies have taken the fallacy-of-composition argument seriously, and a few of them have concluded that it is potentially a serious flaw in the widespread promotion of export-led growth.

One reason why the idea of demand-side limits to export-led growth has been neglected (or dismissed) by most economists is the lack of a theoretical framework in which this idea makes sense. In neoclassical growth models, for example, long-run growth is always determined on the supply side by the growth of non-produced factor inputs (especially the labor force) and increases in the efficiency of factor use (technological progress and scale economies). Growth models in the neo-Keynesian and neo-Kaleckian traditions allow for demand-side factors (especially the entrepreneurs' desire to invest) to influence long-run growth, but most of these models neglect open economy concerns.[1]

However, there is a post Keynesian theory which emphasizes international trade as a limiting factor in the growth process: the model of balance of payments-constrained growth (BPCG), originally developed by Thirlwall (1979). This chapter will show how the BPCG framework can be extended to model the idea of a fallacy of composition by incorporating an adding-up constraint on the simultaneous growth of a large number of countries that are all targeting the same export markets. The extension of the BPCG model proposed here is an unusual one, in the sense that it emphasizes certain relative price effects (that is, real cross-exchange rates among developing country exporters of manufactures). In contrast, most applications of the BPCG theoretical approach to date usually assume that relative price effects are negligible. The reasons for this focus on certain types of relative price effects will be explained below.

## THE HYPOTHESIS

The hypothesis of a fallacy of composition can be stated briefly as follows. Under a given set of global demand conditions, the market for newly industrializing country (NIC) exports of manufactures is limited by the capacity (and willingness) of the industrialized nations to absorb the corresponding imports. The market for imports of labor-intensive manufactures and other NIC exports can grow only so fast, and as a result the export-led strategy can work only for a limited number of countries at a time. If this market is growing at, say, 7 percent per year, then not all of the NICs can have their exports increase at rates of 10 or 15 percent per year – although a few can, *provided that the market shares of other exporters or domestic producers are falling at the same time*. If all try to grow faster than is possible in the aggregate, the result can only be excess industrial capacity and/or falling prices. And if some countries' export performance is disappointing, they will suffer economic stagnation and become more prone to a currency collapse or financial crisis. A key variable in this process is the exchange rate: countries with low, competitive rates will succeed, while those with high, overvalued rates will lose out. But no amount of competitive devaluations can allow *all* of these countries to succeed in the same game of export-led growth at the same time in the same products.

Of course, total exports of manufactures from the developing countries can grow faster than domestic demand in the industrialized countries, provided that the former countries take away market share from domestic producers in the latter. However, the ability of all developing country exporters to increase their total market share abroad is then limited by two factors: first, by protectionist policies, either previously existing protection or responses to import surges; and second, by the eventual disappearance of domestic import-competing producers (or the survival of only a few 'niche' producers), which then constrains total import growth to the growth rate of the domestic market in the industrialized countries. To the extent that the total market share of developing country exporters cannot be increased further, each new entrant can achieve above-average rates of export growth only if it displaces some other exporting country (or countries), whose export growth will inevitably falter as a result.

There are a number of qualifications to this hypothesis. Most importantly, the growth of global markets for manufactured imports is not exogenously fixed and given.[2] This constraint can be relaxed if the industrialized countries stimulate their domestic economies more and open up their import markets to developing nations' exports. This point applies especially to Japan, which is notoriously closed to manufactured imports (see Lawrence, 1987, 1991) and has been stuck in a chronic growth depression since about 1990. However, the same point applies to Europe, which has thus far mainly opened itself up to more intra-regional trade rather than more trade with outside regions[3] – and has maintained slow growth and high unemployment as a result of both macroeconomic policies and structural obstacles.[4]

Under these conditions, the United States has effectively served as the global 'consumer of last resort' in recent years, due to a combination of relatively open markets, robust economic growth and booming consumer demand. The United States maintains some restrictions on imports of manufactures in particular sectors, as do other industrialized countries, but on the whole it has had more rapid growth of imports of developing country manufactured products than any other major industrialized country. Much of the tension in the international trading system today results from the disproportionate share of global manufactured exports that is absorbed in the US market, which widens the US trade deficit and causes political resentments in the United States, while also restricting export growth in the developing countries.

In principle, simultaneous export expansion can potentially provide increased reciprocal demand for all nations' exports. This is the vision of a prosperous, open international economy promoted by classical liberal economic thinkers since the time of Adam Smith. For such simultaneous export growth to be successful in expanding the global market for all countries' exports, the countries that are promoting their exports must also open their own markets to imports and maintain high domestic demand at the same time. What is not feasible is for all countries to attempt to achieve trade surpluses by promoting their exports while simultaneously restricting their imports or repressing consumer demand. The widespread pursuit of this type of neomercantilist policy only tightens the global constraints on export-led growth – since not enough countries are willing to absorb the corresponding imports – and thus fosters intensified conflict over foreign market shares. In short, the classical liberal vision of a world in which export-led growth solves the demand problem through reciprocal and balanced market expansion is not necessarily flawed as a vision, but rather as a characterization of the real world.

## LITERATURE SURVEY

Much of the literature on export-led growth is curiously silent on the possibility of global demand constraints. For example, the otherwise excellent survey of the prospects for industrial exports from developing countries by Ballance et al. (1982) considers micro-level trade barriers in the industrial countries and structural obstacles in the developing countries, but ignores the possibility of macro-level, global demand limits. Many studies that test for whether exports or openness promote growth in cross-sectional samples of developing countries do not explicitly consider adding-up constraints on the collective growth of all developing country exporters.[5] When this issue is raised, it is usually quickly dismissed.

> Regarding the danger of a 'fallacy of composition' in manufactured exports, while there is some evidence that this could become a constraint on industrial development in the South, particularly if slow growth persists in the advanced industrial countries, the potential scope for developing countries to enter Northern markets for textiles, clothing and other such goods is considerable (Akyüz et al. 1998: 30).

There is a greater awareness of global demand limits to export-led growth in some studies of the 1990s financial crises. One of the most robust findings in empirical studies of financial crises is the importance of real exchange rate overvaluation in explaining speculative attacks or contagion effects.[6] This finding is given theoretical support by Yotopoulos and Sawada (1999), who argue that there is a chronic tendency for 'soft' currencies in developing countries to depreciate relative to 'hard' (reserve) currencies, resulting in 'competitive devaluation trade' that misallocates resources and depresses growth. Radelet and Sachs (1998) concede that pressures from surging Chinese and Mexican exports after 1994 contributed to slowing the growth of exports from Southeast Asian countries in 1994–97, although they argue that the effect was quantitatively 'moderate' in terms of explaining the outbreak of the 1997 Asian financial crisis.

Previous studies that explicitly analyze the possibility of a fallacy of composition in the export-led growth strategy are remarkably scarce. Early advocates of this view included members of the Cambridge Economic Policy Group such as Singh (1984), who argued that

> there is an obvious fallacy in the view that such a strategy can succeed for all or even the leading newly industrializing countries in a slow-growing world economy . . . [These countries] will have to rely much more on their internal dynamics – on the growth of internal demand rather than on world market forces – to generate economic expansion.[7]

Another notable exception is Cline's (1982) study of whether the East Asian growth model could be generalized. Cline concluded that 'generalization of the East Asian model of export-led development across all developing countries would result in untenable market penetration into industrial countries' because it would be likely to generate a protectionist response (Cline 1982, reprinted in Cline 1984: 213). In a later study, Cline (1984) argued that moderate manufactured export growth in the 10–15 percent per year range would suffice for achieving high growth rates in most developing countries without inducing a likely protectionist response, although faster export growth rates would run that risk.

Balassa (1989) provided a counter-critique of the idea of limits to export-led growth. He criticized Cline's projections of large shares of developing country imports into industrialized countries' markets for manufactures as unrealistic. Balassa argued that competition among the developing countries would be ameliorated by a shift of the more advanced ones into more capital-intensive exports. He claimed that increased exports of manufactures from the developing countries would not have a negative effect on total industrial employment in the industrialized countries, because successful developing country exporters would also tend to increase their imports of high skill-intensive manufactured goods from the industrialized countries. Basically, Balassa claimed that the classical vision of an unconstrained, balanced expansion of global trade was a more realistic scenario than the pessimistic view of limited export markets.

A few recent papers have studied the problem of excess capacity in specific export-oriented manufacturing industries in developing countries.

Kaplinsky (1993) discusses the export-processing zones in countries like the Dominican Republic, which export labor-intensive commodities such as apparel.[8] Kaplinsky characterizes such countries as experiencing 'immiserizing employment growth, that is employment growth which is contingent upon wages falling in international purchasing power' (p. 1861). Kaplinsky (1999) applies a similar argument to the explanation of the Asian financial crisis:

> most of the East Asian economies locked themselves into a growth trajectory in which specialization in factor and product markets associated with low barriers to entry led to high rates of competition. This has led to falling terms of trade and persistent currency realignments, placing long-term pressures on real exchange rates (Kaplinsky 1999: 2–3).

Erturk (1999) argues that overinvestment occurred in East Asia in the 1990s, as the former 'flying geese formation' broke apart. In the flying geese model, the more advanced countries (that is, first Japan, followed by Korea and Taiwan) moved on to more capital-intensive and technologically sophisticated products as newer low-wage competitors entered the market for more labor-intensive, standardized manufactures. Erturk argues that too many countries entered the more advanced product categories at once in the 1990s, thus creating excess capacity and fostering falling prices for those goods, contrary to the optimistic expectations of Balassa.

## A MODEL OF THE CONSTRAINTS TO EXPORT-LED GROWTH

This section will show how the BPCG model can be extended to incorporate an adding-up constraint on the simultaneous growth of a number of competing countries. Since the basic BPCG model has been explicated numerous times (for example, by McCombie and Thirlwall 1994), a brief summary will suffice here. In the simplest version, assuming that countries are forced to maintain balanced trade in the long run, and assuming that imports and exports are determined by Cobb–Douglas-type demand functions with constant price and income elasticities,[9] a country's long-run average growth rate must equal:[10]

$$\hat{y} = \frac{(-\varepsilon_x - \varepsilon_m - 1)(\hat{e} + \hat{p}^* - \hat{p}) + \eta_x \hat{y}^*}{\eta_m} \tag{1}$$

where $y$ is national income, $\varepsilon_x$ and $\varepsilon_m$ are the price elasticities of export and import demand (expressed as negative numbers, that is, *not* their absolute values), $p$ and $p^*$ are the domestic and foreign price levels, $e$ is the exchange rate (domestic currency per unit of foreign currency), $\eta_x$ and $\eta_m$ are the income elasticities of export and import demand, and a caret over a variable indicates its instantaneous rate of change (logarithmic time derivative).

In the conventional BPCG framework, it is usually assumed that relative price effects are negligible because either (i) the Marshall–Lerner elasticities condition is not satisfied in the sense that $|\varepsilon_x + \varepsilon_m| \approx 1$; or else (ii) relative purchasing power parity (PPP) holds in the long run so that $\hat{e} + \hat{p}^* - \hat{p} = 0$. Under either of these assumptions, (1) reduces to

$$\hat{y}_B = \frac{\eta_x \hat{y}^*}{\eta_m} = \frac{\hat{x}}{\eta_m} \qquad (2)$$

where $\hat{y}_B$ is the BPCG rate and $\hat{x}$ is the growth rate of exports.[11]

The novelty of this approach – aside from its stark parsimony of explanation and neglect of 'natural' supply-side factors – lies in its emphasis on the *negative* effects of excessive openness to imports (as reflected in a high income elasticity of import demand, $\eta_m$) on output growth, in addition to the positive effects of rapid export growth $\hat{x}$. This emphasis accords with the view that the East Asian countries' success can be attributed to a *limited* form of openness, in which exports were promoted but imports were selectively restricted (Singh 1998). Moreover, this model implies a *reason* why exports are so critical in the growth process, that is, they relieve the balance of payments constraint imposed by the high import requirements of rapid growth.

But the BPCG model assumes that export growth rates of individual countries ($\hat{x}$) are independent of each other, when in fact they are related insofar as total world exports must add up to equal total world imports, and the growth of the latter is not unlimited. It is at this point that relative prices between the competing exports of different countries become significant for determining which countries' exports absorb greater or lesser shares of total global imports. Thus, real cross-exchange rates among the developing countries that are exporting similar manufactured products must be important determinants of their export growth, even if their demand for imports is relatively price-inelastic and depends mainly on income variables.[12] Such relative price effects are likely to be more significant in the short run than in the long run, since real exchange rate changes do not necessarily persist over time (for example, the Mexican depreciation of 1994–95 was later offset by the Asian depreciations of 1997–98). Nevertheless, there is no clear evidence for whether PPP holds in developing countries even over very long periods of time (see Rogoff 1996), and hence such relative price effects cannot be ruled out even in the long run.

In order to incorporate such an adding-up constraint into the BPCG model, one can borrow techniques that have been commonly used in multi-country trade models. For reasons explained in more detail in Blecker (1999), the demand for nationally differentiated products will be modeled using the 'almost ideal demand system' (known by its rather unfortunate acronym, AIDS) developed by Deaton and Muellbauer (1980).[13] The AIDS model has certain admirable properties of generality, including (for skeptics of neoclassical consumer choice theory) that it does not require (although it does not rule out) the assumption of utility maximization.

The AIDS model can be integrated with the BPCG model as follows. For convenience, the industrialized countries are treated as a single trading bloc. It is also assumed for simplicity that the developing country exporters do not consume any of their own (or each others') exported manufactured goods. The industrialized countries' demand is modeled using a 'non-nested' specification, which allows a change in the price of one developing country's exports to affect demand for domestic products in the industrialized countries directly, not just through its effect on the average import price in the latter.[14] All the developing countries are assumed to export one type of manufactured good, which is nationally differentiated; thus the model abstracts from changes in the composition of developing countries' exports.[15]

Suppose there are $n-1$ developing or newly industrializing countries exporting manufactured products to the industrialized countries, which are collectively counted as the $n$th country. Let the market share of the $i$th country ($i=1, 2, \ldots, n$) in the industrialized countries' market for manufactured commodities be defined as

$$w_i = p_i x_i / z_n,$$

where $p_i$ is the price of the $i$th country's exports measured in the currency of the $n$th country (say, US dollars), $x_i$ is the quantity of the $i$th country's exports (or, in the case of country $n$, the quantity of home products that compete with imports), and

$$z_n = \sum_{i=1}^{n} p_i x_i$$

is total expenditures on manufactured commodities in country $n$ (including consumption of domestic products as well as imports), and thus $\sum_i w_i = 1$. It can be shown that the AIDS model implies an expenditure share function for each country's exports of the following form:

$$w_i(\mathbf{p}, z_n) = \alpha_i + \sum_{j=1}^{n} \gamma_{ij} \ln p_j + \beta_i \ln(z_n/P) \tag{3}$$

where $\mathbf{p}$ is the vector of all $n$ prices $(p_i)$ and $P$ is a weighted average world price determined by

$$P = \alpha_0 + \sum_{k=1}^{n} \alpha_k \ln p_k + \tfrac{1}{2} \sum_{k=1}^{n} \sum_{j=1}^{n} \gamma_{kj} \ln p_k \ln p_j$$

The parameters $\alpha_i$, $\gamma_{ij}$ and $\beta_i$ must obey certain adding-up constraints for consistency:[16]

$$\sum_{i=1}^{n} \alpha_i = 1 \qquad \sum_{i=1}^{n} \gamma_{ij} = 0 \qquad \sum_{i=1}^{n} \beta_i = 0$$

Although these parameters are not standard elasticities, they are related to standard price and income elasticities as follows.[17] The (uncompensated) price elasticity of demand is

$$\varepsilon_{ij} = \frac{\partial x_i(\mathbf{p}, z_n)}{\partial p_j} \cdot \frac{p_j}{x_i} = \frac{\gamma_{ij} + \beta_i \beta_j \ln(z_n/P) - \beta_i w_j}{w_i} - \delta_{ij}$$

where $\delta_{ij}$ is the Kronecker delta (that is, $\delta_{ij} = 1$ if $i = j$ and $\delta_{ij} = 0$ otherwise). The $\gamma_{ij}$ parameters can be interpreted intuitively as follows. For own-price effects $(i = j)$, assuming that $\beta_i^2$ and $\beta_i w_i$ are relatively small, second-order effects, it is approximately true that demand is relatively elastic $(\varepsilon_{ii} < -1)$ when $\gamma_{ii} < 0$ and relatively inelastic $(\varepsilon_{ii} > -1)$ when $\gamma_{ii} > 0$. For cross-price effects $(i \neq j)$, assuming that the second-order effects $(\beta_i \beta_j$ and $\beta_i w_j)$ are relatively small, it is approximately true that two national goods are gross substitutes if $\gamma_{ij} > 0$ and gross complements if $\gamma_{ij} < 0$. The 'income' elasticity of demand (or, more precisely, the elasticity of the demand for the $i$th country's exports with respect to total industrial-country expenditures on similar goods) is

$$\eta_i = \frac{\partial x_i(\mathbf{p}, z_n)}{\partial z_n} \cdot \frac{z_n}{x_i} = \frac{\beta_i}{w_i} + 1$$

Thus, demand for country $i$'s exports is relatively income-elastic $(\eta_i > 1)$ when $\beta_i > 0$ and inelastic $(\eta_i < 1)$ when $\beta_i < 0$. Note that these elasticities are not constant, but vary with the underlying prices and expenditures.

Similarly – although this is a somewhat 'loose' usage of the AIDS functional form – for each developing country $i = 1, 2, \ldots, n-1$ (that is, not including country $n$, the industrialized countries), let the share of imports in its national income be denoted by

$$v_i = e_i p_n^m m_i / y_i$$

where $p_n^m$ is the industrialized countries' domestic-currency ('dollar') price of their exports (that is, the foreign currency price of the developing country's imports), $m_i$ is the quantity of imported goods, $y_i$ is national income (gross domestic product) measured in domestic currency, and $e_i$ is the exchange rate expressed in units of the $i$th country's domestic currency per unit of the $n$th country's currency (for example, pesos per dollar); thus, $e_n = 1$.

For simplicity, we assume that imports and domestic products (that is, non-exported goods) in the developing countries consist of the same good, but are nationally differentiated, and that all imports are purchased from the $n$th country, which is the bloc of the industrialized countries. Then we can write the import share function for the $i$th developing country as

$$v_i(p_i^m, p_n^m, y_i) = \theta_i + \psi_{ii} \ln p_i^m + \psi_{in} \ln(e_i p_n^m) + \mu_i \ln(y_i/p_i^m) \tag{4}$$

where $p_i^m$ is the domestic price of import-competing goods. The parameters $\psi_{ik}$ ($k = i, n$) and $\mu_i$ are analogous to the $\gamma_{ij}$ and $\beta_i$ parameters, respectively, in equation (2). National income is deflated by the domestic price level for import-competing goods $p_i^m$ in (4), rather than by some ideal price index, for simplicity – and on the assumption that this is the same as the price level for 'home' goods production.

Based on (4), the own-price elasticity of import demand is

$$\varepsilon_{ii}^m = \frac{\partial m_i(p_i^m, p_n^m, y_i)}{\partial p_i^m} \cdot \frac{p_i^m}{m_i} = \frac{\psi_{ii} - \mu_i}{v_i} - 1$$

while the cross-price elasticity is

$$\varepsilon_{ii}^m = \frac{\partial m_i(p_i^m, p_n^m, y_i)}{\partial(e_i p_n^m)} \cdot \frac{e_i p_n^m}{m_i} = \frac{\psi_{in}}{v_i}$$

and the income elasticity of import demand in country $i$ is

$$\eta_i^m = \frac{\partial m_i(p_i^m, p_n^m, y_i)}{\partial y_i} \cdot \frac{y_i}{m_i} = \frac{\mu_i}{v_i} + 1$$

The dollar price of exports from each country (except the $n$th country) is equal to

$$p_i = p_i^d/e_i \tag{5}$$

where $p_i^d$ is the domestic currency price of exports produced in the $i$th country.[18]

The balance of payments constraint, without net capital flows,[19] is simply the requirement that the value of exports equal the value of imports.

Writing this condition for each developing country $i$ $(i=1, 2, \ldots, n-1)$ in 'dollar' terms (that is, in terms of the $n$th currency),

$$p_i x_i = p_n^m m_i$$

or, equivalently,

$$w_i z_n = v_i y_i / e_i \qquad (6)$$

Substituting (3), (4) and (5) into (6), using the definitions of $w_i$ and $v_i$, taking logarithmic derivatives with respect to time, expressing the variables in growth rates and rearranging terms, we can write the solution for the BPCG rate of the $i$th country in real terms as follows:

$$\hat{y}_i - \hat{p}_i^m = \frac{\dfrac{1}{w_i}\displaystyle\sum_{j=1}^{n}[\gamma_{ij}(\hat{p}_j^d - \hat{e}_j)] + (\hat{P} - \hat{p}_i^m + \hat{e}_i) - \dfrac{\psi_{ii}}{v_i}\hat{p}_i^m - \dfrac{\psi_{in}}{v_i}(\hat{e}_i + \hat{p}_n^m) + \left(\dfrac{\beta_i}{w_i} + 1\right)(\hat{z}_n - \hat{P})}{\left(\dfrac{\mu_i}{v_i} + 1\right)}$$

$$(7)$$

If all of the price changes and exchange rate changes are zero, then equation (7) reduces to the traditional solution of the BPCG model, i.e.,

$$\hat{y}_i = \frac{\left(\dfrac{\beta_i}{w_i} + 1\right)}{\left(\dfrac{\mu_i}{v_i} + 1\right)}\hat{z}_n \qquad (7')$$

which is analogous to equation (2) above. However, if the price and exchange rate changes are non-zero, then the real growth rate $\hat{y}_i - \hat{p}_i^m$ must be determined by (7) and is affected by those changes, particularly (in the first term in the numerator) by changes in home-country export prices $(\hat{p}_j^d - \hat{e}_j, j = i)$ relative to export prices of other countries $(\hat{p}_j^d - \hat{e}_j, -j \neq i)$. These cross-price (and cross-exchange-rate) effects, captured by the parameters $\gamma_{ij}$, represent the additional constraint of international competition among developing country exporters of manufactures for a given amount of growth of the industrialized countries' market for their exports.

In addition, the more that a developing country has liberalized its imports, the tighter will be the constraint imposed by the relative price sensitivity of demand for imports, represented by the parameters $\psi_{ik}$ in the numerator of (7), and the higher will be the income elasticity of import demand in the denominator. At the same time, the more that the industrialized countries expand their import markets for developing country exports, and the more that the latter countries move 'up the ladder' into higher-quality products, the greater will be the income (total expenditure) elasticity of export demand in the numerator, and the more the augmented balance-of-payments constraint on developing countries' growth will be relaxed.

## EMPIRICAL PLAUSIBILITY: A PRELIMINARY ANALYSIS

The empirical plausibility of the fallacy-of-composition hypothesis can be assessed in light of some simple, aggregated measures of developing country exports into the US market, as shown in Table 4.1.[20] These data are for total exports, not just manufactures, and do not include other OECD export markets besides the United States. Nevertheless, as discussed earlier, the United States has been the largest and most open market for developing country exports of manufactures, and the developing countries selected for this table are mostly countries with a high proportion of manufactured exports. As Table 4.1 shows, total US imports (in current dollars) grew at average annual rates of 8.5 percent in 1979–89, 7 percent in 1989–94 and 9.5 percent in 1994–97. Countries whose growth rates of exports exceeded these rates were gaining market share in the United States, while those whose export growth rates were lower were losing market share.

The data for the 1980s show rapid growth of US imports from all of the leading developing country exporters of manufactures at that time, including the Four Tigers (with average annual growth rates of 17.2 percent for Korea, 15.7 percent for Taiwan, 9.2 percent for Hong Kong and 19.8 percent for Singapore). China and Thailand also have spectacular growth rates in the 1980s (35 percent and 20 percent respectively), albeit from a very low base in the former case. Japanese exports to the United States continued to boom throughout the 1980s, growing at a 13.5 percent annual rate on top of previous rapid growth in the 1970s. Mexico's exports grew at a respectable 11.9 percent clip in the 1980s, during which (after the debt crisis and oil bust) Mexico reduced its import restrictions, opened up more to foreign direct investment and devalued its currency. As a result of this above-average growth of their exports to the United States, all of these countries increased their shares of the overall US import market between 1979 and 1989 at the expense of other countries.[21]

The 1990s were then marked by a series of notable shifts in relative growth rates and market shares. First, Japanese export growth fell off, to a 5 percent annual growth rate in 1989–94 and a mere 0.7 percent in 1994–97; as a result, Japan's share of the US import market plummeted from 19.6

Table 4.1 US merchandise imports, by country of origin, selected countries and years, 1979–1997 (average annual growth rates of nominal values and shares of total US imports)

| | Average Annual Change (%) | | | Shares (% of total imports**) | | | |
|---|---|---|---|---|---|---|---|
| | 1979–89 | 1989–94 | 1994–97 | 1979 | 1989 | 1994 | 1997 |
| European Union | 10.0 | 7.2 | 9.8 | 15.6 | 17.9 | 18.1 | 18.3 |
| Japan | 13.5 | 5.0 | 0.7 | 12.4 | 19.6 | 17.8 | 13.9 |
| Canada | 8.6 | 7.8 | 9.3 | 18.5 | 18.8 | 19.6 | 19.5 |
| Mexico | 11.9 | 13.0 | 20.1 | 4.2 | 5.7 | 7.5 | 9.9 |
| Argentina* | 5.9 | 7.7 | 6.1 | 0.3 | 0.3 | 0.3 | 0.3 |
| Brazil* | 9.8 | 1.6 | 1.6 | 1.5 | 1.9 | 1.4 | 1.1 |
| Chile* | 12.7 | 6.3 | 8.7 | 0.2 | 0.3 | 0.3 | 0.3 |
| Korea | 17.2 | −0.2 | 5.7 | 1.9 | 4.1 | 2.9 | 2.6 |
| Taiwan | 15.7 | 0.9 | 6.9 | 2.8 | 5.3 | 4.0 | 3.7 |
| Hong Kong | 9.2 | 0.0 | 2.0 | 1.9 | 2.0 | 1.5 | 1.2 |
| Singapore | 19.8 | 11.4 | 9.3 | 0.7 | 1.9 | 2.3 | 2.3 |
| China | 35.0 | 26.4 | 17.3 | 0.3 | 2.5 | 5.8 | 7.1 |
| Indonesia* | −2.8 | 9.3 | 8.0 | 2.2 | 0.9 | 1.0 | 0.9 |
| Malaysia* | 8.6 | 21.2 | 5.9 | 0.9 | 1.0 | 1.8 | 1.7 |
| Philippines* | 7.4 | 9.7 | 20.0 | 0.7 | 0.7 | 0.8 | 1.0 |
| Thailand* | 20.0 | 16.1 | 6.8 | 0.4 | 1.0 | 1.4 | 1.3 |
| Total imports** | 8.5 | 7.0 | 9.5 | 8.3 | 8.8 | 9.6 | 10.8 |
| Memo: nominal GDP | 7.8 | 5.0 | 5.3 | | | | |

Notes:
Based on underlying data in current US dollars.
* Data for these countries begin in 1980.
** The shares shown for total imports are total imports as a share of GDP.

Sources: US Department of Commerce, Bureau of Economic Analysis, US International Transactions and National Income and Product Accounts, Survey of Current Business (various issues); Statistics Canada, World Trade Analyzer Suite; and author's calculations.

percent in 1989 to 13.9 percent in 1997. Not coincidentally, this sharp drop-off in Japanese export performance followed a major appreciation of the yen in the late 1980s and coincided with the country's slide into chronically depressed conditions.

All of the Four Tigers' export growth rates slowed down in the 1990s compared with the 1980s. The exports of Korea, Taiwan and Hong Kong to the United States were completely stagnant between 1989 and 1994. Exports from the first two of these countries recovered somewhat in 1994–97, but only to growth rates in the 5–7 percent range – far below their performance in the 1980s, and below the average growth in total US imports of 9.5 percent per year during the strong economic recovery of the 1994–97 period. Three of the Four Tigers (all except Singapore) lost market share in the United States in the 1990s.

Countries with high export growth rates and rising US market shares throughout the 1990s include, above all, China and Mexico.[22] Mexico's exports to the US grew at a 13 percent annual rate in 1989–94, as the country moved from unilateral trade liberalization toward membership in the North American Free Trade Agreement (NAFTA). Nevertheless, Mexico had a rising current account deficit throughout those years because, with liberalized trade and an overvalued peso, imports rose even faster than exports (see Blecker 1996). After NAFTA went into effect and the peso was devalued in 1994, Mexican export growth shot up to a 20.1 percent annual rate in 1994–97. Meanwhile, China's exports continued to grow at a very rapid 17.3 percent annual rate in 1994–97, down from the astronomical growth rates recorded earlier, but still about double the average growth rate for US imports, resulting in a further increase in China's market share.

A key country whose export growth slowed down in 1994–97 is Thailand, whose currency collapse sparked the 1997–98 Asian financial crisis. Thailand was widely expected to be one of the next 'Tigers' (see, for example, Smith 1991), but in fact its export growth slowed from a healthy 16.1 percent annual rate in 1989–94 to a mere 6.8 percent in 1994–97, below the average growth rate of US imports of 9.5 percent at that time.[23] One reason usually cited for Thailand's disappointing export performance and rising current account deficit in 1994–97 is the effective appreciation of the baht, which occurred because the baht was pegged to the US dollar and the dollar was rising relative to the European and Japanese currencies. But this factor cannot explain why Thailand's exports *to the United States* stag-nated. This can only be explained by the surging exports of *other* countries whose currencies had been devalued, which exported similar types of products, and whose market shares were rising, such as China and Mexico.

The point is not that slowing export growth caused all the financial crises of the 1990s, which it did not, although it seems to have been an important contributing factor in the case of Thailand. The point, rather, is to confirm that the 'fallacy of composition' began to hit home in the 1990s, when a large number of countries had begun to compete with the original Four Tigers, and surging exports and rising market shares for some countries meant sluggish exports and falling market shares for others. The issue for the 2000s, then, is how the developing nations can escape from this trap in which some can only succeed at the expense of others.

## POLICY ALTERNATIVES

Under present conditions, much could be done to expand global export markets and allow all countries to provide more reciprocal demand for each other's products. It is possible to imagine an optimistic scenario of economic recovery in Europe and Japan, along with continued robust growth in the United States and market-opening initiatives by all the industrialized countries, as well as increased south–south trade among the developing countries. But the probability of such an optimistic scenario occurring in reality appears low at present. The problems of high European unemployment and sluggish Japanese growth are longstanding; Europe is only beginning to recover and Japan is still mired in stagnation. Global trade imbalances, especially the US deficit and the European and Japanese surpluses, are getting worse and not better. The opposite scenario of global deflation and depression, while looking less likely in mid-2000 than it did at the peak of the Asian crisis in 1998, still cannot be ruled out.

Moreover, the prospects for further multilateral trade liberalization seem quite limited at present. Industrial workers in the industrialized countries understandably resent being asked to bear the adjustment burdens of allowing more manufactured imports from low-wage countries, while their employers can easily shift production facilities to those countries and increase their profits in the process. This is especially true in the United States, where the record trade deficits of the late 1990s and early 2000s imply that manufacturing jobs *are* being lost – the composition of employment is shifting toward non-tradeables, rather than toward export-oriented manufactures. At the same time, developing nations resent being asked to open their markets ever more to foreign trade and investment without seeing comparable gains in access to the industrialized countries' market. This dilemma has resulted in a political impasse over the direction that future trade negotiations should take, especially regarding whether they should incorporate labor rights, environmental standards and other social concerns.

For these reasons, the constraints on export-led growth are not likely to be relaxed in the near future. Probably the most likely scenario is that the global economy will continue to muddle along with uneven growth, sputtering recoveries, ad hoc regional trade agreements, more unbalanced trade and periodic financial crises. If this is the case, then continued reliance on export-led growth will only result in more of the same problems: recurrent balance of payments problems, unstable currencies, competitive devaluations and conflictive trade relations.

In this situation, the only way forward for the developing countries is to pursue more internally-oriented development,[24] with less reliance on export markets especially in the United States, and more acceptance of the need for rising domestic wages in order to create a mass consumer market. Greater labor bargaining rights and upgraded labor standards could enable workers to win wages more commensurate with their productivity and raise their living standards. Regional trade arrangements among developing countries (for example, MERCOSUR) could also be strengthened, although this will require resolving the financial and macroeconomic problems of those regions. Especially, all the high-saving countries in East Asia (including Japan) need to move away from the excessive saving rates they have achieved and start spending more on consumption, in order to avert the Keynesian paradox of thrift when export demand ceases to be a reliable stimulus.

## NOTES

\* The author would like to thank the Economic Policy Institute (EPI) and the Center for Economic Policy Analysis (CEPA), New School University, for financial support. He would also like to acknowledge helpful comments from Robert Scott and John Williamson, as well as participants in seminars at CEPA and the Workshop on Post Keynesian Economics at the University of Tennessee, Knoxville, on earlier drafts. The usual disclaimers apply.

1. An exception is Dutt (1990), who incorporates international demand constraints on growth in the context of asymmetrical north–south trade (for example, in his model of a neo-Kaleckian north and a neo-Marxian south).

2. Other qualifications include the possibility of expanding south–south trade, and the fact that even the most successful cases of export-led growth (especially in East Asia) also included other types of policies, such as land reform, education, fiscal prudence and targeted industrial policies (including financial incentives) favoring exporters.

3. According to Kleinknecht and ter Wengel (1998), only the United States has a significantly higher ratio of trade to GDP today than it did in the pre-World War I epoch, while the major European countries' openness to trade has barely returned to about its pre-1914 level and Japan's overall openness is notably lower today than it was at that time. Although the individual European countries appear more open to trade than either the United States or Japan, most of their trade is with each other, and the external trade of the EU countries as a group is about the same order of magnitude as that of the United States (and higher than Japan's).

4.  In this author's view, the restrictive macroeconomic policies adopted under the Maastricht Plan for monetary union are the primary cause of high European unemployment, rather than the alleged structural problems in European labor markets (rigid real wages, lack of 'flexibility') – but whatever one's view, it is clear that European economies have been unnaturally depressed and are not providing rapidly growing markets for developing country exports of manufactures.

5.  See, for example, Michaely (1977), Balassa (1978), McCarthy et al. (1987), Sprout and Weaver (1993), and Sachs and Warner (1995). See Blecker (1999, 2000) for more detailed discussion.

6.  See, for example, Kaminsky and Reinhart (1999), Radelet and Sachs (1998), and Sachs et al. (1996).

7.  Singh (1984: 58, 56), quoted in Balassa (1989: 65–6).

8.  In a similar vein, Scott (1999) argues that the slower growth of textile and apparel exports from Central America and the Caribbean in the late 1990s was caused by a surge in competitive exports from the East Asian countries following their currency depreciations in 1997–98.

9.  For some recent extensions of this model that incorporate mark-up pricing behavior, partial exchange rate pass-through and labor market dynamics, see Blecker (1998) and Pugno (1998).

10. Implicitly, this analysis also makes the standard Marshall–Lerner assumption that supplies of exports and imports are infinitely elastic and are priced in the seller's currency.

11. See McCombie and Thirlwall (1994) and McCombie (1997) for surveys of empirical tests of this model and extensions thereof. See Alonso and Garcimartín (1998–99) for a critique of earlier empirical tests and a new empirical methodology for this approach.

12. From this perspective, the export boost that most developing countries get following a devaluation is explained primarily by relative price effects, even though the import contraction that follows a devaluation usually results more from negative income effects (for example, reduced real wages) and asset valuation effects (for example, the increased domestic currency value of foreign currency debt service) rather than from relative price effects.

13. The AIDS model has been applied to international trade by Shiells et al. (1993) and Burfisher et al. (1994), among others.

14. In the alternative, 'nested' specification, consumers first choose between domestic products and imports, and then allocate their import expenditures between different export suppliers. This seems unrealistic, because actual consumers have to choose between products supplied from various individual countries (including the home country), and do not think of 'imports' as a distinct category.

15. Nevertheless, in this framework, a country's position on the industrial 'ladder' could be proxied by the income elasticity of demand for its exports, that is, countries producing basic, labor-intensive commodities would have lower income elasticities than countries producing more complex capital-intensive or skill-intensive goods. Also, countries with different product mixes can be proxied by having a low elasticity of substitution between their exports.

16. Assuming utility maximization imposes certain additional restrictions on the AIDS model, such as the homogeneity and symmetry conditions on the parameters of the expenditure functions. See Deaton and Muellbauer (1980) and Shiells et al. (1993) for details.

17. This presentation largely follows Shiells et al. (1993).

18. In general, we assume that exported goods are different from import-competing goods, and hence $p_i^d \neq p_i^m$. Similarly, we assume that the prices of industrialized country products imported by the developing countries are different from the prices of industrialized country products that compete with exports from the developing countries (that is, $p_n^m \neq p_n$).

19. Net capital flows could easily be added into the model, following the approach of either Thirlwall and Hussain (1982) or Moreno-Brid (1998–99), and in each case would allow for growth to exceed the rate shown in equation (7) provided that certain conditions are

met. This complication is not added here, in order to focus on the issue of cross-price competitive effects.

20.  The data in Table 4.1 were collected for 1979 (1980 for some countries), 1989, 1994 and 1997. The first two years bracket the decade of the 1980s, while eliminating business cycle effects in the US economy, since the starting and ending years were both cyclical peaks. The years 1994 and 1997 correspond to the outbreaks of the Mexican and Thai currency crises, respectively.
21.  Since the data in Table 4.1 are in nominal terms, they are affected by changes in prices of oil exports. The fact that oil prices were falling in 1979–89 makes Mexico's overall export growth in that period all the more spectacular, since Mexico had become a major oil exporter by 1979.
22.  The apparent slowdown in China's export growth in these data is misleading, since China's exports started from a very low base and the absolute growth of Chinese exports continues to be spectacular (resulting in steadily rising market shares) in spite of falling percentage growth rates.
23.  The only other Asian developing country that shows the same pattern as Thailand (that is, with a major slowdown in exports to the United States between 1989–94 and 1994–97) is Malaysia, whose export growth fell from 21.2 percent per year to 5.9 percent per year between those two periods.
24.  For related ideas on policy alternatives to the export-led growth model, see Mead (1999).

# REFERENCES

Akyüz, Y., H. Chang, and R. Kozul-Wright (1998), 'New perspectives on East Asian development', *Journal of Development Studies*, 34(6): 4–36.

Alonso, J. and C. Garcimartín (1998–99), 'A new approach to the balance-of-payments constraint: some empirical evidence', *Journal of Post Keynesian Economics*, 21(2): 259–82.

Balassa, B. (1978), 'Exports and economic growth: further evidence', *Journal of Development Economics*, 5, June: 181–9.

Balassa, B.A. (1989), *New Directions in the World Economy*, New York: New York University Press.

Ballance, R.H., J.A. Ansari and H.W. Singer (1982), *The International Economy and Industrial Development: The Impact of Trade and Investment on the Third World*, Totowa, NJ: Allanheld, Osmun.

Blecker, R.A. (1996), 'NAFTA, the peso crisis, and the contradictions of the Mexican economic growth strategy', *Center for Economic Policy Analysis, New School University, Working Paper Series I, No. 3*, July.

Blecker, R.A. (1998), 'International competition, relative wages, and the balance-of-payments constraint', *Journal of Post Keynesian Economics*, 20(4): 495–526.

Blecker, R.A. (1999), 'The fallacy of composition and the limits of export-led growth', Paper presented at the Meeting on the World Financial Authority, Center for Economic Policy Analysis, New School University, New York, July.

Blecker, R.A. (2000), *The Diminishing Returns to Export-led Growth*, Occasional Paper, New York: Council on Foreign Relations.

Burfisher, M.E., S. Robinson and K.E. Thierfelder (1994), 'Wage changes in a U.S.–Mexico free trade area: migration vs. Stolper–Samuelson effects', in J.F. Francois and C.R. Shiells (eds), *Modelling Trade Policy: Applied General Equilibrium Models of North American Free Trade*, Cambridge, UK: Cambridge University Press.

Cline, W.R. (1982), 'Can the East Asian export model of development be generalized?', *World Development*, 10(2): 81–90.

Cline, W.R. (1984), *Exports of Manufactures from Developing Countries*, Washington DC: Brookings Institution.

Deaton, A. and J. Muellbauer (1980), 'An almost ideal demand system', *American Economic Review*, 70(3): 312–26.

Dutt, A.K. (1990), *Growth, Distribution, and Uneven Development*, Cambridge, UK: Cambridge University Press.

Erturk, K. (1999), 'Worldwide Intersectoral Balance, Overcapacity and the East Asian Crisis', New School University and University of Utah, September, copy.

Greider, W. (1997), *One World, Ready or Not: The Manic Logic of Global Capitalism*, New York: Simon & Schuster.

Kaminsky, G.L. and C.M. Reinhart (1999), 'The twin crises: the causes of banking and balance-of-payments problems', *American Economic Review*, 89(3): 473–500.

Kaplinsky, R. (1993), 'Export processing zones in the Dominican Republic: transforming manufactures into commodities', *World Development*, 21(11): 1851–65.

Kaplinsky, R. (1999), '"If you want to get somewhere else, you must run at least twice as fast as that!": the roots of the East Asian crisis', *Competition & Change*, 4: 1–30.

Kleinknecht, A. and J. ter Wengel (1998), 'The myth of economic globalisation', *Cambridge Journal of Economics*, 22(5): 637–47.

Lawrence, R.Z. (1987), 'Imports in Japan: closed markets or minds?', *Brookings Papers on Economic Activity, 2:1987*, 517–54.

Lawrence, R.Z. (1991), 'Efficient or exclusionist? The import behavior of Japanese corporate groups', *Brookings Papers on Economic Activity, 1:1991*, 311–41.

McCarthy, F.D., L. Taylor and C. Talati (1987), 'Trade patterns in developing countries, 1964–82', *Journal of Development Economics*, 27: 5–39.

McCombie, J.S.L. (1997), 'Empirics of balance-of-payments-constrained growth', *Journal of Post Keynesian Economics*, 19(3): 345–75.

McCombie, J.S.L. and A.P. Thirlwall (1994), *Economic Growth and the Balance-of-Payments Constraint*, New York: St. Martin's.

Mead, W.R. (1999), 'The third way to economic development: how to reach beyond export-led growth', *Milken Institute Review*, 1(4): 30–40.

Michaely, M. (1977), 'Exports and growth: an empirical investigation', *Journal of Development Economics*, 4, March: 49–53.

Moreno-Brid, J.C. (1998–99), 'On capital flows and the balance-of-payments-constrained growth model', *Journal of Post Keynesian Economics*, 21(2): 283–98.

Pugno, M. (1998), 'The stability of Thirlwall's model of economic growth and the balance-of-payments constraint', *Journal of Post Keynesian Economics*, 20(4): 559–81.

Radelet, S., and J.D. Sachs (1998), 'The East Asian financial crisis: diagnosis, remedies, prospects', *Brookings Papers on Economic Activity, 1:1998*, 1–90.

Rogoff, K. (1996), 'The purchasing power parity puzzle,' *Journal of Economic Literature*, 34(2): 647–68.

Sachs, J.D., A. Tornell and A. Velasco (1996), 'Financial crises in emerging markets: the lessons from 1995', *Brookings Papers on Economic Activity, 1:1996*, 147–215.

Sachs, J.D., and A. Warner (1995), 'Economic reform and the process of global integration', *Brookings Papers on Economic Activity 1:1995*, 1–118.

Scott, R.E. (1999), 'Rebuilding the Caribbean: a better foundation for sustainable growth', Briefing Paper, Economic Policy Institute, Washington DC.

Shiells, C.R., D.W. Roland-Holst and K.A. Reinert (1993), 'Modeling a North American Free Trade Area: estimation of flexible functional forms', *Weltwirtschaftliches Archiv*, 129(1): 55–77.

Singh, A. (1984), 'The interrupted industrial revolution of the third world: prospects and policies for resumption', *Industry and Development*, 12: 43–68.

Singh, A. (1998), '"Asian Capitalism" and the Financial Crisis', *Working Paper Series III, No. 10*, Center for Economic Policy Analysis, New School University, August.

Smith, S.C. (1991), *Industrial Policy in Developing Countries: Reconsidering the Real Sources of Export-Led Growth*, Washington DC: Economic Policy Institute.

Sprout, R.V.A. and J.H. Weaver (1993), 'Exports and economic growth in a simultaneous equations model', *Journal of Developing Areas*, 27, April: 289–306.

Thirlwall, A.P. (1979), 'The balance of payments constraint as an explanation of international growth rate differences', *Banca Nazionale del Lavoro Quarterly Review*, 128, March: 45–53.

Thirlwall, A.P. and M.N. Hussain (1982), 'The balance of payments constraint, capital flows and growth rate differences between developing countries', *Oxford Economic Papers*, 34(3): 498–510.

Yotopoulos, P.A. and Y. Sawada (1999), 'Free currency markets and financial crises: is there a causal relationship?' *Seoul Journal of Economics*, 12, Winter: 419–56.

# 5. A new approach to test the balance of payments-constrained growth model, with reference to the Mexican economy

## Juan Carlos Moreno Brid*

## INTRODUCTION

Within the post Keynesian tradition, external demand is considered to be the dominant constraint on the long-run rate of expansion of domestic activity in most open economies. This perspective has its origin in the seminal contributions of Anthony P. Thirlwall. Based on Harrod's work on the foreign trade multiplier, he built a simple analytical model that, under the assumption that the current account deficit in the balance of payments cannot be indefinitely financed, shows that the long-run rate of economic growth is determined by the dynamism of exports and import demand (Thirlwall 1979). This analytical framework, referred to here as the BPCG model, was later revised to allow for the influence of foreign capital flows on long-term economic growth (Thirlwall and Hussain 1982). This second generation of the BPCG model, however, failed to ensure that the economy's long-run rate of growth is accompanied by an accumulation of external debt that is not on an explosive track.

To overcome this limitation, a third generation of BPCG models has recently been developed that captures potential effects of capital flows on long-run economic growth and, simultaneously, ensures a sustainable trajectory of external debt accumulation (McCombie and Thirlwall 1997; Moreno-Brid 1998–99). This new version establishes firmer theoretical foundations for the BPCG model and, at the same time, ratifies the main claims concerning the role of external demand as a binding constraint on long-run economic expansion. The analytical relevance of this third generation of the BPCG model has already been recognized (see Blecker 1999; McCombie and Thirlwall 1999). But its empirical adequacy has not yet been tested. This paper intends to verify its empirical pertinence by applying it to analyze Mexico's economic growth in the last 30 years.

The chapter is organized as follows. After this introduction, the second section gives a brief presentation of the analytical framework of the BPCG model, in its original and in its most recent formulation (here referred to as the third generation of such models). It also describes the methodology followed in the empirical analysis here carried out. This methodology – known as McCombie's test – is by now the standard econometric procedure to assess the BPCG model, and relies on the estimation of the country's long-run income elasticity of import demand and of its hypothetical equilibrium level (Thirlwall 1998; McCombie 1997). The third section presents the results of estimating such values for the income elasticity of Mexico's long-run import demand. The fourth section shows the results of McCombie's tests of the empirical relevance, for the Mexican case, of the BPCG model in its original expression as Thirlwall's Law and in its most recent formulation. The conclusions are presented in the final section.

## ANALYTICAL MODEL OF BALANCE OF PAYMENTS-CONSTRAINED ECONOMIC GROWTH

The third generation of BPCG models was launched by McCombie and Thirlwall (1997) and Moreno-Brid (1998–99). As mentioned above, the key characteristic of their analytical contributions is to revise the model so that it guarantees that the economy's long-run growth is associated with a sustainable path of external indebtedness. In McCombie and Thirlwall's contribution this result is achieved by imposing in the standard BPCG model a long-run balance-of-payments equilibrium condition defined in terms of a constant ratio of the *stock* of external debt relative to nominal income. In Moreno-Brid (1998–99), the equilibrium condition is instead defined as a constant proportion of the current account deficit relative to nominal income.[1] Following his specifications, the economy's long-run rate of BPCG growth may be derived from the following system of equations.

$$dx/x = \eta \, (dp/p - dp^*/p^*) + \pi dw/w \tag{1}$$

$$dm/m = \phi \, (dp^*/p^* - dp/p) + \xi \, dy/y \tag{2}$$

$$B = (p^* m - p \, x) \, / \, (py) \tag{3}$$

$$dB/dt = 0 \tag{4}$$

Equations (1) and (2) are standard export and import demand functions, but expressed in terms of their annual rates of growth; $x$ stands for real exports, $m$ for real imports, $w$ for world's real income, $y$ for real domestic income, $\eta < 0$ and $\pi > 0$ for the price and income elasticities of exports, $\phi < 0$, $\xi > 0$ for the respective elasticities of imports, and $p$ for domestic prices and $p^*$ for foreign prices expressed in a common currency. To simplify the analysis, a constant nominal exchange rate, equal to one, is assumed. Equation (3) is the balance of payments identity, but expressing the current account deficit as a proportion of domestic income. Equation (4) imposes the long-run equilibrium condition for the balance of payments defined as a constant ratio of the current account deficit to nominal income.

Substituting the first three equations in equation (4) defining $\theta$ as the initial year's export/import ratio measured at nominal prices, and solving for $dy/y$, leads to the following specification of the long-run rate of economic growth compatible with a sustainable path of foreign indebtedness (denoted as $\hat{y}_b$):

$$\hat{y}_b = \frac{\theta\pi(dw/w) + (\theta\eta + \phi + 1)(dp/p - dp^*/p^*)}{\xi - (1 - 0)} \tag{5}$$

This equation shows that, if the economy satisfies the long-run equilibrium conditions stipulated in equation (4), then the long-run rate of growth of *real* income $\hat{y}_b$ is given by the initial proportion of foreign exchange requirements supplied by exports, the income and price elasticities of export and imports, and the rates of expansion of the world economy and of the terms of trade. If, in addition, the terms of trade are assumed constant, then equation (5) is simplified to

$$\hat{y}_b = \frac{\theta\pi(dxw/w)}{\xi - (1 - 0)} \tag{6}$$

Or equivalently:[2]

$$\hat{y}_b = \frac{\theta dx/x}{\xi - (1 - 0)} \tag{7}$$

The original formulation of the BPCG model referred to as 'Thirlwall's Law' is easily derived as the special case of equation (7) by assuming that the long-run equilibrium of the current account deficit is zero:

$$\hat{y}_b = \frac{dx/x}{\xi} \tag{8}$$

The empirical analysis for this paper relied on the methodology recommended in two of the most recent comprehensive surveys of applied work on balance of payments-constrained growth economies (Thirlwall 1998; McCombie 1997). This methodology checks the empirical validity of the BPCG model for any given economy by examining whether the long-run income elasticity of import demand, $\xi$, does not significantly differ from its hypothetical equilibrium value, $\xi_H$.[3] The value of $\xi$ should be estimated using time-series techniques that are adequate for the study of long-run phenomena. In turn, $\xi_H$ is defined as the value of the income elasticity of import demand that would equate the actual growth rate of the economy $dy/y$ with its BPCG growth rate $\hat{y}_b$ in the period under consideration. If there is no significant difference between $\xi$ and $\xi_H$, the BPCG model is empirically relevant for the case in point.

The test's conclusions are contingent on the underlying formulation of the BPCG growth rate, $\hat{y}_b$. In this paper we consider the alternative versions of it given by equations (7) and (8). The former corresponds to the revised version of Thirlwall's Law that guarantees a sustainable path of foreign indebtedness. The latter represents its original formulation, based on the assumption of no long-run current account deficit.

The corresponding hypothetical equilibrium values of the income elasticity of imports are obtained as follows. For the revised version of Thirlwall's Law, it is derived by substituting in equation (7) the actual average growth rate of GDP, $dy/y$, for the BPCG growth rate, $\hat{y}_b$, and then solving for $\xi$. This value is denoted as $\xi_x$ and equals:

$$\xi_x = (1 - \theta) + [(\theta \, dx/x) \, / \, dy/y] \tag{9}$$

In turn, the hypothetical equilibrium income elasticity consistent with the original version of Thirlwall's Law is similarly derived by substituting in equation (8) the actual value of $dy/y$ instead of the BPCG rate $\hat{y}_b$, and again solving for $\xi$. It is here referred to as $\xi_T$:

$$\xi_T = (dx/x) \, / \, (dy/y) \tag{10}$$

Note that the calculations of $\xi_T$ as well as of $\xi_x$ are based on the assumption that relative prices and non-tariff constraints are not important influences on the economy's long-run growth rate in the relevant period of analysis. $\xi_T$ may be interpreted as a special case of $\xi_x$ when the values of exports and imports are equal ($\theta = 1$).

# ESTIMATION OF MEXICO'S LONG-RUN IMPORT DEMAND

## Methodological Framework and Overview of Previous Studies

Econometric studies of imports are typically based on the theoretical framework known as the 'imperfect substitutes' model. The model is built on the assumption that domestic and foreign goods are not perfect substitutes and concludes that import demand is determined by the importing country's income, the own price of imports, and the domestic price of locally produced tradeable goods and services. In addition, monetary illusion is frequently assumed away and a zero-homogeneity restriction is imposed to guarantee that the foreign and the domestic price-elasticity of import demand have the same magnitude in absolute terms. Furthermore, an infinite elasticity of supply is generally taken for granted, thus validating the use of single-equation econometric methods to estimate import flows.[4] The standard functional specification of long-run import demand is

$$\ln(m_t) = \beta_0 + \beta_y \ln(y_t) + \beta_p \ln (Pm_t / Pd_t) + \upsilon_t \qquad (11)$$

where $\upsilon_t$ stands for a white noise disturbance term, $m_t$ for real imports and $y_t$ for the real domestic income of the importing country. $Pd_t$ and $Pm_t$ stand respectively for domestic price indices of locally produced tradable output and of imported goods and services expressed in local currency. The parameters $\beta_y \geq 0$ and $\beta_p \leq 0$ correspond to the long-run income and price elasticities of import demand. Being an expression of a long-run equilibrium relation, the log-linear function in equation (11) does not consider any short-run lagged influences.[5]

Most empirical studies of Mexico's import demand have adopted this framework. However, some have modified it to capture the effects of trade protection on import demand. This concern is rooted in the country's historic reliance on tariff and non-tariff barriers to shield its domestic market from foreign competition, as a way to stimulate industrialization via the substitution of imports. Mexico's trade protectionism was brought to an end in the aftermath of the collapse in 1982 of its oil-driven dash for growth. Indeed, soon after the nation embarked on a process of radical macroeconomic reform, systematically phasing out non-tariff barriers on imports and reducing the average level and dispersion of import tariffs. Its trade liberalization ultimately culminated in the North American Free Trade Agreement (NAFTA), the trilateral agreement signed between Mexico, the United States and Canada that went into effect on 1 January 1994 to eliminate, over the next ten years, tariff and non-tariff barriers to most intra-regional trade as well as to ease restrictions on foreign investment (SECOFI 1994; OECD 1996). Moreover, by the year 2000 it had signed a similar trade agreement with the European Union.

Two methodologies have typically been followed to capture the effects of non-price restrictions on Mexico's demand for imports. The first is to include 'dummy' variables as regressors to capture the hysteresis effects on import demand of changes in trade protectionist measures (see, inter alia, Dornbusch and Werner 1994; Sarmiento 1999). The second approach is to include as regressors variables that may mirror the incidence of non-tariff restrictions on trade flows (Salas 1982, 1988; Ize 1992; López and Guerrero 1998; Sotomayor 1997). Despite differences in samples and estimation techniques, studies of the Mexican case have concluded that non-tariff barriers significantly influenced its imports.

Notwithstanding their merits, earlier studies of Mexican imports have shortcomings that limit their usefulness for the purpose of the present investigation. One of their limitations is their concern with rather short periods. These fail to adequately cover the country's transition from trade protectionism (until the early 1980s) to being today one of the most open economies to foreign trade. Another of their shortcomings is their use of econometric methods that pay insufficient attention to the stationary properties of time series (see, for example, Alberro 1998; Carvajal and Loria 1994; Sarmiento 1999). Such neglect implies that their results may suffer problems of spurious correlation, bias and inconsistency of the estimated parameters, and their statistical inferences may be erroneous (Carone 1996; Enders 1995; Rao 1994).

Galindo and Cardero (1999), López and Guerrero (1998) Senhadji (1998) and Sotomayor (1997) are the only published econometric studies of Mexican import demand that consider the non-stationary properties of the relevant variables. The first two contributions used Johansen's cointegration techniques to examine Mexican imports during 1989–95 and 1982–93, respectively. These samples cover the period when Mexico's domestic market opened to foreign competition but capture none, or very few, years of NAFTA's operation. Thus it is unwise to take their results as reasonable estimates for Mexico's long-run import demand. Senhadji (1998) applied cointegration techniques to estimate Mexico's import demand during 1960–93, thus covering years before NAFTA was put in place. Sotomayor (1997) focused on long-run demand for Mexican imports during 1950–94; covering only one year of operations of NAFTA. Moreover, the cointegration analysis was conducted applying Engle and Granger single-equation methods, a procedure that ignores the possibility of multiple cointegrating relations and whose results critically depend on the variable chosen to normalize the cointegrating relation (Maddala and Kim 1998). Furthermore, its findings are questionable because, by including as a regressor a trade-weighted index of the coverage of import licenses, it introduced the endogenous variable on both sides of the regression equation of import demand.

Our analysis of Mexico's long-term import demand tries to overcome the above-mentioned limitations. It applies Johansen's cointegration methods and covers a period that extends from Mexico's trade protectionist era in the 1960s, through the implementation of trade liberalization in the mid-1980s, up until 1999 with NAFTA in its sixth year of operation. Also, it explicitly allows for the effects of non-tariff restrictions on import demand. Given the evidence collected in earlier studies of Mexican imports, *a priori* omitting such restrictions may introduce a misspecification bias and lead to unreliable estimates and statistical inferences (Greene 1993). The *a priori* exclusion of a relevant variable would lead the tests to reject the hypothesis of cointegration among the remaining variables (Kennedy 1998).

Identifying a variable that accurately measures a country's policy stance regarding its restrictions to foreign trade is not trivial. In the case of Mexico, there is consensus that prior permit requirements – that is, import licenses – were its main instrument to shield its domestic market from foreign competition (Balassa 1983; De Mateo 1988; Ten Kate 1992; Ros 1994). Lists of official import reference prices were also used to protect local producers from foreign competition, but their coverage and relevance was much lower. Mexico's ministry of industry (SECOFI) has been calculating an index of the production-weighted coverage of import licenses. This index may be a good indicator to capture the effects of trade restrictions on imports. It avoids the downward bias inherent in the use of trade-weighted average coverage of licenses in situations where trade protection is very severe (Cameron et al. 1999).[6]

Other indicators of trade restrictions, such as the average and dispersion of tariff rates or the indicators of the degree of exchange rate controls, may not be so useful for the present case. First, the impact of tariff rates is already taken into account in the estimation of import demand, through their effect on relative prices.[7] Second, in the Mexican case, exchange rate controls were relevant only for a few years. In August 1982, in the aftermath of the collapse of the international oil market, and faced with massive capital flight and a severe balance of payments crisis, the Mexican government imposed a dual exchange rate: a 'controlled' rate to be used only for authorized transactions related to foreign trade or debt payments, and a 'free-rate' to operate for the other transactions. In September full exchange rate controls on all capital flows were imposed and the banking system was expropriated by the state. Exchange rate controls began to be relaxed by President Miguel de la Madrid, who took office in December of that year. In practice, they were eliminated in July 1985, when a new exchange rate regime was put in place based on a managed float in the controlled tier and banks were authorized to buy and sell dollars at the 'black' market rate (Lustig and Ros 1987).

Denoting the index of the production-weighted coverage of import licenses as $q$ and introducing it directly in the right-hand side of equation (11) leads to the following specification of long-run import demand:

$$\ln(m_t) = \beta_0 + \beta_y \ln(y_t) + \beta_p \ln(p_t) + \beta_q q_t + v_t \tag{12}$$

where, for simplification purposes, the ratio of relative prices $Pm_t / Pd_t$ expressed in common local currency is denoted as $p_t$. By construction the value of $q$ falls between zero and one ($0 \leq q \leq 1$). It equals zero when all license requirements on imports have been eliminated, and it equals one when they are mandatory on every importable good or service. Given Mexico's commitment in the last 15 years to liberalize its domestic market to foreign competitors, it seems reasonable to assume that the long-run value of $q$ is zero. The expected sign of $\beta_q$ is negative. To interpret this parameter, it is useful to differentiate equation (12) with respect to time, and thus obtain the following expression for the long-run rate of growth of import demand:

$$\frac{dm}{m} = \beta_y \frac{dy}{y} + \beta_p \frac{dp}{p} + \beta_q \frac{dq}{dt} \tag{13}$$

Therefore $\beta_q$ represents the increase in the long-run rate of growth of import demand ($dm/m$) that *ceteris paribus* would be caused by the elimination of import licensing in a fully protected domestic market; that is, when $dq$ takes its minimum value ($dq = -1$).

Equation (12) is the basis for the estimation of Mexico's long-run import demand conducted here.[8] It was carried out with annual data because no quarterly data were available for some variables before 1980. The time series for real imports and real GDP and in nominal terms were derived from national accounts data published by the Instituto Nacional de Estadística, Geografía e Informática. The relative price was computed as the ratio of the implicit price deflators of imports and of GDP. Data for $q$, the production-weighted index of the coverage of import permits for 1967–94, were obtained from Secretaría de Comercio y Fomento Industrial (SECOFI). For 1995–99, the index was calculated by the author based on official information from Banco de Mexico. Lack of information on the incidence of import licenses on Mexico's tradable output prior to 1967 impeded tracing the index $q$ further back; thus limiting the estimation of Mexico's long-run import demand to 1967–99.

## Cointegration Tests of Mexico's Demand for Imports: 1967–99

The first step for the cointegration analysis of Mexico's long-run import demand via Johansen cointegration methods was to apply Dickey–Fuller

and augmented Dickey–Fuller (DF and ADF) tests to examine the stationary properties during 1967–99 of the time series considered in equation
(12).[9] Selection of the optimum lag $k$ for the ADF tests was done with the
Akaike information criteria (AIC) and the Schwarz Bayesian criteria
(SBC). The findings indicate that all four variables – that is, the production-
weighted coverage of import permits, and the log levels of real GDP, real
imports and relative prices – are I(1) processes, and their first differences are
I(0) processes (Table 5.1).

Applying the Akaike information and Schwartz Bayesian criteria, an

*Table 5.1    Mexico: Dickey–Fuller and augmented Dickey–Fuller tests on
selected variables to estimate long-run import demand, 1967–99*

(A)  $\Delta z_t = \alpha + \rho z_{t-i} + \Sigma^k(\gamma_i \Delta z_{t-i}) + \xi_t$

(B)  $\Delta z_t = \alpha + \lambda_t + \rho z_{t-i} + \Sigma^k(\gamma_i \Delta z_{t-i}) + \xi_t$

|  | Lag $k$ Selected by AIC | | Lag $k$ Selected by SBC | |
|---|---|---|---|---|
| Equation A: | lag $k$ | ADF | lag $k$ | ADF |
| ln($y$) | 0 | −3.187* | Same as AIC | |
| $\Delta$ ln($y$) | 0 | −3.800* | Same as AIC | |
| ln($m$) | 2 | −0.042 | 0 | −0.099 |
| $\Delta$ ln($m$) | 1 | −4.668* | Same as AIC | |
| ln($p$) | 1 | −2.652 | 0 | −2.139 |
| $\Delta$ ln($p$) | 1 | −5.355* | Same as AIC | |
| $q$ | 1 | −1.112 | Same as AIC | |
| $\Delta q$ | 0 | −3.531* | Same as AIC | |
| | | | | |
| Equation B: | | | | |
| ln($y$) | 0 | −1.774 | Same as AIC | |
| $\Delta$ ln($y$) | 0 | −4.338* | Same as AIC | |
| ln($m$) | 1 | −2.867 | Same as AIC | |
| $\Delta$ ln($m$) | 1 | −4.651* | Same as AIC | |
| ln($p$) | 3 | −2.095 | 0 | −2.015 |
| $\Delta$ ln($p$) | 1 | −5.345* | Same as AIC | |
| $q$ | 1 | −2.454 | Same as AIC | |
| $\Delta q$ | 0 | −3.489* | Same as AIC | |

*Notes:*
AIC = Akaike Information criteria, SBC = Schwarz Bayesian criteria, $y$ = real GDP, $m$ = real
imports, $p$ = ratio of implicit price deflators of imports relative to domestic output, $q$ =
production-weighted coverage of prior import licensing requirements. $\Delta$ stands for first
differences. An asterisk denotes significance with Dickey–Fuller's 5 percent critical values.

*Source:*    Own calculations with Microfit 4.0.

optimum one-year lag was identified for the unrestricted VAR system for import demand under the assumption of no deterministic trends (Table 5.2). The variable $q$ was assumed to be an exogenous I(1) process in the VAR. Such an assumption does not rule out short-run effects among all the variables in the VAR system (Pesaran and Pesaran 1997) but implies that in the long run the imposition of prior permit requirements on imports is not determined by the evolution of the endogenous variables (real GDP, real imports or relative prices). This assumption may be justified by the fact that in the last 15 years, and independently of the evolution of domestic economic activity, Mexico has been persistently eliminating its licenses and quantitative restrictions on imports and refraining from imposing additional barriers to foreign trade. As a matter of fact, even in the midst of the acute balance of payments crisis suffered in 1995, Mexico moved ahead in its trade liberalization strategy and continued honoring its commitments to NAFTA.

*Table 5.2    Mexico: Statistical specification of VAR system to estimate long-run import demand (based on annual data, 1967–99)*

| Period | Test Statistics and Optimal Order for VAR System | | | Order chosen | LM Serial Correlation Tests for Individual Equations of of VAR(1) System ($p$ values) | | |
|---|---|---|---|---|---|---|---|
| | AIC | SBC | ALR | $k$ | $\ln(m)$ | $\ln(y)$ | $\ln(p)$ |
| 1967–99 | 143.6 $k=1$ | 132.4 $k=1$ | 0.477 $k=1$ | 1 | 0.260 | 0.405 | 0.054 |

*Notes:*
The VAR system was estimated taking the production-weighted coverage of import licenses as an I(1) exogenous variable.
AIC = Akaike information criteria, SBC = Schwarz Bayesian criteria, ALR = adjusted likelihood ratio, LM = Lagrange multiplier test, $y$ = real GDP, $x$ = real exports, $p$ = ratio of implicit price deflators of imports relative to domestic output.

*Source:*   Own calculations with Microfit 4.0.

Lagrange multiplier tests were conducted to check for residual serial correlation of the individual equations of the VAR(1) system. In all cases, the results could not reject the hypothesis of no serial correlation with a 5 percent critical level (see again Table 5.2). Johansen tests were applied on this VAR(1) system to estimate a cointegrating vector for Mexico's import demand. No deterministic trend was assumed, but two different specifications for the intercept were explored. Under the assumption of an unrestricted intercept, the tests identified one cointegration vector for import demand. But two vectors were identified when the intercept was restricted to the cointegrating space. In such instances, the vector corresponding to the largest eigenvalue was chosen as the adequate estimate of Mexico's long-run import demand, once it had been checked that its cointegrating coefficients were consistent with the theoretical model of import demand.

The assumption regarding the intercept's specification, as restricted or unrestricted, did not lead to qualitatively different estimates for Mexico's long-run import demand in 1967–99 (Table 5.3). Under either specification at least one cointegrating vector was identified. And the respective coefficients were very similar, reporting an estimated long-run income elasticity, $\beta_y$, of around 1.8, a long-run price elasticity, $\beta_p$, of close to –0.5, and an estimated parameter for the long-run effect of import permits, $\beta_q$, of around –1.0. Individual significance of the cointegrating coefficients was tested by imposing over-identifying restrictions equalizing each one to zero. The results of the respective tests based on the likelihood ratio statistics (LRS) always rejected the null hypothesis of a zero income elasticity, $\beta_y = 0$. They also rejected the null hypothesis of non-significant effects of import licenses, $\beta_q = 0$. However, the tests could not reject the hypothesis that the price elasticity of Mexico's import demand during 1967–99 was not significantly different from zero, $\beta_p = 0$.[10] (Table 5.3, part A).

The lack of a significant long-run effect of relative prices on import demand satisfies one condition to validate the BPCG hypothesis. As McCombie and Thirlwall argue:

> for a country to be potentially balance-of-payments constrained, the change in relative prices cannot have a significant effect on the growth of exports or imports (McCombie and Thirlwall 1999: 49).

It remains to be tested whether relative prices do not have a significant long-run impact on Mexican exports.[11]

Given this result, Mexico's long-run import demand was again estimated for 1967–99 but excluding the relative price variable from the VAR system. The results of Johansen's tests assuming an unrestricted intercept identified one cointegrating vector among the log levels of GDP and of imports and the index of non-tariff restrictions $q$ (Table 5.3, part B). The estimated cointegrating coefficient for the long-run income elasticity of import demand was $\beta_y = 1.772$, practically the same as the corresponding estimate obtained using the larger VAR system. The estimated coefficient for the long-run response of imports to changes in non-tariff restrictions was $\beta_q = -1.269$; not too different from its previous estimate ($-1.044$).

The estimates for the long-run income elasticity here obtained are well within the range of earlier findings on Mexican import demand. However,

*Table 5.3    Mexico's long-term import demand, 1967–99 (estimated with Johansen's cointegration procedures)*

$$\ln(m) = \alpha + \rho_y \ln(y) + \rho_p \ln(p) + \rho_q q + v$$

Part A: Results for VAR(1) system with three endogenous variables: $\ln(m)$, $\ln(v)$ and $\ln(p)$

| | Test on max eigenvalue | | | Test on trace | | | Cointegration vector and $\chi^2$ test on the significance of $\rho_p$ and $\rho_q$ |
|---|---|---|---|---|---|---|---|
| | $H_0$ $r=0$ | $H_1$ $r=1$ | LRS 48.7* | $H_0$ $r=0$ | $H_1$ $r\geq1$ | LRS 67.7* | $A_1$. $\ln(m)=1.777\ln(y)-0.536\ln(p)-1.044\,(q)$ |
| Unrestricted intercept ($\alpha=0$) | $r\leq1$ $r=2$ | | 14.1 | $r\leq1$ $r\geq2$ | | 19.0 | $\quad\quad\quad\quad(0.12)\quad\quad\quad(0.27)\quad\quad\quad(0.16)$ |
| | $r\leq2$ $r=3$ | | 4.9 | $r\leq2$ $r=3$ | | 4.9 | $\chi^2[\rho_p=0]\,p\text{ value}=0.193\quad\chi^2[\rho_q=0]\,p\text{ value}=0.000$ |
| | $r=0$ $r=1$ | | 72.2* | $r=0$ $r\geq1$ | | 103.9* | $A_2$. $\ln(m)=1.872\ln(y)-0.577\ln(p)-0.983\,q-6.52$ |
| Restricted intercept ($\alpha\neq0$) | $r\leq1$ $r=2$ | | 20.8* | $r\leq1$ $r\geq2$ | | 31.8* | $\quad\quad\quad\quad(0.15)\quad\quad\quad(0.28)\quad\quad\quad(0.15)\quad\quad(2.16)$ |
| | $r\leq2$ $r=3$ | | 11.0 | $r\leq2$ $r=3$ | | 11.0 | $\chi^2[\rho_p=0]\,p\text{ value}=0.187\quad\chi^2[\rho_q=0]\,p\text{ value}=0.000$ |

Part B: Results for VAR(1) system excluding the relative price of imports ln($p$)

| | *Test on max eigenvalue* | | | *Test on trace* | | | Cointegration vector |
|---|---|---|---|---|---|---|---|
| | $H_0$ | $H_1$ | LRS | $H_0$ | $H_1$ | LRS | |
| Unrestricted intercept ($\alpha=0$) | $r=0$ | $r=1$ | 41.7* | $r=0$ | $r=1$ | 49.9* | $B_1$. ln($m$) = 1.772 ln($y$) − 1.269 $q$ |
| | $r\leq1$ | $r=2$ | 8.3 | $r\leq1$ | $r=2$ | 8.3 | (0.18)  (0.19) |
| Restricted intercept ($\alpha\neq0$) | $r=0$ | $r=1$ | 56.9* | $r=0$ | $r=1$ | 75.2* | Not available |
| | $r\leq1$ | $r=2$ | 18.3* | $r\leq1$ | $r=2$ | 18.3* | |

*Notes:*
Tests are carried out assuming no deterministic trend and taking the coverage of import license requirements ($q$) as an exogenous I(1) process. In Part A, when two cointegrating vectors were identified, the one associated with the largest eigenvalue is reported here. In Part B, since there are only two endogenous variables, there can be at most one linearly independent cointegrating relation between them. The identification of two such vectors by Johansen tests may reflect specification errors in the VAR system.
$H_0$ = null hypothesis, $H_1$ = alternative hypothesis, $r$ = number of cointegrating vectors, LRS = likelihood ratio statistics, $y$ = real GDP, $m$ = real imports, $p$ = ratio of the implicit price deflators of imports relative to domestic output, $q$ = production-weighted coverage of import licenses. An asterisk (*) denotes significance with a 5 percent critical level. Asymptotic standard errors of the estimated cointegration coefficients are reported in parentheses.

*Source:*   Own calculations with Microfit 4.0.

the non-significance of the price elasticity contrasts with previous results. Such contrast may be due to the fact that earlier studies of Mexican imports focused on rather short periods, in which the influence of relative prices may have been relevant. Finally, our findings concerning the significantly negative influence of quantitative trade restrictions on import demand are consistent with the results of earlier studies of Mexican imports.

For the VAR system that excluded relative prices, the application of Johansen's tests under the assumption of a restricted intercept led to results that were not satisfactory. They suggested the presence of specification problems in the VAR system. Therefore the cointegrating vector estimated under the assumption of an unrestricted intercept for the trivariate VAR system was considered as our preferred results for Mexico's long-run import demand during 1967–99.

## TESTING THE BPCG MODEL FOR THE MEXICAN ECONOMY

This section applies McCombie's procedure to examine the comparative adequacy, for the Mexican case, of Thirlwall's Law in its original version and in its revised form as put forward in the third generation of BPCG models. Essentially it tests whether the long-run income elasticity of Mexican imports, $\xi$ – estimated via cointegration analysis in the previous section – is significantly different from the hypothetical equilibrium value as given either by $\xi_T$ or by $\xi_x$.

Using official data on the average annual rate of growth of Mexico's real GDP and real exports, equations (9) and (10) lead to the following estimates for the hypothetical equilibrium value of the income elasticity of import demand during 1967–99: $\xi_T$ is equal to 2.189 and $\xi_x$ to 1.991. Both estimated figures are, apparently, not too distant from the estimate of 1.777 for the long-run income elasticity of import demand derived with Johansen's techniques applied on the full sample for 1967–99 (Table 5.4). Obviously they do not differ very much from the alternative estimate of the long-run income elasticity, $\xi = 1.772$, derived by the cointegration tests applied on the trivariate VAR system that excluded relative prices. The significance of the differences must be formally tested.

The likelihood ratio statistics calculated to test the over-identifying restriction $H_0$: $\xi = \xi_T$ imposed on the cointegrating vector for the full VAR system (including relative prices) reject the null hypothesis at a 5 percent critical level of significance (see again Table 5.3). Such a result suggests that Thirlwall's Law, in its original formulation, does not offer an adequate interpretation of Mexico's long-run economic growth during 1967–99. On

*Table 5.4  Test of the empirical relevance of Thirlwall's Law (original and extended versions) for the Mexican economy, 1967–99 (based on McCombie's procedure)*

| | Income Elasticity of Import Demand | | | | | | |
| | Johansen's cointegration coefficient | Hypothetical equilibria consistent with Thirlwall's Law as expressed in the: | | | LRS Tests of Equality of the Long-run Income Elasticity and Its Hypothetical Equilibrium Values (p values) [a] | | |
| | | original BPCG model [b] | extended BPCG model [c] | | Null hypothesis | | |
| VAR system for import demand | $\xi$ | $\xi_T$ | $\xi_x$ | $\xi_{xm}$ | $\xi = \xi_T$ | $\xi = \xi_x$ | $\xi = \xi_{xm}$ |
| A. With four variables ln($m$), ln($y$), ln($p$) and $q$ | 1.777 | 2.189 | 1.991 | 2.058 | 0.048 | 0.177 | 0.108 |
| B. With three variables [d] ln($m$), ln($y$) and $q$ | 1.772 | 2.189 | 1.991 | 2.058 | 0.072 | 0.282 | 0.178 |

*Notes:*

a  The $p$ values of the $\chi^2$ corresponding to the LRS to test the over-identifying restriction equalizing the cointegrating coefficient for the income elasticity of import demand to its hypothetical equilibrium derived from different versions of Thirlwall's Law.

b  $\xi_T$ is derived from equation (10).

c  $\xi_x$ is derived from equation (9) taking $\theta$ (the export/import ratio) reported for 1967. $\xi_{xm}$ is calculated with the value of $\theta$ given by the ratio of the sums of exports and imports for the whole period 1967–99.

d  The tests were conducted using the results derived by Johansen's cointegration tests on the trivariate VAR system (excluding relative prices) because the coefficient for price elasticity in the cointegrating vector in the full VAR system for 1967–99 was not significant.

*Source:*  Own calculations with Microfit 4.0.

the other hand, when the alternative definition of the long-run balance of payments equilibrium is adopted, the conclusions of the LRS tests are the opposite. Indeed, their results could not reject the null hypothesis $\xi = \xi_x$ even at a 10 percent level of significance. Thus they give strong support to the modified version of Thirlwall's Law given by equation (7) as a relevant hypothesis for the Mexican case. The result gives some grounds to claim that the third generation of BPCG models recently introduced may strengthen the empirical relevance of the theory of balance of payments-constrained growth economies.

The results of the LRS tests on the cointegrating vector identified in the analysis of the trivariate VAR system for 1967–99 (excluding relative prices) also suggest that, for the Mexican case, the third generation BPCG model may be more relevant than the original one (see again Table 5.4). Indeed, they did not reject the null hypothesis $H_0$: $\xi = \xi_x$. With a $p$ value of 0.282, they strongly confirm the adequacy of the modified version of Thirlwall's Law given by equation (7) for the empirical analysis of Mexico's long-run economic growth. Substituting the actual rate of expansion achieved by real exports during 1967–99 in equation (7) gives an estimate of 4.4 percent for the balance of payments-constrained rate of annual expansion of the Mexican economy. This rate is very close to the 3.8 percent annual average increase achieved by Mexico's real GDP in those years.

The LRS test of the null hypothesis $H_0$: $\xi = \xi_T$ using the cointegrating vector estimated for the trivariate VAR system – that is, excluding relative prices – reported a $p$ value of 0.072. This result rejects the null hypothesis at the 10 percent critical level, though not at the 5 percent level. It gives support to the empirical adequacy of Thirlwall's Law in its original version given by equation (8); but somewhat weaker than that given to its revised version expressed in equation (7). In its original version, Thirlwall's Law indicates that Mexico's BPCG average annual rate of growth during 1967–99 was 4.8 percent. This figure is 0.4 percent higher than the previous estimate, and one point above the actual rate of growth of real GDP.

## CONCLUSIONS

The paper's findings show that the balance of payments was a binding constraint on Mexico's long-run economic growth in 1967–99. In addition, they indicate that during these years the terms of trade played no significant role in determining Mexico's long-run economic growth. More importantly, the results prove that the introduction of an alternative definition of balance-of-payments long-run equilibrium (as a constant ratio of the current account deficit relative to income) may enhance the empirical relevance of the BPCG model. Hopefully, this extended version of the BPCG model – what we have called here the third generation – will be useful for the empirical study of long-run growth in other economies.

## NOTES

\*   This paper is an abridged version of chapter 4 of the author's PhD dissertation: 'Essays on economic growth and the balance-of-payments constraint, with special reference to the case of Mexico', Faculty of Economics and Politics, University of Cambridge, 2001. The comments of Jesus Felipe, John McCombie, Carlo Panico and Martín Puchet on earlier versions of this paper are gratefully acknowledged.

1.   The model in McCombie and Thirlwall (1997) has the limitations of assuming away changes in the terms of trade and of not analyzing the stability properties of the economy's long-run equilibrium. These limitations are overcome in Moreno-Brid (1998–99).

2.   Equation 7 coincides with the expression derived by McCombie and Thirlwall (1997) by imposing the alternative long-run equilibrium condition in terms of a fixed ratio of the stock of external debt to GDP, and constant terms of trade.

3.   For a comparative evaluation of the alternative procedures to test the BPCG model, see Thirlwall (1998) and McCombie (1997).

4.   Goldstein and Khan (1985) present a synthetic view of the imperfect and the perfect substitutes theoretical models. Houthakker and Magee (1969) is the classic work on the empirical estimation of long-run export and import functions. Caporale and Chui (1999), Krugman (1989), Márquez (1999) and Hooper et al. (1998) estimate trade elasticities for OECD and other countries in recent periods.

5.   The concept of long-run equilibrium adopted in the BPCG literature is not the same as the theoretical notion of a steady-state growth path. The latter requires a unitary income elasticity of import demand to keep a constant import/output ratio in the steady state when relative prices $Pm / Pd$ remain unaltered.

6.   Use of production-weighted indices of coverage of import licenses to mirror quantitative restrictions on foreign trade was common practice in the World Bank's Trade Policy Loans to Mexico in the 1980s (Ten Kate 1992).

7.   Alternative measures of trade policy openness based on *ex post* outcomes include the export/output or import/output ratios (Cameron et al. 1999). These are frequently used in analysis of the relation of trade openness and economic growth.

8.   The inclusion of $q$ in log-level form in equation (11) is not recommended because it would imply that, unless $\beta_q = 0$, the elimination of import licenses *a fortiori* causes an unbounded increase in the long-run demand for imports in real terms, even assuming constant domestic income and relative prices.

9.   A synthetic description of Johansen's testing procedure may be found in Enders (1995).

10.  If the null hypothesis formulated as an over-identifying restriction on the coefficients of the normalized cointegration vector holds, the likelihood ratio statistic (LRS) is asymptotically distributed as $\chi^2$ with one degree of freedom (Pesaran and Pesaran 1997).

11.  However, Alonso and Garcimartin (1998–99) suggest that the BPCG model may be valid even if relative prices influence the long-run rate of economic growth.

## REFERENCES

Alberro, J.L. (1998), 'Productivity, trade liberalization and productive restructuring', in NAFTA's Commission for Labor Cooperation (ed.), *Incomes and Productivity in North America: papers from the 1997 seminar*, Dallas, TX.

Alonso, J. and C. Garcimartin (1998–99), 'A new approach to balance-of-payments constraint: some empirical evidence', *Journal of Post Keynesian Economics*, 21, Winter–Fall: 259–82.

Balassa, Bela (1983), 'Trade Policy in Mexico', World Development, 11(9) 795–811.

Blecker, R. (1999), *Taming Global Finance: A Better Architecture for Growth and Equity*, Washington DC: Economic Policy Institute.

Cameron, G., J. Proudman and S. Redding (1999), 'Openness and its association with productivity growth in UK manufacturing industry', *Working Paper*, ISSN 1368–5562, Bank of England, London.

Caporale, G. and M.K.F. Chui (1999), 'Estimating income and price elasticities in a cointegration framework', *Review of International Economics*, 7: 254–64.

Carone, G. (1996), 'Modeling the U.S. demand for imports through cointegration and error correction', *Journal of Policy Modeling*, 18: 1–48.

Carvajal, L. and E. Loría (1994), 'Ingreso y balanza comercial de la industria manufacturera mexicana 1970–1992', *Comercio Exterior*, 44: 417–23.

De Mateo, F. (1988), 'La política comercial de México y el GATT', *El Trimestre Económico*, 55: 175–216.

Dornbusch, R. and A. Werner (1994), 'Mexico: stabilization, reform, and no growth', *Brookings Papers on Economic Activity, I*, 253–315.

Enders, W. (1995), *Applied Econometric Time Series*, New York: John Wiley.

Galindo, L.M. and M.E. Cardero (1999), 'La demanda de importaciones en México: un enfoque de elasticidades', *Comercio Exterior*, 49: 481–8.

Goldstein, M. and M. Kahn (1985), 'Income and price effects in foreign trade', in R. Jones and P. Kenen (eds), *Handbook of International Economics*, Vol. II, Amsterdam: North Holland.

Greene, W.H. (1993), *Econometric Analysis*, New York: Macmillan.

Hooper, P., K. Johnson and J. Márquez (1998), 'Trade elasticities for G-7 countries', *International Finance Discussion Papers No. 609*, Board of Governors of the Federal Reserve System, Washington.

Houthakker, H.S. and S.P. Magee (1969), 'Income and price elasticities in world trade', *Review of Economics and Statistics*, 51: 111–25.

Ize, A. (1992), 'Liberalización comercial, estabilización y crecimiento', in C. Bazdresch and N. Lustig (eds), *Mexico, Crisis y Ajuste,* Lecturas No. 73, Mexico: Fondo de Cultura Económica.

Kennedy, P. (1998), *A Guide to Econometrics*, 4th edition, Cambridge, MA: MIT Press.

Krugman, P. (1989), 'Differences in income elasticities and trends in real exchange rates', *European Economic Review*, 33: 1031–54.

López, J. and C. Guerrero (1998), 'Crisis externa y competitividad de la economía mexicana', *El Trimestre Económico*, 65: 582–98.

Lustig, N. and J. Ros (1987), 'Mexico', *Stabilization and Adjustment Policies and Programmes,* World Institute for Development Economics Research, Helsinki.

Maddala, G.S. and I.M. Kim (1998), *Unit Roots, Cointegration and Structural Change*, Cambridge: Cambridge University Press.

Márquez, J. (1999), 'Long-period stable trade elasticities for Canada, Japan and the United States', *Review of International Economics*, 7: 102–16.

McCombie, J.S.L. (1997), 'On the empirics of balance-of-payments-constrained growth', *Journal of Post Keynesian Economics*, 19: 345–75.

McCombie, J.S.L. and A.P. Thirlwall (1997), 'Economic growth and the balance-of-payments constraint revisited', in P. Arestis et al. (eds), *Markets, Unemployment and Economic Policy*, New York: Routledge.

McCombie, J.S.L. and A.P. Thirlwall (1999), 'Growth in an international context: a post Keynesian view', in J. Deprez and J.T. Harvey (eds), *Foundations of International Economics: Post Keynesian Perspectives*, London: Routledge.

Moreno-Brid, J.C. (1998–99), 'On capital flows and the balance-of-payments constrained growth model', *Journal of Post Keynesian Economics*, 21: 283–9.

OECD (Organization for Economic Cooperation and Development) (1996), *Trade Liberalization Policies in Mexico*, Paris: OECD.

Pesaran, M.H. and B. Pesaran (1997), *Working with Microfit 4.0: Interactive Econometric Analysis*, Trowbridge: Redwood Books.

Quantitative Micro Software (1997), *Eviews: Econometric Views*, Irvine, CA: QMS.

Rao, B. (ed.) (1994), *Cointegration for the Applied Economist*, New York: St. Martin's Press.

Ros, J. (1994), 'Mexico's trade and industrialization experience since 1960', in G. Helleiner (ed.), *Trade Policy and Industrialization in Turbulent Times*, London: Routledge.

Salas, J. (1982), 'Estimación de la función de importaciones para México', *El Trimestre Económico*, 49: 292–335.

Salas, J. (1988), 'Estimación de la función de importaciones para México: una revisión 1961–1986', *El Trimestre Económico*, 55: 818–46.

Sarmiento, H. (1999), 'Repercusiones de la apertura comercial en la economía mexicana', *Comercio Exterior*, 49: 930–9.

SECOFI (1994), *Tratado de Libre Comercio entre México, Canadá y Estados Unidos*, México: Secretaría de Comercio y Fomento Industrial.

Senhadji, A. (1998), 'Time series estimation of structural import demand equations: a cross country analysis', *IMF Staff Papers*, 45: 236–64.

Sotomayor, M. (1997), 'Estimación de funciones de exportación y de importación para la economía mexicana', *Documento de Trabajo*, Mexico: Colegio de la Frontera Norte.

Ten Kate, A. (1992), 'Trade liberalization and economic stabilization in Mexico: lessons of experience', *World Development*, 20: 659–72.

Thirlwall, A.P. (1979), 'The balance of payments constraint as an explanation of international growth rate differences', *Banca Nazionale del Lavoro Quarterly Review*, 128: 45–53.

Thirlwall, A.P. (1998), 'The balance of payments and growth: from mercantilism to Keynes to Harrod and beyond', in G. Rampa et al. (eds), *Economic Dynamics, Trade and Growth*, London: Macmillan.

Thirlwall, A.P. and M.N. Hussain (1982), 'The balance of payments constraint, capital flows and growth rate differences between developing countries', *Oxford Economic Papers*, 34: 498–509.

# 6. Banks' liquidity preference and financial provision

**Penelope Hawkins***

## INTRODUCTION

This chapter explores the liquidity preference of banks as an explanation for differential financial provision to borrowers. While some borrowers may have first call on a bank's resources, others are unable to obtain credit, and hence are constrained by financial exclusion. Still others may remain on the fringe, with capricious access to credit leaving them financially vulnerable. The paper suggests that liquidity preference presents a possible conceptual framework within which to develop a model of banks' distributive behavior toward different types of borrowers within the framework of an endogenous money supply. The spectrum of financial provision presented below may also provide insight into the transmission of monetary policy.

The spectrum of financial exclusion may be seen against the background of an endogenous money supply where the banks seek profits through actively managing their balance sheets, as guided by their preference for liquidity. This approach, which may be termed the conditionally endogenous approach to the money supply, is associated with the work of Minsky (1982), Chick (1983), Dow (1993, 1996), Dow and Dow (1989) and Carvalho (1992, 1999) and contrasts with the passive accommodation attributed to the banking sector by the horizontalists.

The spectrum of financial provision suggests that at one extreme will be those who are excluded from financial provision. To be financially excluded means to be denied access to command over liquidity. In a monetary economy, with a developed banking sector, this can mean exclusion from financial services, such as saving accounts, chequing deposits, credit cards, and credit extension. Households are excluded from access to mortgages, credit for household durables and education expenditure. Firms and start-up businesses are excluded from access to capital good purchases or overdraft facilities. The paper distinguishes between those who are financially excluded and those who are financially vulnerable. The financially vulnerable are on the fringe of financial provision and may be included at times, but may find it difficult to roll over loans at other times. Access to credit may wax and wane as the banking sector develops over time, and as differential development of the financial sector takes place between regions. In addition, the liquidity preference of banks may change over the business cycle, which may lead to the financial vulnerability of firms.

In a monetary economy, with uncertainty, those who do not have access to banking services and credit flows are at a disadvantage, and financial exclusion may add to their difficulties of survival. Lack of cheque accounts, for example, may make ensuring payment unwieldy and expensive. In addition, the ability to withstand the shocks associated with volatile income receipts is likely to be lower where access to credit is denied. The disparities that lead to individuals, neighborhoods or regions being excluded from some or all of the financial services of the monetary economy are exacerbated by their exclusion. The argument extends readily to the international context, but is explained here primarily in a domestic context.

The discussion of financial provision presented here suggests that the evaluation of creditworthiness influences and is influenced by the banks' liquidity preference. The liquidity preference of banks at any time can be seen as a combination of their evaluation of their existing loan portfolio as well as perceptions of potential new clients. Liquidity preference traditionally refers to portfolio choice among the range of liquid and illiquid assets. For banks, it has come to refer also to the size of the balance sheet. Hence liquidity preference of banks embraces both the composition and size of the asset portfolio held. It is suggested here that the valuation of the liquidity (or creditworthiness) of particular clients, which in turn affects the composition of the portfolio held, should also be incorporated into the concept of banks' liquidity preference.

The spectrum of financial provision embraces what Keynes called the 'fringe of unsatisfied borrowers', which is used as the point of entry in section 2. In the third section of the chapter, the explicit incorporation of the evaluation of creditworthiness into banks' liquidity preference is discussed. It is suggested that banks' perception of systemic and borrower risk are interdependent. In the context of uncertainty, borrower risk is evaluated by means of rules of thumb, which may disadvantage the unconventional borrower. In section 4, the spectrum of financial provision is presented. In section 5, the policy implications of the variability of banks' standards of eligibility and the existence of the fringe are briefly examined. It is suggested that this framework contributes to our understanding of the influence of the banking sector on economic activity.

## THE FRINGE OF UNSATISFIED BORROWERS

In his *Treatise of Money* (1930) Keynes (1971: 59) emphasized that banks have a range of options in terms of holding assets, with assets differing in terms of their expected returns and liquidity premiums. Keynes considered bills of exchange or call loans to the money market, investments and advances to customers. In general, advances to customers were the most profitable of these assets, but the least liquid. Examining the 'advances to customers' category more closely reveals that there are different classes of borrower from the banks' point of view. In particular, Keynes (1971: 327) referred to a 'fringe of unsatisfied borrowers' who were excluded from financial provision on the grounds of eligibility rather than lack of security or the rate of interest. These were borrowers who met the explicit criteria of lending but, on the basis of the purpose of the loan or their lack of standing or influence with the bank, were relegated behind those who had 'first claims on a bank's favours' (1971: 327). Nonetheless, they could be seen as eligible borrowers, should the bank find itself in a position to lend more.

In Keynes's view, it was the existence of this fringe of eligible but excluded borrowers, together with the variability of the eligibility criteria, that meant that banks could influence the rate of investment over and above their influence through the mechanism of short-term interest rates (1971: 327). Hence banks could be seen as holding a key position in terms of influencing the rate of investment, by tightening and expanding credit to the fringe.

It is suggested here that the variable standards of eligibility can be seen as reflecting changes in banks' liquidity preference. The attitude of banks to the fringe of unsatisfied borrowers is a function of the view they take of their existing loans (current assets) and of new borrowing (future assets). Their attitude to new borrowing is influenced both by the perceived systemic risk of the economy and the industry as well as the perceived risk (or creditworthiness) of the individual firm or entrepreneur. At times when the liquidity preference of banks is low, they are willing to accommodate these marginal clients. Hence banks' attitude to the fringe (and hence their evaluation of creditworthiness) appears to change with their liquidity preference. Keynes's discussion of the Federal Reserve System in the United States suggests that the treatment of the fringe is not necessarily consistent:

> [I]t makes a great difference to the practical help which the member banks accord to projects for new investment whether the volume of Federal Reserve credit existing at the moment is based on member-bank discounting or on gold and open-market operations by the Reserve Banks themselves. In the former case the member banks will be struggling to lend less and to fob off borrowers of margi-

nal eligibility; in the latter case they will be eagerly seeking an outlet for their funds (Keynes 1971(1930): 329).

At the time Keynes was writing, it appears that banks would primarily find themselves in a position to lend more if their liquidity improved, perhaps due to some change in their reserve position. Hence the focus was on the *forms* in which they would hold assets, rather than on *how much* (Keynes 1971/1930: 59). In modern banking systems, the capacity of banks to extend credit becomes more elastic as they proceed through the stages of development. Hence, the eligibility of those on the fringe appears to be driven more by the changing liquidity preference of banks than by some quantitative rule involving reserves. Both the *form* and the *quantity* of bank lending are variable. But banks will not, in general, extend credit unless the borrower is considered creditworthy. Hence it appears that when liquidity preference is low, there is a shift to accommodate marginal clients because evaluation of their creditworthiness may have changed at the same time that there is a shift to relatively illiquid assets. Hence standards of credit-worthiness may fall together with the lower liquidity preference of banks. While creditworthiness and liquidity preference are discussed separately here, their interrelatedness is considered in the next section.

The existence of the fringe of unsatisfied borrowers has come to be explained in mainstream theory by credit rationing. This occurs when an individual cannot borrow as much as she would like to at the going rate, or when, among identical borrowers, some are able to borrow and others are excluded (Blanchard and Fischer 1989: 489). In this view, the market for credit does not clear like other markets, where prices do all the adjusting to keep markets cleared, as there are market imperfections. In credit markets, asymmetric information and incentive problems are the spanners in the works, confounding the price allocation system. There is the explicit assumption that borrowers know their risk but conceal this knowledge from banks. Because adverse selection and moral hazard can exist in these markets, if lenders raise loan rates to curtail the demand for credit, they might drive off the risk-averse borrowers. This leaves the least creditworthy clients, who may be encouraged to undertake risky projects. Hence, banks use other criteria to ration credit and distinguish between those on the fringe. Because of the spanners in the works, the credit market may not produce an optimal solution, and some investment that should be under-taken may not be (Blanchard and Fischer 1989: 486).

The credit-rationing view sees the problem as being one of asymmetric information, which could be remedied by full information on the project and borrower. The view presented here is that there is an unavoidable lack of knowledge in an uncertain world, which prevents both borrowers and lenders from quantifying risk. The fringe exists because of the liquidity preference of banks within this environment of unquantifiable risk. Although the borrowers in the fringe are 'observationally equivalent' (Fazzari et al. 1988:152) in the sense that they all meet the collateral requirements; banks' loan officers discriminate between them. Keynes suggests that borrowers with a lack of standing with the bank or lack of influence are excluded in times of tight credit and included in times of easy credit. While this suggests that there are implicit or qualitative criteria, the collateral standards of banks may also change.

Traditionally, liquidity preference has come to refer to the preferred constitution of portfolio assets (Keynes 1936:166). With the extension of the concept of liquidity preference to banks (which has the capacity to create liabilities as it creates assets), the concept has also come to embrace the size of the portfolio (Dow 1993:165). Hence the size of the portfolio can be seen as a decision taken after the assessment of the liquidity of different assets has taken place. It is being suggested here that the evaluations that inform decisions regarding the preferred constitution of the portfolio, or the process of liquidity assessment, may also be incorporated in a bank's liquidity preference.

The liquidity preference of banks eases when they perceive a change in their relative liquidity and are willing to accommodate more of the needs of the fringe. This may occur, for example, as the economy enters the upturn in a business cycle. This is generally associated with improved expectations, increased confidence in these expectations, and lower liquidity preference on the part of banks and firms alike. Hence banks are more inclined to create credit at the same time that firms are more inclined to borrow to buy capital goods. Hence low liquidity preference, as it is seen here, involves a shift from liquid to relatively more illiquid assets (that is, a composition shift), a greater willingness to meet loan requests (that is, growth of the portfolio) and a more favorable evaluation of marginal clients (that is, a re-evaluation of their creditworthiness). This suggests that potential borrowers who were refused credit in the downturn of the previous cycle may find themselves, now, being judged as creditworthy.

## EVALUATION OF CREDITWORTHINESS AND BANKS' LIQUIDITY PREFERENCE

The notion that banks' evaluation of the creditworthiness of borrowers is bound up in their liquidity preference has not been explicitly set out before. However, there are a number of potentially supportive ideas that can be seen as the background against which the notion can be evaluated.

First, Dymski (1998) points to the thinness of the New Keynesian analysis of credit rationing; thin because, among other things, it lacks analysis of power relations between lender and borrower. He suggests instead that creditworthiness is socially constructed and 'that market opportunities themselves are endogenous and socially constructed at any point in time' (p. 251). This suggests that the perceived creditworthiness of a firm and/or a project is not 'objective' in any absolute sense.

Second, uncertainty may be seen as a relative concept (Dow 1993: 166). Hence liquidity preference may be higher if the degree of uncertainty is higher, as well as if there is a higher incidence of uncertainty. If the degree or incidence of uncertainty changes, projects may be re-evaluated by banks. While a reduction in uncertainty may increase the riskiness associated with some projects, it may improve the evaluation of creditworthiness of others. Hence as the banks' uncertainty about the future changes, this may improve their evaluation of some projects, at the same time that their liquidity preference is falling.

Third, Davidson (1978: 330) suggests that when financial intermediaries seek to float new issues, they 'may "beat the bushes" in order to flush out additional investment projects from entrepreneurs, particularly from those who might, under other circumstances, be part of the unsatisfied fringe of borrowers'. This suggests that banks and financial institutions may seek out borrowers, depending on their liquidity preference. This view seems to suggest that, at times, the attitude of banks toward the fringe can be speculative, where they seek short-term profits from capital gains rather than income from committed investment (Chick 1983: 215). While this change may be associated with the business cycle, it may occur systematically, too, due to a reaction to competition from non-bank financial institutions – as in the fifth stage of banking development (Chick 1986).

In order to justify the incorporation of assessment of creditworthiness within banks' liquidity preference, the three motives for holding liquid assets, the transactions, speculative and precautionary motives, are examined. Banks' *transactions motive* for money is essentially reflected in their reserves. Reserves or transaction balances represent the expected daily call for liquid balances by the banks' clients. Since the banks have to estimate this daily requirement, even this motive is affected by uncertainty. (This contrasts with Runde 1994: 133, who suggests that the transactions motive has no connection with uncertainty). Holding adequate reserves prevents banks from having to resort to interbank loans or call on the central bank's discount window to meet daily transactions demand. The daily shortage in the market is traditionally met by the central bank, but is also a means by which central banks exert control over commercial banks. Banks will tend to attempt to minimize this exposure to the central bank's influence by holding adequate reserves, and so banks balance the need for holding reserves against the potential return to holding alternative assets. Changes in perceptions of systemic risk may affect the expected daily call on reserves, which may affect this motive. An example might be the expected demand for cash over the millennium period, which involved a worldwide increase in banks' cash reserves in order to meet expected demand (which did not eventuate to the degree anticipated).

The association of the *speculative motive* with banks has become more prominent in the light of the liability management of banks associated with the fifth stage of banking development (Chick 1986). As banks become more active liability managers, seeking to attract deposits in the wake of having extended credit, they appear to be more like speculators, seeking profits, than long-term investors seeking income. Banks become more active in securitized lending, and the range of assets that banks finance, such as consumer loans, property deals and takeovers, becomes more speculative in nature (Chick 1997: 540). Like speculators, when banks expect a downturn in the economy, they are likely to shift into more liquid assets. This may mean that they offer fewer loans and that the loans they do offer are for shorter time periods. Assets that were previously judged creditworthy no longer appear so in the light of the banks' new assessment of the economy. Hence expectations of a downturn in the economy are likely to affect the assessment of individual borrowers, with firms' projections of returns duly discounted downward.

Stage 6 of banking development captures the secular trend toward increased securitization, where banks attempt to avoid capital adequacy ratios and bad debts by converting loans into tradable securities. While the speculative nature of banking is inherent in the process of lending long and borrowing short (Minsky, quoted in Dymski 1988: 518), securitization allows banks to manage the liquidity of loans. If a downturn in the business cycle is expected, the speculative motive for holding liquid assets may be reflected in a move into short-term securities by selling off relatively illiquid loans. Short-term securities have the advantage of ease of convertibility. In the same way, when liquidity preference falls, the banks may shift out of short-term securities back into loans, in expectation of greater returns.

Whereas speculative demand is associated with being liquid because of expectations that holding illiquid assets would result in a capital loss, *precautionary demand* for liquid holdings is associated with increasing uncertainty about outcomes. The greater the uncertainty of banks, the less weight they are likely to attach to expectations regarding the redeemability of illiquid assets. Hence, with their confidence in their expectations eroded (Crotty 1994: 114), banks are less likely to extend credit, and more likely to increase their holdings of short-term securities and treasury bills and reserves. The onset of an increase in uncertainty may result in a sudden tightening of the bank's standards of creditworthiness. In the wake of the Asian crisis, for example, when lenders in the United States reported a substantial tightening of standards and extension of credit (Lown et al. 2000: 3). In the same way, the general increase in the liquidity of banks' assets in the 1980s was associated with a general increase in uncertainty generated by floating exchange rates and money supply targeting (Strange 1986).

The description of the banks' liquidity preference offered here suggests that banks' perceptions of systemic and borrower risk are interdependent. An expected fall in wealth, for example, may cause banks to re-evaluate borrowers' creditworthiness on the basis of the speculative motive. An increase in uncertainty may cause banks to re-evaluate borrowers on the basis of their precautionary motive. In the same way, an improvement in expectations of economic activity and growth is likely to improve the perceptions of borrower risk and creditworthiness, as is a general reduction in uncertainty.

The liquidity preference of banks in an environment characterized by uncertainty challenges the mainstream view of an orderly assessment of borrower risk with as many borrowers served as is permitted by the deposits of the system, apart from the degree to which credit rationing is assumed to occur. In an environment of uncertainty, however, risk cannot be quantified and ranked, with appropriate premiums applied (Dow and Dow 1989: 154). Rather, the notion of an objectively quantifiable risk or creditworthiness gives way to a reasoned assessment by bankers influenced by perceptions of systemic and individual risk, and recourse to rules of thumb. These rules of thumb can be seen to reflect convention as captured by the 'expectations formation and decision making process based on custom, habit, tradition, instinct and other socially constructed practices' (Crotty 1994: 121). The endogenous money supply view suggests that banks respond to borrower demand but are not necessarily unconditionally accommodating. Perceptions of individual creditworthiness may change in response to external factors and changing perceptions of systemic risk. Rather than being ranked according to some quantifiable assessment of risk, clients and their risk are ranked according to conventional rules of thumb influenced by factors such as individual wealth, status and standing. Standards may implicitly vary along the spectrum of borrowers.

This view of the spectrum of borrowers contrasts also with the New Keynesian view where risk is essentially knowable and quantifiable. Risk can be captured by probability calculus and information can, in principle, be complete. However, although borrowers are assumed to have complete knowledge of the risk they present to the lender, it is in their interest to conceal this. The discontinuity in knowledge and incompleteness of risk is introduced by incomplete revelation by borrowers. Because of the incomplete revelation of information, borrowers are grouped into cohorts that cannot be distinguished from each other. Asymmetric information is the spanner in the works, and this is a story of providing incentives to achieve greater cooperation between principle and agent and hence better (more complete) risk assessment. By contrast, the story here is one of lack of attainability of complete knowledge under conditions of uncertainty (Dow 1999: 222). Neither firm nor banker has complete knowledge of the future, and while an entrepreneur may underrate risks relative to how a banker may perceive them, this may have more to do with lack of experience or differences in perception than deliberate masking on the part of the entrepreneur.

The New Keynesian system allows a neat ordering of risk and borrowers through quantifiable risk calculations based on potentially continuous information because the future is given – and independent of the choices of transactors (Crotty 1994: 111). This contrasts with the post Keynesian system where incompleteness and discontinuity of information is a feature of the system. The future is in principle unknowable, as it is affected by the choices of transactors. There is an awareness that assessment of the future is likely to be incomplete. Hence, at times of particular uncertainty, confidence in the incomplete forecasts of the future is eroded. In this scheme, information is by nature partial, 'lumpy' and at times contradictory. Faced with a situation of unquantifiable risk, lenders tend to categorize borrowers according to rules of thumb that may require subsequent revision, and that may exclude certain cohorts of potential borrowers. Within the post Keynesian scheme, financial exclusion is to be expected rather than being surprising.

Rules of thumb imply that certain categories of borrower will be excluded; for example, illiterate or enumerate borrowers are likely to be summarily excluded. However, as regards the fringe, banks' evaluation of creditworthiness is unlikely to be objectively quantifiable and may have to adjust to different situations and clientele. Where conventional standards are employed across diverse groups, this may lead to exclusion of the 'unconventional' borrower. This may involve the disparate treatment associated with discrimination by race or gender (Dymski 2000). The standards of credit scoring may reflect this, as standards may shift and similar client responses may receive different scores, depending on the particular institutional and historical position of the banks. Standards of assessment of creditworthiness appear to be integral to banks' allocation decisions regarding credit, and hence it is argued that it is reasonable for the evaluation of borrowers to be incorporated conceptually in banks' liquidity preference, as reflected in the size and composition of their asset portfolios and how they deal with the fringe.

The importance of variable standards of eligibility appears to be reflected in the Federal Reserve's Senior Loan Officer Opinion Survey, which is conducted quarterly and embraces 8000 banks in the United States. In this survey, loan officers are asked whether they tightened or eased credit creation in the previous quarter. The survey confirms the role of banks in allocating loans not simply by raising and lowering rates, but by tightening and loosening other non-price standards (Lown et al. 2000: 7). The changes in the evaluation of creditworthiness may account for the abrupt tightening of credit availability associated with a credit crunch. When liquidity is tightened, loan officers quickly adjust their standards upward, curtailing the extension of credit and effectively expanding the number of those excluded, and on the fringe, assuming demand for credit is unchanged.

If the perception of borrowers' creditworthiness shifts during the cycle, it makes marginal clients particularly vulnerable when the cycle enters a downturn. It is this group, who do not have first call on the banks' resources and whose access to credit extension was predicated by easy money conditions, that is likely to be the first to be denied credit extension when it most needs it. The analogy of a trendy nightclub has been used: one has to clear the velvet rope before getting a chance to pay the door charge (Lown et al. 2000: 4). Those who are included when the 'velvet rope' is lowered are likely to be particularly sensitive to a credit crunch because the 'velvet rope' may also rise, excluding them when they need credit most. Their susceptibility to credit withdrawal, as banks' liquidity preference and standards change, makes them financially vulnerable. The cyclical nature of bank lending is examined further below.

## THE SPECTRUM OF FINANCIAL PROVISION

At one extreme of the spectrum of financial provision are those who have first call on the bank's services, and who may receive preferential treatment, including preferential rates and waived charges. They have been referred to as the 'super-included' (Dymski 1996: 93). Next along the spectrum is the 'included' category. This cohort includes the vast majority of the banks' clients, who meet the banks' collateral requirements but also have to meet their bureaucratic requirements, fill in forms and so on. The next category includes those who are on the fringe and potentially eligible for financial inclusion. Since their inclusion is not guaranteed, they are financially vulnerable to credit withdrawal. Beyond the fringe are those who do not meet the basic collateral requirements of loan finance. Even when banks adopt their most inclusive stance toward fringe borrowers, this cohort remains excluded. Only extreme circumstances would cause the banks even to consider a process of evaluation of this cohort of potential borrowers. The events leading up to the loans made to less developed countries (LDCs) in the 1970s could constitute such an extraordinary situation. This issue is taken up again later.

1: High liquidity preference
2: Medium liquidity preference
3: Low liquidity preference

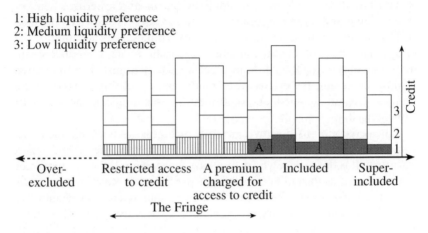

*Figure 6.1    Spectrum of financial provision during a period of high liquidity preference*

The spectrum of financial exclusion (Figures 6.1 and 6.2) is drawn with a view to expressing the spectrum of borrowers, the elasticity of inclusion of those on the fringe and the concept of an endogenous, but conditional, money supply. The vertical scale attempts to capture the notion of the demand and supply of credit and to capture the liquidity preference of borrowers and bankers alike. The layered bar charts represent the demand for credit by borrowers during periods of high (1), medium (2) and low (3) liquidity preference. When borrowers have high liquidity preference, they are less likely to seek loans to purchase capital goods. When their liquidity preference is low, borrowers are likely to enter into new ventures that require high levels of finance; hence their demand for credit is likely to be higher.

The notion of the endogeneity of the money supply is seen by assuming that the curve of the banks' supply of credit follows the top of each successive layer of the bar chart, depending on whether liquidity preference is high or low. The shaded portion of each bar represents the volume of credit extended to each cohort. Hence the banks respond to the demand for credit, but do not necessarily serve the whole spectrum of borrowers. The extent of the accommodation along the spectrum (horizontal axis), and how far the banks extend credit to those on the fringe, depends on their liquidity preference, including their evaluation of the creditworthiness of different borrowers. In Figure 6.1, credit is extended to those borrowers encompassed by the shaded area to A. The partially shaded area beyond A represents expressed, but unfulfilled, credit demand. As the cycle improves and the liquidity preference of banks and borrowers falls, banks accommodate at a higher level of demand, but again not necessarily across the spectrum.

Assume that banks are accommodating credit demand in the economy as represented by the bars ending at A (Figure 6.1). Some part of the fringe is accommodated. If expectations of firms and banks alike improve, the banks may now accommodate at point C rather than only at B (Figure 6.2). Hence the improvement in expectations and a changing perception of liquidity results in the shift to illiquid assets, increasing the size of the loan portfolio and bringing about a re-evaluation of marginal borrowers. Hence there is an expansion along both dimensions, resulting in a larger extension of credit to more clients. If, later in the cycle, expectations deteriorate, this part of the fringe may now be excluded, which makes them financially vulnerable to credit withdrawal.

1: High liquidity preference
2: Medium liquidity preference
3: Low liquidity preference

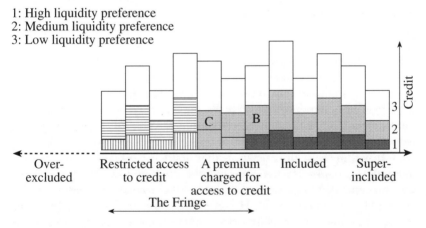

*Figure 6.2   Spectrum of financial provision during a period of lower liquidity preference*

The spectrum along the horizontal axis expresses the differential treatment of borrowers. The super-included have first call on the banks and may receive unsolicited services and waived charges. The included group, who are not super-included but represent the majority of the banks' clients, still have to apply for financial services and credit extension through the banks' bureaucratic procedures. Those marginal clients that constitute the fringe may shift in and out of inclusion. Some may be required to pay a premium and others may have restricted access.

The discontinuity between the fringe and the over-excluded, indicated by the break in the horizontal axis of Figures 6.1 and 6.2, indicates the wide divide between the fringe and the over-excluded. The over-excluded are deemed uncreditworthy and would not, in the normal course of events, even be evaluated as potential clients. The lack of knowledge of this cohort is indicated by the absence of a bar for this group in the charts. The theory of liquidity preference suggests, however, that the over-excluded are likely to have high liquidity preference, maintaining some level of reserves – expressed as cash under the mattress in the case of an individual, or reserves with foreign banks in the case of a small country (Dow 1995: 9). The chasm between the fringe and the over-excluded is only breached under extraordinary circumstances.

The lack of credit provision for the over-excluded may be seen to reflect the operation of the rules of thumb employed by bankers to deal with unquantifiable risk. Borrowers may fall into this cohort because they are poor, unemployed, discriminated against or lack familiarity with the financial system, among other reasons. Although in general banks do not deal with the over-excluded, there are times when they appear to make a strategic decision to span the breach. It is possible to interpret the extension of credit to LDCs by the international banks after the first oil shock of 1973 in terms of this framework.

The recessionary adjustment of 1973–74 in developed countries led to a shortage of traditional borrowers at the same time that banks in developed countries were receiving the cash surpluses of oil-exporting countries. Banks in the City of London received around 30 percent of these surpluses, but were unwilling to involve themselves in domestic industry (Palma 1995: 115). It was in these circumstances that first Citibank and then a host of international banks declared their intention to loan to LDCs. These loans were not extended to the poorest of nations, but to the newly industrialized and middle-income countries. However, the nature and scope of the loans to countries previously excluded from private finance was unprecedented.

Between 1974 and 1982, US$275 billion was dispersed to non-oil LDCs (Palma 1995), in a process often referred to as the recycling of petrodollars. It has been suggested that part of the culpability for the crisis outcome must fall on the banks that loaned to LDCs without any real sense of the capacity of these countries, or the firms within them, to repay debt. In the light of the model developed here, since these LDCs had previously been excluded, there was a minimal research base upon which to evaluate their creditworthiness. The lack of familiarity with these peripheral countries suggests that banks could give only a partial evaluation at best. The banks failed sufficiently to take into account systemic risk associated with such large capital inflows, but could not have foreseen the subsequent oil price increases and the devaluation of the currencies of LDCs. However, the banks also do not seem to have adopted new techniques or creditworthiness standards in order to evaluate these countries, as only 18 months before the debt crisis became obvious to all, there was still talk of confidence underpinning banks' activities in LDCs (Palma 1995: 122). This suggests that if credit is extended to unconventional or over-excluded borrowers, and if evaluation methods remain static, the banks may expose themselves to bad debt. In the case of the LDC debt crisis, banks' evaluation of creditworthiness may have been clouded by their strategic commitment to the new order they had put in place. Loans to LDCs continued even after the crisis of 1982, with banks attempting to rescue the situation.

## MONETARY POLICY AND THE FRINGE

Implicit in the preceding discussion has been the suggestion that, in the aggregate, banks' liquidity preference and the existence of the fringe has consequences for the influence of monetary policy on economic activity. This was one of the reasons for Keynes attributing banks with a key role in the economy. Keynes (1971(1930): 327) saw the existence of the unsatisfied fringe and the variability in the banks' standards of eligibility as allowing the banking system an additional means of influencing the rate of investment (over and above the rate of interest). In this view, as expectations of firms and bankers improve, so too will bank lending (even if the rate of interest is unchanged). Because of the variability in the standards of eligibility, credit extension may increase even when interest rates are perceived to move in a perverse way. At the same time that interest rates are changing, so too may expectations about the future, which in turn may affect evaluations of creditworthiness as reflected in banks' liquidity preference. Such a case occurred in the United States in 1994, when an interest rate hike was accompanied by an increase in bank lending.[1]

In Figure 6.3, the ratio of credit extension to GDP (on the right-hand axis) and the annual discount rate (on the left-hand axis) are shown for the US economy between 1980 and 1998. The cyclical nature of the ratio of credit to GDP is apparent. Our focus of attention is the period following 1990.

In the early 1990s, the domestic credit to nominal GDP ratio declined, from a peak of 89.1 percent in 1987 to 76.6 percent in 1993 and 76.3 percent in 1994. In 1994 the discount rate was raised from 3 percent to 4.75 percent,

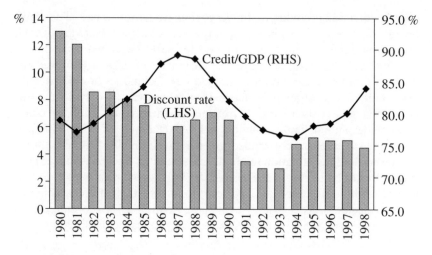

*Source:*   IFS Country Statistics, United States, with acknowledgement to WEFA for access to their Time Series Explorer database.

*Figure 6.3     US credit extension/GDP ratio and the discount rate*

and again to 5.25 percent in 1995. While this hike in interest rates may have been criticized from the perspective of cost of credit, the rise in credit extension which accompanied the interest rate hike can be explained in terms of the variable standards of eligibility for financial provision and the existence of a fringe of unsatisfied borrowers. At the time that interest rates increased, growth in the US economy was establishing new levels, after the relatively low growth rate of 1991 (Figure 6.4). Hence the increase in credit extension may be seen to be the result of higher expectations on the part of households and firms, leading to a greater willingness on the part of banks to extend credit. The 'advances to customers' category of assets became relatively more profitable as interest rates increased, at the same time that liquidity preference eased, allowing an extension of a greater volume of credit to a larger spectrum of clients. Hence, given the change in the assessment of creditworthiness associated with the upswing, credit extension as a ratio to GDP increased. Some would argue that this has contributed to the maintenance of the current strong cycle in the United States.

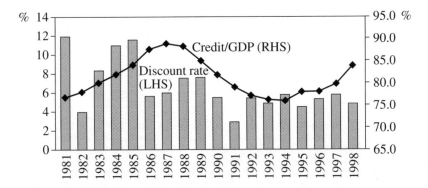

*Source:* IFS Country Statistics, United States, with acknowledgement to WEFA for access to their Time Series Explorer database.

*Figure 6.4 US credit extension/GDP ratio and GDP growth*

## CONCLUSION

This chapter has attempted to build on the theory of liquidity preference of banks by developing a model of banks' distributive behavior toward different borrowers in a conditionally endogenous money system. This approach suggests that while bankers respond to borrower demand, they do not meet the demands of all borrowers. The model suggests that the post Keynesian view of uncertainty and discontinuity of information allows for the identification not only of a fringe of unsatisfied borrowers, but of an over-excluded cohort. The three motives associated with the demand for money are explicitly related to the liquidity preference of banks. It is argued that the banks' evaluation of creditworthiness may be incorporated into their liquidity preference.

A distributive model of banks' lending behavior is then presented, along a spectrum of borrowers, all differentially affected by the banks' liquidity preference and evaluation of creditworthiness. The model suggests that when liquidity preference changes, the composition and size of banks' assets change, as does their evaluation of the creditworthiness of borrowers. Hence borrowers on the fringe may be included in times of low liquidity preference. The threat of credit withdrawal, should banks' liquidity preference change, makes the fringe cohort financially vulnerable. By contrast, those beyond the fringe are financially excluded, unless banks make a strategic decision to span the breach.

The existence of the fringe of unsatisfied borrowers, together with the variable standards of eligibility as reflected in the liquidity preference of banks, provides insight into how an increase in credit extension to a broader spectrum of clientele may accompany an interest rate hike.

## NOTES

\*    This chapter was prepared for the Sixth International Post Keynesian Conference in Knoxville, Tennessee, June 2000. It is part of my thesis, entitled 'Financial Constraints and the Small Open Economy'. My thanks go to Sheila Dow for mentoring me in this process. The comments of the participants at the conference were welcome and my thanks go particularly to Jamie Galbraith, Gary Dymski and Fernando Carvalho. Financial support from the Centre for Full Employment and Price Stability and the JPKE, as well as the Royal Economic Society Conference Grant Scheme, is gratefully acknowledged.
1.    My thanks to Jamie Galbraith for drawing this to my attention.

## REFERENCES

Blanchard, O. and S. Fischer (1989), *Lectures on Macroeconomics*, Cambridge, MA: MIT Press.

Carvalho, F. (1992), *Mr Keynes and the Post Keynesians*, Cheltenham: Elgar.

Carvalho, F. (1999), 'On banks' liquidity preference', in P. Davidson and J. Kregel (eds), *Full Employment and Price Stability in a Global Economy*, Cheltenham: Elgar, 123–38.

Chick, V. (1983), *Macroeconomics after Keynes*, Cambridge, MA: MIT Press.

Chick, V. (1986), 'The evolution of the banking system and the theory of saving, investment and interest', *Economics et Sociétiés*, 20: 111–26.

Chick, V. (1997), 'Some reflections on financial fragility in banking and finance', *Journal of Economic Issues* XXXI(2): 535–41.

Crotty, J. (1994), 'Are Keynesian uncertainty and macrotheory compatible? Conventional decision making, institutional structures and conditional stability in Keynesian macromodels', in G. Dymski, and R. Pollin (eds), *New Perspectives in Monetary Economics*, Ann Arbor: University of Michigan, 105–39.

Davidson, P. (1978), *Money and the real world*. Second edition. London: Macmillan.

Dow, A.C. and S.C. Dow (1989), 'Endogenous money creation and idle balances', in J. Pheby (ed.), *New Directions in Post-Keynesian Economics*, Aldershot: Elgar, 147–64.

Dow, S.C. (1993), *Money and the Economic Process*, Aldershot: Elgar.

Dow, S.C. (1995), 'Liquidity preference in international finance: the case of developing countries', in P. Wells (ed.), *Post Keynesian Economic Theory*, Norwell, MA: Kluwer, 1–15.

Dow, S.C. (1996), 'Horizontalism: a critique', *Cambridge Journal of Economics*, 20: 497–508.

Dow, S.C. (1999), 'The stages of banking development and the spatial evolution of financial systems', in R. Martin (ed.), *Money and the Space Economy*, New York: Wiley, 31–48.

Dymski, G.A. (1988), 'A Keynesian theory of bank behaviour', *Journal of Post Keynesian Economics*, X(4) 499–526.

Dymski, G.A. (1996), 'Money as a "time-machine" in the new financial world', in P. Arestis. (ed.), *Keynes, Money and the Open Economy: Essays in Honour of Paul Davidson*, Vol. I, Cheltenham: Elgar, 85–104.

Dymski, G.A. (1998), 'Disembodied risk or the social construction of creditworthiness?', in R.J. Rotheim (ed.), *New Keynesian Economics/Post Keynesian Alternatives*, London: Routledge, 241–61.

Dymski, G.A. (2000), 'Is discrimination disappearing? Residential credit market evidence, 1992–98. Paper presented at the January 2000 meeting of the Association for Social Economics.

Fazzari, S., R. Hubbard and B. Petersen (1988), 'Financing constraints and corporate investment', *Brookings Papers on Economic Activity*, 1: 141–206.

Keynes, J. M. (1936), *The General Theory of Employment, Interest and Money*, London: Macmillan.

Keynes, J.M. (1971), *A Treatise on Money: The Applied Theory of Money*, The Collected Writings of John Maynard Keynes Volume VI, London: Macmillan for the Royal Economic Society.

Lown, C.S., D.P. Morgan and Rohatgi (2000), 'Listening to loan officers: the impact of commercial credit standards on lending and output', *Federal Reserve Bank of New York Economic Policy Review*, July: 1–16.

Minsky, H. (1982), *Can 'it' happen again?* Armonk: M.E. Sharpe.

Palma, G. (1995), 'UK lending to the Third World from the 1973 oil shock to the 1980s debt crisis: on financial "manias, panics and (near) crashes"', in P. Arestis, and V. Chick (eds), *Finance Development and Structural Change*, Aldershot: Edward Elgar, 113–46.

Runde, J. (1994), 'Keynesian uncertainty and liquidity preference', *Cambridge Journal of Economics*, 18: 129–44.

Strange, S. (1986), *Casino Capitalism*, Oxford: Basil Blackwell.

# 7. Racial/ethnic disparity and economic development

## William Darity, Jr

Research undertaken by Jessica Gordon Nembhard and myself (Darity and Nembhard 2000a, 2000b) provides a preliminary investigation into the relationship between inter-group disparity and levels of economic development. We utilized a data set of 12 countries with reliable data on intergroup differences. Our findings are presented in two papers, including an extremely compact summary in the May 2000 proceedings issue of the *American Economic Review* (Darity and Nembhard 2000b).

The 12 countries are Australia, Belize, Brazil, Canada, India, Israel, Japan, Malaysia, New Zealand, South Africa, Trinidad and Tobago, and the United States of America. Race, caste or ethnicity each serves as the basis for group division and differences in economic outcomes. In 1998 the range in per capita incomes across the 12 countries varied from a low of US$430 for India to a high of US$32,380 for Japan (World Bank 2000b). The range in scores on the United Nations Development Program's (UNDP's) Human Development Index (HDI) varied from a low of .545 for India to a high of .932 for Canada (UNDP 2000).

We found that countries with a lower general level of inequality do not necessarily have lower levels of intergroup inequality. Nor does disparity across groups evaporate as levels of development, whether measured by per capita income or by the HDI, rise.

Generally positive social effects are associated with increasing dignity for women. Even in very low-income regions or societies, if women are highly literate and comparatively involved in the political process, other indicators of well-being typically come out quite well. For example, in the south Indian state of Kerala and in the adjacent country of Sri Lanka there is high longevity and low infant and maternal mortality by international standards. In fact, men and women in Kerala live longer than black men and women in Harlem in New York City (Sen 1997). Still, this provides little insulation against inter-caste or inter-ethnic conflict and disparity.

Research by Deshpande (2000) using data from India's 1993–94 National Sample Survey demonstrates the persistence of a high degree of inter-caste (scheduled castes versus others) inequality in Kerala with respect to land ownership, consumption and schooling. Deshpande concludes (p. 325) that 'even in a relatively egalitarian state like Kerala, intercaste disparity continues to underlie overall disparity'. And it is well known that the Tamil separatist movement continues to be a source of deep communal conflict and violence in Sri Lanka. In the ten years following 1983, it is estimated that 14,000 people died in the conflict between the Tamils and the Sinhalese (UNDP 1994: 32).

With respect to the 12 countries in our sample, Nembhard and I also considered whether inter-group economic disparity was perceptibly lower in the countries with higher values of the UNDP's Gender Enpowerment Index, a measure that captures the degree of equality in women's participation in a nation's political processes. We found no systematic relationship.

In the 1994 volume of the UNDP's *Human Development Report* (pp. 98–101), inter-group disparity within countries in 1992 is captured by disaggregated HDIs, disaggregated in some cases along spatial lines and in other cases directly along ethnic/racial lines. South Africa, the United States, Brazil, Canada and Malaysia are countries examined in the report that overlap with our sample of 12.

South Africa's overall HDI in 1992, toward the close of apartheid, was calculated to be .65. However, white South Africa's HDI was .88. If one were to treat whites in South Africa as a separate country – which they actively sought to be – they would have ranked 24th out of approximately 180 countries (at the level of Spain). Blacks in South Africa had an HDI of a mere .46, placing them at 123rd out of 180 countries, just above the Congo (UNDP 1994: 98).

The racial differential in HDIs was not as wide, but still substantial, for the United States. While the overall HDI for the United States was .93, the eighth highest in the world, for whites it was .98 but for blacks it was 10 percent lower at .88 (UNDP 1994: 98). Thus, American blacks had an HDI value in 1992 at the level of countries like Spain, Uruguay, Hungary, Lithuania and, ironically, South African whites.

The Brazilian estimates of HDIs were disaggregated by region, specifically for the south and the northeast of Brazil. The population of the south of Brazil is disproportionately white, consisting largely of Euro-Brazilians, while the northeast is disproportionately black and mulatto or Afro-Brazilian. In general Brazil is a country with a population largely of African descent, but the north is considerably darker-hued than the south (Twine 1998). Brazil's overall HDI was .76, giving Brazil a ranking of 63rd in the world. But the South of Brazil's HDI was .84, which would have placed that region 20 positions higher on the world's rankings; the northeast of Brazil, which includes the state of Salvador, had a markedly lower

HDI of .55. The gap in HDI between south and northeast is attributable to a 17-year differential in life expectancy, a 33 percent difference in adult literacy rates and a 40 percent difference in real per capita GDP (UNDP 1994: 100).

In 1992, Canada had the highest HDI in the world at .93. But even in Canada there still was sharp evidence of gaps between groups, especially a rift between the social conditions of the majority of the population and the indigenous racial and ethnic minority. UNDP (1994: 100) reports:

> The available data do not allow the construction of separate HDI for different social groups in Canada. But they do show that the 'aboriginals' (the Indians, the Inuit, and the Metis, constituting 2.3% of the population) have a life expectancy 5.6 years lower than the rest of the population, and their real income is one-third less.

Indigenous Canadians were six times as likely to be murdered and more likely to suffer from depression; in 1988, there were 40 suicides per 100000 indigenous persons, three times the national rate (UNDP 1994: 32). The indigenous unemployment rate was 20 percent, two times the rate across the entire Canadian population (UNDP 1994: 25). Nearly 50 percent of indigenous people living on reservations depended on transfer payments to subsist (UNDP 1994: 26).

On the other hand, Malaysia is not characterized by a 'minority problem'. The economically subaltern group, the native Malays or *bumiputra*, is a numerical and political majority. Native Malays constitute more than 55 percent of the population, while the ethnic Chinese are about 30 percent and the ethnic East Indians are slightly less than 10 percent. Separate HDIs were calculated based upon 1992 data for the native Malays and the Chinese-Malaysians. While the overall Malaysian HDI was .79, the native Malay HDI was .73 while the Chinese-Malaysian HDI was .90. The Chinese-Malaysian HDI would place their standard of well-being among that of the top 20 countries in the world (UNDP 1994: 100).

The country not in our sample with information indicative of intergroup disparity in the 1994 *Human Development Report* is Nigeria. There are no direct reports on income or well-being by ethnicity in Nigeria. Instead, UNDP (1994: 99) ranks each of the 19 Nigerian states by HDI scores. Since there is a relatively high degree of internal ethnic homogeneity in each of the states, ranking the states by HDI also provides a rough measure of the relative welfare of the various ethnic groups that comprise the country.

Nigeria's overall HDI was .348 in 1992, a very low score that placed the country 139th in the world. But there still were very wide spatial disparities. The state of Bendel ranked the highest among the 19 states with an HDI of

.67, even placing it ahead of Sri Lanka and Cuba. At the opposite extreme, Borno had an HDI of only .16, lower than any country in the world (UNDP 1994: 99).

Does economic growth reduce inter-group disparity? The answer: economic growth is not a sufficient condition to close the gap. In the Darity–Nembhard sample of 12 countries, the comparatively high-growth countries are Malaysia, Japan, India and Belize. At first glance, Malaysia seems to provide the best example that rapid growth reduces inter-group disparity.

The first phase of affirmative action on behalf of the native Malay majority was conducted under the auspices of the New Economic Policy (NEP) between 1971 and 1990, during an interval of rapid economic growth. Government statistics indicate that the monthly income ratio for native Malay men relative to Chinese men rose from .46 to .57 between 1970 and 1984 (Darity and Deshpande 2000: 77–8). In the 1994 *Human Development Report* (p. 100), Malaysia was applauded for the effectiveness of its program of social integration, including 'carefully-crafted affirmative action' (p. 38).

Estimates of the ratio of HDI for native Malays to Chinese-Malaysians rose from 70 percent in 1970 to 81 percent in 1981 (UNDP 1994: 100). Those estimates were made using Malaysian government data on per capita income. The problem is that data from the retrospective work histories in the Second Malaysian Family Life Survey (MFLS2) completed in 1989 indicate exactly the opposite pattern over the 20-year course of the NEP. The MFLS2 data display a widening gap: Malay men's earnings fell markedly behind those of Chinese men and slightly behind those of East Indian men (Gallup 1997). The government data and the MFLS2 data do not appear to be reconcilable.

In the case of a second relatively high-growth country, Japan, Nembhard and I (Darity and Nembhard 2000a) were able to find only two observations on *burakumin* to non-*burakumin* income. The *burakumin* historically have been the Japanese equivalent of the 'untouchables' in India. Circa 1983–84, the *buraku* male to non-*buraku* male income ratio was .59. In 1997 the *buraku* to non-*buraku* per capita income ratio was .73. Unfortunately these estimates are not strictly comparable since the former ratio is driven by male earnings while the latter is based on per head calculations. Therefore, it is impossible to determine whether or not economic growth in Japan was associated with an improvement in the relative economic status of the *burakumin* (Darity and Nembhard 2000a).

A third comparatively high-growth country is India. Nevertheless, throughout the 1980s there was a high degree of stability in the ratio of per capita consumption expenditure between the scheduled castes (primarily the Dalits or former untouchables) and all others. Thus, there was no sub-stantive evidence of a narrowing of the gap (Darity and Nembhard 2000a). Dalits continue to work for considerably less than US$1 per day on average and are murdered routinely by the police; Dalit women frequently are targets of sexual abuse by men from other caste groups (Human Rights Watch 1998).

Did the gap invariably widen between groups in countries with low growth rates where we could obtain multiple observations at different points in time? South Africa (–0.6 percent), Brazil (1.1 percent) and New Zealand (0.8 percent) are three slow-growth countries over the interval 1975–94 with data on inter-group disparity over time. Actually South Africa displayed a sharp rise in relative incomes for blacks, coloreds and Asians relative to whites between 1980 and 1994, despite the negative growth rate during that period. The disparities were staggering in 1980: black income was 13 percent of white income, colored income was 23 percent of white income, and Asian income was 37 percent of white income (Darity and Nembhard 2000a, 2000b).

By 1991 there was not much of a change: black income was still a meager 16 percent of white income, colored income remained 23 percent of white income, and Asian income had risen slightly to 43 percent of white income. Three years later, in 1994, a dramatic change had occurred in racial income gaps in South Africa. Black income now was estimated to be 42 percent of white income, colored income was 47 percent of white income, and Asian income was 63 percent of white income (Darity and Nembhard 2000a, 2000b). What was different about 1994 versus 1991? An enormous policy change had taken place with the onset of majority rule in South Africa – the dismantling of apartheid.

At first blush, New Zealand seems to fit the conventional story. Slower growth was accompanied by a widening gap between Maori and non-Maori incomes. Even an inverted trickle-down effect seems to be part of the mechanism accounting for the pattern of divergence. Slower growth had a disproportionately negative impact on Maori employment. But as in South Africa, there was also a policy basis for the increase in inter-group dispar-ity. New Zealand officialdom embraced IMF-style austerity measures in the 1980s, thereby slashing income going to Maori families, who were more reliant on transfer payments than non-Maori families (Darity and Nembhard 2000a, 2000b).

Brazil was a third low-growth country in our sample where we could examine inter-group inequality over the interval 1976–95. Although there are still substantial disparities, the black–white and mulatto–white income ratios narrowed over these two decades (Darity and Nembhard 2000a). Between 1976 and 1995 the black–white income ratio rose from .35 to .61

and the mulatto–white ratio from .50 to .73 (.63, if one relies on interviewer classification rather than self-classification of race).

Does market-based discrimination play a role in the maintenance of inter-group inequality? Or does discrimination decline in importance over time as a factor explaining inter-group disparity in market-based economies, as neoclassical economics would have us believe? The answer to the first question is that market-based discrimination against subaltern groups is a global phenomenon. The answer to the second question is that there is no consistent evidence of a decline in discrimination in market-based economies.

Statistical inquiries have demonstrated that Sephardic Jews in Israel have suffered discriminatory losses in earnings and that blacks and mulattos suffer such losses in Brazil (see discussion in Darity and Nembhard 2000a). A recent investigation by George Sherer (2000) indicates that labor market discrimination against black South Africans actually may be increasing in the post-apartheid era. Market-based discrimination against blacks was substantial in South Africa under the apartheid regime, in spite of the dismal levels of schooling imposed upon blacks that rendered them generally less competitive in the labor market.

In New Zealand, labor market studies demonstrate that discrimination against Maoris continues to be an important factor explaining the Maori/non-Maori earnings gap (for discussion, see Darity and Nembhard 2000a, 2000b). And despite the low literacy levels of the scheduled castes and tribes in India, there is evidence of persistent labor market discrimination against them as well (Deshpande 2000: 82).

Furthermore, although the native Malays control the Malaysian civil service, there is pronounced evidence of labor market discrimination against them. In Trinidad and Tobago, men and women of African and East Indian ancestry have incurred discriminatory losses in earnings relative to whites of both genders. In Canada, statistical research consistently finds evidence of discrimination against blacks (Darity and Nembhard 2000a).

Today in the United States, black male wages are 12–15 percent lower than white male wages due to labor market discrimination. The sharpest fall in measured discrimination against blacks took place in the decade immediately following the passage of the Civil Rights Act in 1964. Thereafter, national estimates of discriminatory losses stabilized in the 12–15 percent range. Audit studies continue to detect discrimination in direct fashion in employment and hiring processes against both blacks and Latinos. Statistical evidence suggests that measured discrimination increased against Puerto Rican, Mexican and native American men between 1980 and 1990 (Darity 1998).

What is the relationship between inter-group division and economic development? Does a greater degree of inter-racial or interactive disparity lower the performance of a national economy? Easterly and Levine (1997) consider the low growth rates characteristic of African economies over the past 35–40 years and contend that slow growth in that region is due to ethnic diversity there. They argue that African nations are more ethnically diverse than countries in any other region of the world. Ethnic heterogeneity, according to Easterly and Levine, leads to growth-reducing, rent-seeking practices by dominant groups through the state and a bloated government sector. It is noteworthy that Dani Rodrik (2001) has shown that African state sectors actually are not exceptionally large by international standards. Indeed, Rodrik demonstrates that the correlation between the size of the public sector and the extent of rent-seeking activity or corruption is very weak.

Easterly and Levine use an index of ethno-linguistic variation to capture the degree of ethnic diversity in a country. The index has a minimum value of one for the least fractionalized countries and a maximum value of 100 for the most fractionalized countries. Paradoxes abound with this measure; the extent of ethno-linguistic variation certainly does not capture the extent of social tension or violence. For example, Haiti has an index score of one due to linguistic homogeneity, but there is a high degree of conflict between the social elite and military versus the majority of civil society: 2100 people were killed in 1992 and 1993 alone (UNDP 1994: 41–2).

Burundi scores a mere four on the ethno-linguistic variation index due to the universality of the use of French. The index never would have predicted genocidal violence conducted by the Tutsis against the Hutus there. The same problem with the efficacy of the index occurs in the case of Rwanda, where the 1994 genocide was conducted by the Hutus against the Tutsis. Everyone speaks French in Rwanda also.

What Easterly and Levine really should be seeking to capture is inter-ethnic tension cum violence, and its relationship to economic growth. They do consider an alternative measure, an ethnic conflict index developed by Ted Gurr (1993) at the Minorities at Risk Project at the University of Maryland at College Park. Note that in Gurr's research, groups at risk are not always 'minorities' in a numerical sense; the term 'minorities' is a very Americo-centric construct and is problematic even in the United States. For Gurr, a 'minority at risk' is a communal ethnic group that is (1) subject to political and/or economic discrimination, and (2) acting politically on behalf of its own collective interests. Nevertheless, Easterly and Levine still use the ethno-linguistic variation index in their statistical inquiry despite its emptiness of content.

On the Gurr scale the whole population is at risk in Burundi, Chad and South Africa. Here the particularism of the African case becomes more apparent. Gurr shows that Africa taken as a whole has the largest share of population consisting of minorities at risk in a global sample. But in a new study, Robert Bates (2000) shows that the presence of 'minorities at risk' and corresponding high levels of inter-ethnic tension in Africa (and elsewhere for that matter) are not generally associated with the destruction produced by political violence.

Indeed, Bates (2000: 133) argues that political violence as measured by riots, demonstrations, revolts and assassinations is lower than one might expect in Africa, given the large presence of minorities at risk. Political violence inhibits economic growth, not ethnic diversity per se. Moreover, Bates (2000: 131) argues that ethnic groups can play a key positive role in the growth process via 'credible contracts between generations' in human capital formation; this is the nexus between ethnic group social capital and individual human capital acquisition.

Obviously waves of genocidal violence or inter-ethnic disputes leading to civil war are not associated with prosperity or growth in the near or intermediate term, particularly if the violence is not confined spatially. Such violence results in societal dysfunction, destruction of normal day-to-day productive activities, discouragement of investment and generalized economic collapse. But this is not a uniquely African phenomenon.

Communal divisions leading to inter-ethnic strife in Eastern Europe, especially the former Yugoslavia, Indonesia in 1997 and 1998, and Cambodia under the Khmer Rouge have all contributed to economic decline. Other non-African nations where ethnic divisions have played a key role in armed strife in recent years include Turkey, the United Kingdom, Iraq, Iran, Israel, Lebanon, Colombia, Guatemala, Bangladesh, India, Laos, Myanmar, Pakistan, the Philippines, Sri Lanka and Tajikstan (UNDP 1994: 47).

But in the longer term the effects of inter-group violence on economic performance are less obviously negative. Even a genocidal process of ethnic homogenization of population or ethnic homogenization of control over a nation's resources is not inimical to prosperity, at least for the 'winners' and their descendants. Indeed, wealth seizures in the form of conquest of native peoples and appropriation of their lands, coupled with the use of captive and slave labor, laid the basis for the affluence of today's richest nations, for example, the United States, Australia, Britain, France, Belgium and the whites of southern Africa.

Theft via conquest has long constituted an effective mechanism for achieving redistribution of wealth among groups. Industrialization, by destruction of the lives of indigenous peoples, has been a commonplace event during the past half millennium. Violence is the historic adjunct to compulsory wealth redistributions across racial or ethnic lines.

Rarely does an inter-group wealth redistribution ever occur under what might be construed broadly as democratic or consensual processes. The rare exception is the inter-racial wealth redistribution that took place in Malaysia between 1971 and 1990, when the share of Malaysian corporate assets owned by the *bumi* (more than 55 percent of Malaysia's population) rose from 2 percent to 20 percent by dint of government interventions on the Malaysian stock exchange. This was perhaps the largest democratically engineered inter-group wealth redistribution ever undertaken. The native Malay numerical majority in the parliamentary system was essential to the implementation of this policy as a part of the NEP.

Moreover, communal violence triggered the introduction of the racial wealth redistribution measure. The riots of 1969 led the Malaysian regime to adopt the NEP, an affirmative action program to benefit the native Malays that included measures to close the inter-racial wealth gap. Over the two decades of the NEP the Chinese ownership share actually rose slightly. This was made possible by the rapid growth in corporate valuation during economic 'good times' coupled with a drop in the foreign ownership share (Darity and Deshpande 2000: 83).

The problem in Malaysia is the *intra*-ethnic distribution of wealth among the native Malays. A *bumiputra* elite apparently has appropriated the lion's share of the wealth redistribution for themselves, leading to somewhat legitimate charges of 'crony capitalism'. But should the redistribution not have taken place because it has not been equitable within the receiving group? Is the intra-ethnic distribution of wealth among the *bumi* different from the intra-ethnic distribution of wealth among the ethnic Chinese-Malaysians?

The images of transnational wealth-sharing activities among some diasporized populations, such as the Chinese, the Jews, the South Asians and the Palestinians, may give the impression of greater intra-group equality of wealth among them than among other ethnic and racial groups (World Bank 2000a: 39–40). But we have no direct evidence to establish that this is true.

A substantial inter-racial redistribution of wealth in the United States is a target of some advocates of reparations for blacks. A key ethical foundation for such a policy lies in the systematic destruction of black wealth in the past, especially loss of land ownership, and the fact that the major source of wealth today is inheritance (Oliver and Shapiro 1989). American blacks have little wealth today because their parents have had little to endow upon them. Studies of the American pattern of ownership of financial assets by race have placed the median wealth of black Americans at close to zero while that of whites exceeds US$10,000 (Chiteji and Stafford 1999).

Longstanding land reform movements in Mexico, in much of Central

America, in South Africa and in Zimbabwe all amount to efforts to conduct an inter-racial or inter-ethnic redistribution of wealth. Ironically, the *Human Development Report* for 1994 (p. 46) praised Zimbabwe for its 'remarkable progress in social integration . . . raising the human development levels of the black community without restricting opportunities for the white population – thus avoiding social tension'. This laudatory assessment plainly is no longer sustainable in light of the conflicts that have arisen with President Mugabe's recent promotion of the seizure of white-owned farms by Zimbabwean blacks. Regardless of whether such movements are grassroots initiatives or possibly guided for cynical political motives (for example, the controversy over Mugabe and land reform in Zimbabwe), at their base lies a pronounced inter-group disparity in wealth, consistently a disparity much wider than the gap in earnings and income between groups.

Bates (2000) as well as Easterly and Levine (1997) have posed an important question: does ethnic division or tension lower economic growth and prospects for development? The answer: not necessarily for all groups that comprise a nation, and not indefinitely. But there is a reverse relationship to be considered: does lower economic growth exacerbate inter-ethnic divisions or tensions (even if lower economic growth is *not* systematically associated with a widening gap in income between groups)?

The recent East Asian financial traumas would provide an affirmative answer. In Malaysia and especially in Indonesia, economic crisis is implicated directly in a sharp rise in communal violence. On the other hand, inter-racial conflict in Brazil seems to be low, despite the high level of inter-racial economic inequality, regardless of national economic conditions.

The upshot is that there are few, if any, strongly unqualified claims that can be made about the relationship between inter-group inequality and economic development. However, a substantial number of claims can be made about the international pattern of inter-group inequality itself: (1) it is a global phenomenon; (2) it continues, seemingly impervious to high rates of economic growth, lower levels of general inequality in a society and the improved social status of women; (3) it encompasses both income and wealth gaps and is more severe with respect to the latter; (4) it is consistently supported and maintained by the mechanisms of labor market discrimination; (5) the global empirical persistence and trajectory of discrimination is inconsistent with the tenets of neoclassical economics; and (6) measures to remedy inter-group disparity, such as affirmative action, often afford greatest benefit to the most well-placed members of the subaltern group and, unsurprisingly, are most strongly opposed by the less competitive members of the dominant group.

# REFERENCES

Bates, Robert H. (2000), 'Ethnicity and development in Africa: a reappraisal', *American Economic Review: Papers and Proceedings*, 90(2): 131–4.

Chiteji, Ngina and Frank Stafford (1999), 'Portfolio choices of parents and their children as young adults: asset accumulation by African-American families', *American Economic Review*, 89(2): 377–80.

Darity, William, Jr (1998), 'Intergroup disparity: economic theory and social science evidence', 64(4): 805–26.

Darity, William, Jr and Ashwini Deshpande (2000), 'Tracing the divide: intergroup disparity across countries', *Eastern Economic Journal*, 26(1): 75–86.

Darity, William, Jr and Jessica Gordon Nembhard (2000a), 'Racial and ethnic inequality: cross national comparisons' *Working Paper*, Morgan State University, January.

Darity, William, Jr and Jessica Gordon Nembhard (2000b), 'Racial and ethnic inequality: the international record', *American Economic Review*, 90(2): 308–11.

Deshpande, Ashwini (2000), 'Does caste still define disparity?: A look at inequality in Kerala, India', *American Economic Review*, 90(2): 322–5.

Deshpande, Ashwini (forthcoming), 'Caste at birth? Redefining disparity in India', *Review of Development Economics*.

Easterly, William and Ross Levine (1997), 'Africa's growth tragedy: policies and ethnic divisions', *Quarterly Journal of Economics*, 112(4): 1203–50.

Gallup, John (1997), 'Ethnicity and earnings in Malaysia', *Development Discussion Paper No. 593*, Harvard Institute of International Development, Cambridge, MA, July.

Gurr, Ted Robert (1993), *Minorities at Risk*, Washington DC: United States Institute of Peace Press.

Human Rights Watch (1998), *Broken People: Caste Violence against India's Untouchables*, New York: Human Rights Watch.

Oliver, Melvin and Thomas Shapiro (1989), 'Race and wealth', *Review of Black Political Economy*, Spring: 4–25.

Rodrik, Dani (2001), 'What drives public employment in developing countries?', *Review of Development Economics*, October.

Sherer, George (2000), 'Intergroup economic inequality in South Africa: the post-apartheid era', *American Economic Review*, 90(2): 317–21.

Twine, Frances Winddance (1998), *Racism in a Racial Democracy*, New Brunswick: Rutgers University Press.

UNDP (United Nations Development Program) (1994), *Human Development Report 1994*, New York: Oxford University Press.

UNDP (United Nations Development Program) (2000), *Human Development Report 2000*, New York: Oxford University Press.

World Bank (2000a), *World Development Report 1999*, New York: Oxford University Press.

World Bank (2000b), *Entering the 21st Century: World Development Report 1999/2000*, New York: Oxford University Press.

# 8. Saving and investment: the theoretical case for lower interest rates

**Basil Moore**

## INTRODUCTION

The economics profession has not yet absorbed the full implications of perhaps the most important policy insight of Post Keynesian theory: in modern overdraft economies, the level of short-term interest rates is exogenous. Monetary authorities administer the interest rate as their chief policy instrument, so as to affect the rate of growth of aggregate demand (AD) in an attempt to guide the economy toward their stabilization targets.

Interest rates are raised and lowered procyclically, but central bankers have a wide range of discretion over the particular rates set. The levels chosen depend on the authorities' perception of the state of the economy, and their policy objectives, theoretical model and 'policy reaction function'. Most central banks have recently made price stability their central objective. Inflation targetting has supplied the justification for not reducing interest rates, even in the face of unemployment, excess capacity and AD deficiency.

A number of major theoretical issues currently divide the profession. One important difference concerns whether economies are demand constrained, and the underlying causal relationship between saving and investment. Mainstream economists adopt the classical position that economics is about scarcity. *Income and output are resource-constrained.* Since resources are normally fully employed, saving must first be available to provide the resources necessary for investment.[1] *Saving 'causes' investment.*[2]

The heterodox Post Keynesian minority vociferously adopts Keynes's vision that macroeconomics is centrally about uncertainty. In the real world the production possibility frontier is a wide band. Excess capacity is built in, since firms are price-setters and quantity-takers and cannot be sure of their future demand. As a result economies operate well below their full capacity output. *Income and output are demand-constrained.* Investment creates the saving necessary to finance itself. *Investment 'causes' saving.*[3]

As a National Accounting concept, there is general agreement that saving and investment are identical *ex post*. It is impossible to sort out the direction of causality in the S-I relationship by empirical analysis.[4] What is required is a clear theoretical elucidation of how saving and investment are causally interrelated.

The aim of this chapter is to resolve this controversy, by utilizing dynamic process analysis rather than comparative static equilibrium analysis. It concludes that, in contrast to its transitive colloquial connotation, and the 'trained intuition' of modern economists, 'saving', defined as income, not consumed as measured in the national income accounts, is not an independent behavioral relation but is simply the accounting record of investment, a product of the convention of double-entry bookkeeping.

## PROCESS ANALYSIS

The world is complex beyond human comprehension and should be modeled as a complex system (Moore 2002, Part I). National income like the vast majority of other economic time series appears to have a unit root (Nelson and Plosser 1981; Pindyck and Rubinfield 1991; Moore 2002). There is no empirical support for the common mainstream view that market forces guide income along a trend 'equilibrium path' (Stock and Watson 1988; Moore 2002).

The use of 'equilibrium' as a 'center of gravity' is the conventional and effective way of simplifying economic analysis. It does this by dismissing historical time. But with time goes ontological uncertainty, and the recognition of agents' total inability to predict successfully future states of their world. By focusing on final equilibrium states, equilibrium analysis ignores rather than elucidates the events of the disequilibrium processes within which we are continually enmeshed. The apparatus of equilibrium theory serves to conceal our ignorance, and thereby accentuates our ignorance (Loasby 1976: 220).

Irrespective of whether it is defined as a conceptual state of balance where all change ceases, or as a conceptual state where all markets clear, and all agents' expectations are mutually consistent and congruent, 'equilibrium' can never conceivably occur in the real world. Since its necessary conditions can never be satisfied empirically, its predictions remain purely deductive, and can never be refuted empirically.

As a model of the complex, non-linear and non-ergodic world in which we live, the assumption that there exists some future 'general equilibrium' state of the world cannot contribute to our ability to foresee the future nor to understand the past. A theory which takes complexity and uncertainty seriously must be a theory of processes through time, not a theory of final equilibrium states.

Even stipulating the existence of 'multiple equilibria' is beyond our reach. We must simply accept that the future is closed to us. As a social science economic behavior is more evolutionary than mechanical. Economics is more like biology and history than like physics and engineering. From our perspective, too many things simply 'happen'. Economics must start from the principle that the future *evolves* from the present.

Economics must pay particular attention to the dynamical processes by which economic variables evolve. It is a fatal analytical mistake to attempt to discover unknowable final outcomes. Change is the only constant. Economists must give up prediction, and substitute process analysis, the analysis of how phenomena change through time, for equilibrium analysis, the analysis of final equilibrium states (Moore 2002).

In order to understand macroeconomic phenomena the dynamic processes whereby expenditure investment is financed by saving must be intensively re-examined. Flow of funds analysis must be thoroughly integrated into national income analysis. In a complex world, *ex ante* variables can be explained only as expected ordinal changes from present levels, not as final 'equilibrium' outcomes. Economists' models of the circular flow of income and output must be amended to fit the observable dynamics.

Due to the ontological uncertainty of economic units faced with an unknowable future, and their subsequent desire to reduce future risk exposure by acquiring liquid assets, market economies are demand-constrained, and typically operate well *inside* their production possibility frontiers. It will be argued that aggregate demand insufficiency is at root attributable to the high level of interest rates maintained by most central banks, who in the absence of income policies regard price stability as their central goal, and as a result are predisposed toward tight money and high interest rates.

As a stylized fact in modern economies more than 90 percent of national production is by firms who possess some market power, that is, are price-setters (Marris 1997). They build in excess capacity so as to be able to meet unexpected demand, and also to deter entry. In the short-run, the aggregate supply (AS) curve should be viewed as horizontal in price–output space, at a stable mark-up over average variable costs (Moore 1988, 2002). Once money is recognized as endogenous, there is no wealth, Pigou or 'real balance' effect associated with changes in the price level. The AD curve is vertical in price or inflation-output space. (Moore 1988, 2002).

Nominal and real output are demand-constrained and demand-driven. Production expands or contracts over time, in response to continual changes in AD. Income follows a random walk with drift. It is possible to predict the extent to which economic units in the next period will be deficit or surplus-spenders, that is, the value of their marginal propensity to spend.

The implications of these simple insights from process analysis are extremely destructive, both to the mainstream vision of how the economy works, and to the 'trained intuition' of mainstream economists.

## SAVING IS THE ACCOUNTING RECORD OF INVESTMENT: A DUAL SECTOR ECONOMY

In a two-sector world consisting of only households and business firms, nominal income ($Y$) is defined as the total value of all currently produced final consumption goods ($C$) and investment goods ($I$), as valued at current market prices:

$$Y \equiv C + I \tag{1}$$

Savings ($S$) is defined as all income that is not consumed:

$$S \equiv Y - C \tag{2}$$

Keynes argued that there existed a stable 'fundamental psychological law' between consumption and income, which implied the existence of a behavioral relationship, his so-called 'consumption function' (Keynes 1936). Since the savings–income ratio is the inverse of the consumption–income ratio, from equation (2) it superficially appears that if there exists a behavioral relationship between consumption and income, there must also exist a behavioral relationship between saving and income, the so-called 'savings function'.

But this is a *non sequitur*. Rearranging the above definition of saving, equation (2) may be seen to be not a behavioral relationship, but merely the identity that all income must either be consumed or saved:

$$Y \equiv C + S \tag{2a}$$

Equation (2a) is a simple definitional identity like equation (1). Equation (2a) no more implies the existence of a stable 'savings function' between saving and current income than equation (1) implies the existence of a stable 'consumption function' between consumption and current income.

Income in the sense of total final expenditures comprises only consumption and investment expenditures (equation 1). Similarly, income in the sense of total income earned comprises only consumption and saving (equation 2a). Equating equations (1) and (2a), the logical implication is clear and incontrovertible. Private saving defined as income not consumed is identically equal to private investment.

$$S \equiv I \qquad\qquad (3)$$

This accounting identity holds true at all times, irrespective of the time unit or time period over which it is measured. The implications of this simple identity have not been absorbed by the profession. As an identity it is universally admitted to be true *ex post*. But in the textbooks, *ex post* is viewed as referring to past events. It is not explicitly acknowledged that *ex post* also includes the present.

Investment is widely regarded as forward-looking and exogenous, with a high variance. It moves sharply and irregularly with shifts in 'animal spirits' and is only loosely related to income in the current period. Consumption expenditures, in contrast, change gradually over time. They are well explained by a moving average of past income.

Since saving is simply the accounting record of investment, it varies identically with investment. If investment moves sharply and irregularly over time, so does saving. The fact that consumption expenditures may be explained as a stable moving average over time does not logically imply that saving, income, or the ratio of saving or consumption to income are also stable.

The statement that saving is the accounting record of investment can be demonstrated in several ways. Consider first the following: in national income accounting practice exceptions inevitably must be made on pragmatic grounds. There is always the difficulty of where to draw the line when devising empirical counterparts to theoretical concepts.

Since consumption is the final purpose of economic activity, only 'final' consumption goods and services, as sold by firms to households, are included in national income. All 'intermediate' goods sold to other business firms are excluded, to prevent double counting. It is well known that investment goods are not final goods but intermediate goods, not used up in the current production period. Since they have an expected lifetime longer than one year, they are included in annual current gross output.

Gross investment is conventionally defined as total business expenditures on plant, equipment and inventory accumulation, and household purchases of residences. Net investment is defined as gross investment minus the estimate for depreciation. But since no market transactions are available, official estimates of depreciation are a very inexact estimate of the value of capital actually used up in any year. As a result, net investment and net saving are estimated with greater error than gross investment and gross saving.

What is also well known but not so widely emphasized is that since it is impossible to date objectively and unambiguously the lifetime of services, all business expenditures on investment services, for example, advertising, worker training, computer software and so on, are excluded from investment, and are recorded as a current cost of production (that is, as intermediate goods) in the national income accounts. For similar pragmatic reasons all household acquisitions of long-lived consumer durables, for example, cars, appliances, computers, with the sole exception of residences, and all household expenditures on human capital, for example, education, are arbitrarily considered consumption.

Conventional national income accounting thus clearly underestimates the 'true' amount of investment undertaken in an economy (Eisner 1994: Chs 1, 2). Suppose, in an attempt to better explain productivity growth, investment expenditures were defined more inclusively, to include estimates of all investment services, including households and human capital (Eisner 1989: Chs 2, 4, 6). Recorded 'investment' would then be very significantly higher. Recorded 'saving' would rise by an identical amount, with no change in volitional saving behavior.

Suppose that the price of investment goods were to fall sharply relative to consumption goods, as has been the recent case with computers. The real value of 'investment' spending then increases. Real 'saving' would rise by an identical amount.

Finally, suppose that estimates for depreciation were revised, so that nominal and real measured net investment were higher or lower. Net saving, nominal and real, would then adjust by an identical amount.

'Saving', defined as income that is not consumed, or as the change in net worth, is a magnitude identically equal to investment. As the accounting record of measured investment, its value changes with changes in how investment is measured and defined. Actual 'saving' is not an independent volitional behavioral relationship on the part of household 'savers', as implied by the colloquial use of the verb 'to save', and as construed in mainstream theory or pictured in innumerable diagrams.

Consider a second argument: Keynes defined saving indirectly, as what it is not, income 'not' consumed (abstention), rather than what it is, net asset accumulation. When individuals abstain from spending their income and save, they add to their wealth. If current income is not spent on consumption goods, it must either be held in the form of money, spent on some kind of non-consumption asset, or used to repay debt. Saving may be defined directly as the net accumulation of assets by economic units.

In the national wealth accounts total assets comprise total holdings of all types of assets, both financial and tangible. Financial assets are IOUs, claims of creditor units against debtor units. For every financial asset outstanding there exists an identical financial liability, and for every financial asset holder there exists a financial asset issuer. Apart from differences in valuation by asset issuers and asset holders, total financial assets are identical to total financial liabilities.[5]

In a closed economy, total financial assets and total financial liabilities sum to zero and so cancel out. Net investment represents the net change in total tangible assets. Net saving as the increase in net worth, is identical to net investment. Measured saving, whether defined as income not consumed or as the net accumulation of wealth, is not an independent behavioral relationship, as is commonly held. Its equality with investment is not an 'equilibrium' condition, but merely an accounting identity. Saving is simply the change in net worth in the national balance sheet identity.

*Table 8.1   Components of the national balance sheet*

| National balance sheet | | |
|---|---|---|
| Financial assets | Financial liabilities | |
| Tangible assets (Net investment) | New worth | (Net saving) |
| Total assets | Total liabilities + Net worth | |

## SAVING IS THE ACCOUNTING RECORD OF INVESTMENT: A MULTI-SECTOR ECONOMY

There are numerous reasons why the identity between saving and investment in a dual sector model has not been fully incorporated into macroeconomic theory. One is that when the government and the rest-of-the-world sector are added to the two-sector model, the accounting equations have conventionally been incorrectly extended, without properly allowing for capital budgeting and intermediate goods. It (falsely) appears that in multisector models the simple saving–investment identity no longer holds.

National income accounting for private, public and foreign saving and investment conventionally proceeds as follows:

$$Y \equiv C + I + G + X - M \qquad (4)$$

$$Y \equiv C + S + T \qquad (5)$$

Equating r.h.s:

$$I + G + X \equiv S + T + M \qquad (6)$$

Rearranging:

$$(I - S) + (G - T) + (X - M) \equiv 0 \qquad (7)$$

or:

$$(I - S) \equiv (T - G) + (M - X) \qquad (8)$$

where $G =$ government spending, $T =$ government tax receipts, $X =$ exports and $M =$ imports.

In multi-sector models, saving and investment appear to differ by an amount equal to the size of the government deficit or surplus $(T - G)$ plus the size of the current account surplus or deficit $(M - X)$. Since most governments run budget deficits or surpluses, and most countries have current account deficits or surpluses, saving never appears to be identical to investment. When the government runs a deficit and the economy also has a deficit on current account, as was recently the case in the United States (the 'twin deficits'), the inequality between saving and investment appears to be substantial.

First consider the case of the government sector in isolation, under the provisional assumption of a closed economy. Under conventional national income accounting, saving appears to differ from investment by the size of the government deficit or surplus:

$$(I - S) \equiv (T - G) \qquad (9)$$

To the general public, and to most conservative financial journalists, it appears obvious that whenever the government runs a deficit, the country automatically is suffering from an 'insufficiency' of saving.

Current accounting conventions do not distinguish between government consumption and investment expenditures, on the grounds that for governments such a distinction is particularly arbitrary. As a result, only when government's tax receipts are sufficient to finance all its consumption spending plus all its investment spending, so that the government is running a surplus on current account, will government saving appear as zero. Only when $T = G$ will saving equal investment.

If $G \equiv (Cg + Ig) \equiv T$, or $Ig \equiv (T - Cg)$, from equation (9) $S \equiv I$ (10)

To reach correct conclusions about saving, capital budgeting must be applied consistently to the government sector as well as to the private sector, as the United Nations has long recommended. National income accounts should distinguish between government consumption ($Cg$) and government capital expenditures ($Ig$) as for private expenditures.[6] Once government investment expenditures are estimated, government investment, like private investment, automatically results in an equal increase in total saving, irrespective of how such investment spending is financed (whether by taxes or debt issue).

$$(I + Ig + Cg) \equiv (S + T) \text{ or} \tag{11}$$

$$(I + Ig) \equiv (S + T - Cg) \tag{12}$$

Suppose taxes were zero ($T = 0$) and government spending was solely for public investment goods ($G = Ig$, $Cg = 0$). The government deficit would equal total government investment spending, but saving would still be identical to investment. Alternatively suppose government tax receipts were equal to government consumption expenditures ($T = Cg$), and the government ran a balanced budget on current account. Government investment spending would then be financed completely by borrowing. But total saving would be identical to total (private and public) investment expenditures.

$$(I + Ig) \equiv S \tag{13}$$

Now consider the rest-of-the-world sector. Ignoring the government sector under conventional accounting it appears that saving is less than or greater than investment by the deficit or surplus in the current account:

$$(S - I) \equiv (X - M) \tag{14}$$

Whenever economies grow more rapidly than their neighbors, they tend to suck in imports, particularly of capital goods, and so tend to run a deficit on current account. Financial journalists are then quick to lament the apparent 'fact' that saving is insufficient to finance investment.

But again one must apply national income accounting consistently. For the rest-of-the-world sector one must distinguish between different types of imports: consumption goods ($Cm$), investment goods ($Im$) and non-final (intermediate) goods ($Nm$):

$$M \equiv Cm + Im + Nm \tag{15}$$

Imported intermediate goods (*Nm*) should be excluded from NIPA, since they have already been included in GDP. Imports of capital goods (*Im*) represent investment. Since saving is the accounting record of investment, imports of investment goods are reflected as saving, irrespective of how they are financed. So long as the value of exports is sufficient to pay for imports of consumption goods (*X* = *Cm*), saving is identical to total (domestic and foreign) investment:

$$(I + Im) \equiv S + (X - Cm) \qquad (16)$$

Suppose exports were zero (*X* = 0), and only investment goods were imported (*M* = *Im*, *Cm* = 0). The current account deficit would then equal imports of investment goods. But saving would always be equal to total investment.

## PROCESS ANALYSIS: THE TREATMENT OF SAVING IN NATIONAL INCOME AND FLOW OF FUNDS ACCOUNTS

A more insideous reason why the $I - S$ identity has not been thoroughly recognized is the use of the common verb 'to save' to denote a technical accounting relationship. Many financial asset transactions, widely considered to be saving in the literature – for example, the decision to buy or sell stocks and bonds – are clearly independent from business investment decisions. Such financial transactions do not constitute saving. Most household transactions that are labeled as 'saving' in the textbooks, for example the purchase of previously existing financial and tangible assets, are neither saving nor national income accounting transactions. They are, rather, portfolio transactions, representing shifts in the ownership and allocation of wealth portfolios, and properly recorded in the flow of funds and national wealth accounts, not the national income accounts.

At the level of the individual household, 'saving' is not equal to 'income not consumed'. For individual economic units consumption and investment spending do not exhaust total income. For individual households most 'income not consumed' is not spent on new investment, nor on directly financing new investment. Most 'income not consumed' is allocated to the purchase of previously existing and newly created financial and tangible assets.

Process analysis focuses on the question: how does saving finance investment over each period? Any transaction that does not constitute additional investment does not constitute additional 'saving', for example, the purchase of previously created tangible assets, or previously issued financial assets. It denotes changes in the form and ownership of previously existing real wealth, previously produced tangible assets, and previously issued financial assets and liabilities, that is, claims against existing real wealth.

In the United States over the past few decades, about one-half of total investment spending has been financed internally by retained earnings (business saving), and one-half financed externally by the issue of debt and equities. Most external finance initially takes the form of new bank loans, accompanied by new money creation. During the initial construction process, bank lending is used to finance increases in the working capital needs of the original manufacturers and contractors. 'Saving', the accounting record, is concurrent with investment spending. In this case, saving takes the form of 'convenience lending' by bank depositors of newly created deposits, the non-volitional accumulation of deposit balances (Moore 1988, 2002).

Once the contractor has produced the new investment goods they are sold to the original investor. The contractor can then repay the bank loan with the proceeds of the sale. In the process the newly created deposits are extinguished. The investor acquired the funds with which he paid for the investment either through retained earnings, a transfer of ownership of previously issued deposits, or the proceeds of newly issued financial liabilities.

Through the credit circuit longer-term assets and liabilities gradually displace newly created bank loans and deposits in the national balance sheet. Since roughly one-half of investment in the United States is internally financed out of retained earnings, equity ownership gradually accumulates, amounting to about one-half the value of the new investment. Wealth owners tailor the maturity of their liabilities to the maturity of their assets, to reduce the interest rate risk of their portfolios.

For individual economic units, income not consumed may be spent on acquiring non-reproducable or producible tangible assets, previously existing or newly created financial assets, or repaying past debt. Alternatively, income not consumed may be given away, lost or even destroyed. None of the above constitute an act of investment, and so do not constitute an act of 'saving'.[7] 'Saving' represents the change in net worth for both the individual and the economy. But it is only for the economy, and not for individual economic units that 'saving' may be defined as income that is not consumed.

From the point of view of the economy, saving, defined as income not consumed, must be devoted to the purchase of newly created or previously existing financial assets, or tangible assets, or the repurchase of outstanding liabilities. Transactions that do not directly finance additional investment expenditure do not constitute an act of 'saving'.

The acquisition or hoarding of previously existing assets constitutes temporary resting places for purchasing power, while an increase in saving or abstention reduces AD for currently produced goods and services. The result of an *ex ante* increase in saving is a reduction in AD and, so long as investment is unchanged, is not an increase in 'loanable funds'.

## PLANNED SAVING AND INVESTMENT ARE NEVER IDENTICAL

There is a long and distinguished historical literature on the puzzling identity between saving and investment. This literature invariably accepted the linguistic presumption that saving and investment are separate and independent volitional behavioral relationships, and attempted to establish the underlying causes of their equality (see Lerner 1938, 1939).

When investment and saving are viewed as independent behavioral relationships, this presents a near-insuperable conceptual difficulty to comprehend fully the accounting tautology that saving is necessarily identical to investment. In modern monetary production economies, 'saving' and 'investment' are performed by different economic units. Households are on balance surplus-spenders and specialize in saving decisions, the purchase of financial assets. Firms are on balance deficit-spenders and specialize in investment decisions, the purchase of tangible assets.

If saving and investment were independent *ex ante* behavioral relationships, undertaken by different units, why is the saving independently undertaken by households *precisely identical* to the investment independently undertaken by firms? What forces ensure such a result? If saving and investment were truly independent relationships, only if they were equated through some market mechanism that caused interest rates (loanable funds), incomes (Keynesian multiplier) or prices (monetarism) to adjust, could such an equality possibly occur. But each of the above mechanisms have been logically refuted (Moore 2002).

The conventional (Keynesian) resolution of the problem retains the notion of an independent saving function, but makes a fundamental distinction between saving and investment *ex post*, which are explicitly recognized as an identity, and saving and investment *ex ante*, which are viewed as volitional and unequal. The level of income is presumed to adjust, under comparative static analysis, to the point where planned saving and investment are equated and equilibrium is attained. *Ex post* is commonly misconstrued as pertaining solely to past but not also to current values of saving and investment.

Once saving and investment are viewed as balance sheet identities, the asset and net worth side of a single phenomenon, investment, saving and investment may be shown to be identical by definition. As the accounting record of investment expenditure, the S–I identity becomes apparent. Saving must rise and fall with investment. *Ex post* comprises the present as well as the past.

The volitional connotation attached to the transitive verb 'to save' has served to mislead economists. In everyday speech, saving is regarded from a micro viewpoint as the volitional decision to abstain from spending and to add to one's wealth. But the extension of the micro viewpoint, that saving is a volitional decision, to macro saving behavior represents a classic example of the fallacy of composition. Agents *individually* decide how much they wish to save. But agents *in the aggregate* are logically constrained to save exactly the total amount that other agents have invested.

Individual agents are free to abstain or 'save' the quantity they desire. But in economics, saving is defined from a macroeconomic point of view: the change in net worth the national balance sheet. Since saving by definition is the accounting record of investment, agents collectively are constrained to 'save' to the precise amount that agents collectively invest.

Suppose that investment were independent from current saving, and could be taken as given. This would be the case in a pure service economy where inventories do not exist. The decision by individuals to abstain from consuming would then not result in any increase in aggregate investment or saving. The result of a *ceteris paribus* increase in abstention by savers must then solely be the Keynesian one. Saving as abstention from consumption simply results in an identical reduction in AD.

Suppose that households suddenly planned to save one-half of their income, and that the resulting planned saving of households was substantially in excess of the planned investment of firms. This would imply that for the economy as a whole, the marginal propensity to spend out of income would fall by one half. When the increase in planned saving does not result in an equal addition in investment, it results in a concurrent identical reduction of AD. Income and output would fall by about one-half.

Unless we are dealing with a pure service economy where inventories do not exist, a decision to reduce spending on consumption will concurrently influence investment. An increase in the desire of households to save will reduce AD and result in an unintended increase in firms' inventories. The S–I identity always holds.

Define a 'period' as the length of time before a reduction in AD is recognized by business firms. In such a 'period' the result of an increase in planned saving is a simultaneous identical, involuntary and unplanned increase in inventory accumulation. It may then be concluded that within the short 'period', a change in saving 'causes' an identical change in investment.

But in the next 'period', the Keynesian well-known 'Paradox of Thrift' operates. After firms realize their sales have fallen below expected levels, and their inventories have increased to higher levels than they desire, they cut back on their production, employment and output. This reduces the level of income, investment, AD and saving, leading to the Keynesian 'Paradox of Thrift'. *Ex post*, the level of investment, saving and income will fall. The change in investment thus 'causes' the change in saving.

There is no necessity for the level of prices, incomes, interest rates or any other variable to change to bring about equality between the 'supply' of saving and the 'demand' for investment. The equality between saving and investment is necessarily always true, since it is simply the bookkeeping identity: total assets are identical to total liabilities plus net worth.

The reason why income does not fluctuate more sharply from one period to the next is because consumption spending is relatively stable. Business is able to estimate next period's consumption reasonably accurately as a quantitative distribution based on past behavior. Firms as price-setters and quantity-takers attempt to meet all demand forthcoming. They maintain target inventories and 'build in' excess capacity that attempts to achieve this goal.

When households' planned saving exceeds the level of firms' planned investment, this leads concurrently to unexpected inventory accumulation and unexpected falls in sales, profits, income and planned investment. When households' planned saving is below firms' planned investment, this leads concurrently to unexpected inventory decumulation, and unexpected increases in sales, profits, planned investment and income.

Keynes was correct in stating that the condition for income to remain unchanged over time was that 'planned' saving must exactly equal 'planned' investment. His mistake was in interpreting this conceptual event as defining a potential future point of 'equilibrium'. It should instead be viewed as logical evidence why expectations are perpetually unsatisfied, and so that income changes continually and unpredictably through time.

In the real world the future is unknowable. Firms never exactly realize their 'planned' investment. Since economic time series have a unit root, agents initial expectation is that next period sales will be like this period plus any 'drift'. In boom conditions businesses are pleasantly surprised by greater than expected sales. They persistently experience unplanned inventory decumulation to which they respond by increasing production. Animal spirits soar. In slump conditions the reverse occurs. Firms are continually disappointed by lower than expected sales. They persistently experience unplanned inventory accumulation, to which they respond by reducing output. Animal spirits collapse. The future is always unknowable. Expectations may be regressive or extrapolative, but are never 'rational'.

The total quantity that firms plan to invest is in reality never identical to the total quantity that households plan to save. Alternatively expressed, the economy's marginal propensity to spend is never unity. Some units plan to deficit-spend, causing AD to grow. Other units plan to surplus-spend, causing AD to fall. The two never precisely balance out. The economy is a complex system characterized by ceaseless change, constant novelty, continually unfulfilled expectations, and continual pleasant surprises when they get it right and harsh disappointments when they get it wrong.

## THE THEORETICAL CASE FOR LOWER INTEREST RATES

In market economies households are the ultimate owners of all private wealth. Business firms directly own the tangible assets that comprise the economy's capital stock. Firms are ultimately owned by households, in the form of equity claims. Households own some tangible assets directly, primarily land, real estate and consumer durables. But the majority of their wealth is held in the form of financial claims issued by firms, governments and other households.

Disposable income should be defined more comprehensively as total consumption plus the change in net worth. Household financial wealth represents the liability and net worth side of business balance sheets. The greater the capital gains in the total market value of claims to business assets, the greater the ratio of disposable income to earned income and output, the more secure and confident are households, and the higher will be household utility, GDP and AD.

Due to their inability to forecast their future cash inflows and needs, household wealth owners have a strong preference to increase their holdings of liquid assets. They are all too aware that their lives are uncertain and finite, and their labor income will not continue forever. Wealth enables them to keep their future options open and additional wealth reduces the negative consequences of the risk they continually bear from an unknowable future. By increasing their wealth–income ratio, wealthowners reduce the consequences of unfavorable future outcomes. Liquid assets offer them security against unanticipated future falls in their property values and income streams, and unanticipated future increases in their need for cash.

Households save because of the utility they derive from increases in the value and liquidity of their net wealth. Saving reflects households' demand to increase the value of their wealth, and the ratio of their wealth to their income, by abstaining from current consumption and acquiring liquid financial assets with positive expected returns. Similarly, investment reflects business demand to increase the value of their future sales, profits and wealth, by acquiring tangible positive assets with expected returns.

Since economies are demand-constrained, the amount that households wish to save typically exceeds the amount that business firms wish to invest at the full employment output capacity of the economy. The market signal received by business from an increase in household saving is a reduction in current demand for goods and services. Businesses respond to a perceived reduction in AD by reducing the amount they plan to invest. When AD falls, businesses anticipate less demand for future output, and so plan a lower level of potential AS capacity.

In response to perceived reductions in their wealth and income, households increase their saving. The result is a cumulative downward spiral in consumption, investment, profits, income, output and wealth values. Government policies designed to raise household saving, to the extent they are successful, have the unintended effects of reducing AD, income and output.

So long as economies are demand-constrained the appropriate policy response of monetary authorities is to reduce the short-term rate of interest. A reduction in interest rates reduces the cut-off rate of return required by businesses to undertake additional investment projects. The result is increases in planned investment and in the ratio of capital to income, so actual investment expenditures, income, and output, increases. Disposable income exceeds GDP, so AD rises and the output gap falls.

In addition to encouraging additional real investment, lower interest rates reduce the cost to debtors of servicing past debts, lower interest rates and raise the price–earning ratio of corporate equities and the valuation ratio (the ratio of the market value of equities to the replacement value of the stock of businesses' tangible assets). The effect of a reduction in interest rates is to increase the market value of total wealth, wealth–income ratios, capital gains income associated with asset revaluation, disposable income, AD and current consumption.

Higher wealth–income ratios also increase households' utility. A greater store of purchasing power relieves wealthowner insecurity about adverse future shocks, and encourages increases in current spending. The expansion of AD leads to a further expansion of investment, wealth values and consumption, and a self-sustaining rise in AD. The result is a rise in household consumption, business investment, profits, output and AD. The result of a reduction in interest rates is thus a self-reinforcing expansion of income and wealth.

In contrast, a rise in interest rates raises the required return for investment projects, by reducing the number of attractive investment projects, investment spending declines. A rise in interest rates raises the cost of servicing past debts and reduces the market value of household wealth, utility, and AD. In response wealthowners increase their levels of abstention and reduce their expenditure on current output. The result is to reduce AD and raise planned saving, in an attempt to increase their wealth values. This leads to an unintended contraction of disposable income, business investment, wealth values, household consumption, profits, output, and AD. The result of a rise in interest rates is a self-reinforcing contraction of disposable income, AD, income and output.

The recognition that saving is the accounting record of investment makes clear that saving is not an independent volitional relationship. It is widely believed that a reduction in interest rates increases planned investment in an economy, but it also reduces planned saving. The latter is thought to restrain the amount of resources available to finance investment.

But a rise in planned saving does not imply an increase in funds to finance investment. An increase in planned saving results in the short run in a decrease in consumption and AD. In modern credit money economies, a change in planned saving does not imply an accompanying change in funds available for investment finance. Rather it implies a fall in consumption, investment and AD. There is no behavioral saving relationship for the economy.

Actual saving is the accounting record of actual investment. If a reduction in interest rates increases investment, it necessarily also increases saving. If investment expenditure increases due to a reduction in interest rates, this leads to an increased demand for bank loans to finance producers' increased working capital needs. The resulting increase in the money supply provides an increase in non-volitional saving by all units whose money balances have increased over the period. Investment is never constrained by a lack of saving since the interest rate is set by the central bank.

Most short-run changes in saving are non-volitional. *Ex ante* volitional increases in saving constitute a reduction in expenditure on consumption. If household *ex ante* volitional saving were positively related to the rate of interest, lower interest rates, would increase the consumption spending, reflecting the decline in volitional saving. Increased consumption spending stimulates AD, and results in greater increases in investment, saving, profits, income, output and wealth.

To the extent that government policies to raise domestic resource mobilization are successful in their goal of increasing volitional saving, they will have the unintended effect of raising abstention and reducing AD. In response to the fall in AD, investment and income will decline and output will fall further below the economy's production possibility frontier. Government measures to stimulate savings must be accompanied by a concurrent CB reduction in the level of interest rates. Investment must rise sufficiently to offset any fall in consumption so that AD increases. Otherwise wealth–income, investment–income, saving–income ratios, and the growth rate will all decline. To mainstream economists it always appears that a rise in the saving ratio *permitted* an increase in investment. But the true causality is reversed. Increases in saving are the accounting record of increases in investment.

Providing the monetary authorities were to target full employment, economies with higher propensities to save would have lower interest rates and higher investment and saving ratios. They will be unambiguously better off economically, since they enjoy higher ratios of wealth to income, total utility, disposable income, AD and rates of growth of national income and output. Through appropriate cheap money, low interest rate policy, central banks can indirectly assure the long-run classical result, 'saving causes investment'.

## CONCLUSIONS

1. Measured saving is the accounting record of investment under a system of double-entry bookkeeping.
2. The equating between saving and investment is an accounting identity.
3. Investment and consumption are behavioral relationships, but there is no behavioral saving function.
4. Investment is constrained by the level of interest rates not the 'insufficiency' of saving.
5. Difference between 'planned saving' and 'planned investment' results in concurrent changes in income, output and AD. Measured saving is always identical to measured investment.
6. Saving and investment are not 'equilibrated' by changes in the level of interest rates or prices.
7. An increase in planned household saving may cause a *temporary* increase in investment, in the form of unintended inventory accumulation. But this increase will be reversed by business units as soon as it is discovered. The long-run result will be a reduction in AD, and the Keynesian 'Paradox of Thrift' will lead to consumption spending and lower investment.
8. An increase in planned saving is reflected as a reduction in AD. It implies a reduction in income, investment and saving. An increase in planned investment implies an increase in AD, income, investment and saving.
9. Income changes continuously in every period, depending on whether

planned investment is greater than or less than planned saving or, what is the same thing, whether the marginal propensity to spend is greater or less than unity. Planned saving is *never* identical to planned investment. Expectations are continually refuted and revised. Income has no tendency to move along any 'equilibrium' orbit.

10. 'Loanable funds' and 'liquidity preference' theories of interest are both fallacious. Interest rates are set as an exogenous policy instrument by the central bank.
11. The Keynesian 'multiplier' theory is fallacious. As a stylized 'fact' the short-run AS curve is horizontal and the short-run AD curve is vertical. The level of output changes with changes in AD.
12. When investment is internally financed, the decision to save is jointly determined with the decision to invest. It is then impossible to assign the direction of 'causation' between the two.
13. When investment is externally financed, saving is non-volitional and occurs simultaneously in the form of 'convenience saving' by bank depositors. Investment then 'causes' saving.
14. Household income allocated to the purchase of previously issued tangible or financial assets does not represent an act of 'saving'. It represents rather portfolio transactions, and belongs in the flow of funds and wealth accounts, not the national income accounts.
15. Given the interest rate set by the central bank, changes in the total quantity of money outstanding are made at the initiative of bank borrowers, not bank depositors.
16. The supply of credit money is endogenous. It expands and contracts over time through the 'monetary circuit'. New investment is initially financed by bank loans. Over time these loans are gradually repaid and replaced by the issue of longer-term debt and equity.
17. A *ceteris paribus* rise in household 'abstention' will cause finished goods to remain unsold and profits to fall. In consequence firms will initially increase their bank borrowing to finance unintended and involuntary accumulation of inventories. Subsequently firms volitionally reduce output, investment and employment, so AD and the level of income fall.
18. Equilibrium analysis should be abandoned.
19. Monetary and fiscal policy can never be neutral.
20. One can judge the wealth of an economy and the sagacity of its monetary authorities by the lowness of its interest rates.

# NOTES

1. A classic example is the Solow growth model, where the saving rate ($s$), construed as the thriftiness of economic units, determines the allocation of output between consumption and investment (see, for example, Mankiw 2000; Taylor 1998).
2. Equilibrium analysis cannot be reconciled with causality. Mathematical economists maintain that since everything is interrelated with everything else, the concept of causality is otiose. Such a position is unhelpful for policy advice.
3. See Davidson (1994). Post Keynesians and institutionalists have clearly recognized that additional saving is not beneficial, since it lowers AD. But they have also treated saving as a volitional decision. See Dugger (1984), Foster (1987), Terzi (1986–87) and Wray, (1991).
4. The World Bank is currently pursuing a major international saving study on what factors determine private saving rates. The research project has identified eight factors that purportedly 'drive' saving: income, growth, fiscal policy, pension reform, financial liberalization, external borrowing and foreign aid, demographics and uncertainty. See www.worldbank.org/research/projects/savings/policies.htm.
5. Equities, as financial assets representing ownership claims to business net worth, present a qualification to the above. Their book value equals the accounting value of business net worth, total assets minus total liabilities. Standard accounting practices measure business tangible assets at historical cost, minus estimated depreciation. This constitutes the book value of equities. But shareholders value equities at their market value, as determined on the stock exchange. Share prices represent the stock market's current weighted consensus of the discounted present value of stocks' expected future dividends and capital gains. Whenever stock prices rise, shareholders receive income in the form of capital gains.

   Such capital gains income is excluded in national accounting measures of income, which include only income derived from current output and exclude all income from asset revaluation, although both represent an increased store of purchasing power.

   Measured saving ratios are sensitive to whether capital gains on tangible and financial assets are excluded or included in the definitions of income and wealth. Because capital gains are excluded from income in current national income accounting practices, total saving (volitional and non-volitional) is equal to the accounting record of total investment spending, measured at historical costs, minus any negative government and external dissaving.

   The book value (historical cost) of capital is a poor proxy for how shareholders value their equity portfolios, and so of the role of wealth in consumption behavior. This is particularly the case in a world of general asset inflation. Equities are valued by their owners at their current market price, which considerably exceeds their historical book value. This is particularly the case in the United States at present, when price–earning ratios, and the accompanying capital gains on stock, are at historically unprecedented levels.

   If equities are valued at market value by their owners, and at book value by their issuing firms, their net value will not cancel out. When shareholders choose to realize capital gains, AD will exceed earned income. Measured household 'saving' will then appear negative. A strong case can be made to introduce a comprehensive definition of disposable income in the national accounts, including capital gains and losses from asset revaluations.
6. It should also distinguish government intermediate goods, for example police and defense services, which would reduce measured GDP (Eisner 1989).
7. Disposable income may be increased or reduced by capital gains or losses on the sale of previously existing financial and tangible assets. Such income is currently excluded from the national income accounts. A strong case can be made for including capital gains and losses due to asset price revaluations under a broader definition of disposable income. If this were done, unrealized capital gains would constitute 'saving'.

# REFERENCES

Davidson, P. (1994), *Post Keynesian Macroeconomic Theory*, Aldershot, Hants: Edward Elgar.

Dugger, W. (1984), 'The nature of capital accumulation and technological progress in the modern economy', *Journal of Economic Issues*, 18: 799–823.

Foster, G. (1987), 'Financing investment', *Journal of Economic Issues*, 21: 101–12.

Keynes, J.M. (1936), *The General Theory of Employment, Interest and Money*, Vol. VII, *The Collected Writings of John Maynard Keynes*, 1972, London: Cambridge University Press.

Lerner, A. (1938), 'Saving equals investment', *Quarterly Journal of Economics*, LII(2): 297–309.

Lerner, A. (1939), 'Saving and investment: definitions, assumptions and objectives', *Quarterly Journal of Economics*, LIII(4): 611–19.

Loasby, B. (1976), *Choice, Complexity and Ignorance*, New York: Cambridge University Press.

Mankiw, G. (2000), *Macroeconomics*, 4th edition, New York: Worth.

Moore, B.J. (1988), *Horizontalists and Verticalists: the Macroeconomics of Credit Money*, London: Cambridge University Press.

Moore, B.J. (1994), 'The demise of the Keynesian multiplier: a reply to Cottrell', *Journal of Post Keynesian Economics*, 17: 121–34.

Moore, B.J. (2002), *Complexity and Macroeconomics* (manuscript).

Nelson, C. and C. Plosser (1981), 'Unit roots and random walks in economic time series', *Journal of Monetary Economics*, 10, September: 139–62.

Pindyck R., and D. Rubinfield (1995), *Econometric Models and Economic Forecasts*, New York: McGraw-Hill.

Stock, J. and M. Watson (1988), 'Variable trends in economic time series', *Journal of Economic Perspectives*, 2(4): 611–69.

Taylor, J. (1998), *Macroeconomics*, 2nd edition, New York: Houghton Mifflin.

Terzi, A. (1986–87), 'The independence of finance from saving: a flow of funds interpretation', *Journal of Post Keynesian Economics*, 9, Winter: 188–97.

Wray, L. (1991), 'Saving and profit in capitalist economies', *Journal of Economic Issues*, 25: 951–75.

# 9. Demand constraints and the new economy

## Marc-André Pigeon and L. Randall Wray.

Like the clock that loses a second an hour, the American economy has lost ground so gradually over the past twenty years that we don't realize how far behind we have fallen. The economic expansion of the first half of the 1990s has made it even more difficult for Americans to judge how weak our economy has been over the past two decades compared with the rest of our industrial history. The main reasons for this decline are not inflation, government budget deficits, low levels of investment, faltering education, the irresponsibility of Democrats or Republicans, excessive spending on the military, the aged, or the poor – or the many other explanations for America's economic dilemma that we repeatedly hear. Rather, these presumed causes are themselves largely the consequences of a more persistent problem: a sharp slowdown in economic growth (Madrick 1997: 3–4).

If rapid economic growth returns, most of the acute social issues that worry us today will become manageable. Wages will rise, our Social Security, Medicare, and welfare commitments will be easily met, and we will generate enough resources to invest adequately in our future. Most Americans would once again make the kind of financial progress they had come to expect . . . When workers are in demand in a growing economy, ethnic or sexual prejudice diminishes, and labor unions find it easier to organize and win more benefits for their members. In times of rapid expansion, privilege typically plays a smaller role in determining who gets the better jobs, and more Americans can afford the education that will help them qualify for good jobs (Madrick 1997: 151, 154).

Everyone is aware that US economic growth in the last few years has been robust. Since 1995, real GDP has been growing at close to 5 percent per year. By contrast, from 1972 to 1995, it grew at only 2.75 percent per year. Such a high growth rate contributed to the lowest unemployment rates in a quarter-century, rising real wages and the turn-around of the federal government budget – which moved from chronic deficits to record post-World War II surpluses. Robust growth probably also played a role in producing falling crime rates, in reversing the post-1973 trend toward greater inequality, and in raising consumer confidence and general feelings of well-being. The dire projections about social security's demise have had to be continually revised to postpone the day of reckoning in light of the long-term improvements to its finances that have resulted from higher growth rates. While economic growth is not the answer to all our nation's problems, it certainly ameliorates many of them.

Slow growth, by contrast, compounds many problems. After 1973, the United States (and many other nations) suffered through a quarter-century of growth that was about 1.5 percentage points below the long-term trend. While that may not seem like a large drop, as Madrick has calculated, the accumulated losses suffered between 1973 and 1993 due to lower growth amounted to US$12 trillion – or more than US$40,000 per American (in inflation-adjusted dollars) – with the loss in 1993 alone totaling US$1.2 trillion (Madrick 1997: 4). This is because the impact of slow growth is compounded over time. And these losses are not limited to narrow economic losses that can be measured in dollars. Slow growth contributes to social unrest, the politics of scapegoating, protectionism, 'waning confidence in long-standing institutions, and rising cynicism in our public life that threaten our best convictions as a nation' (Madrick 1997: 4).

In his careful analysis, Madrick went on to claim that the higher, pre-1973, growth rates were a thing of the past – slow growth was here to stay. This was not a fringe view. Indeed, slow-growth projections played a critical role in fueling the debate about social security 'reform'. However, looking back from the perspective of the first year of the new millennium, Madrick and other 'doomsayers' appear to have completely missed the birth of the 'new economy'. Not only did economic growth accelerate, but growth of labor productivity boomed, as was recognized by some even very early in the transition. At the end of 1995, *Business Week* proclaimed on its cover: 'Productivity to the rescue: technology is transforming the American economy into the most productive in the world' (9 October 1995). Chairman Greenspan was an early convert to the view that the rapid pace of technological innovation since the mid-1990s was fueling productivity growth that allowed for rapid economic growth without inflation, and, indeed, this recognition is credited for convincing the Fed to postpone monetary tightening – allowing the economy to continue to grow more robustly than many had thought possible. Where some had shown pessimism, enthusiasts for the new economy view display nearly unbounded optimism. Nowhere is this more in evidence than in President Clinton's budget surplus projections, which rely heavily on a sustained expansion, and seem to grow by the trillions upon every revision. By nearly all accounts, the cornucopia is here to stay.

Proponents of the new economy view generally focus their attention on supposed productivity enhancements due to the 'information technology' (IT) revolution, which has led to an acceleration of technical change in computers and telecommunications. The poster pin-up for the IT revolution is, of course, the internet, which is supposed to revolutionize the way America does business. As Gordon (2000) notes, the IT revolution dates from 1995, coinciding with the acceleration of the Clinton expansion, when unemployment finally began to fall and labor productivity began to grow at a fast clip. It is likened to the industrial revolution, or to the particularly innovative period at the end of the 19th century (the 'second' industrial revolution). Many proclaim that we have entered a new 'long wave' of rapid growth of output and productivity. If true, this means that the slow-growth, post-1973 period, as well as the non-accelerating inflation rate of unemployment (NAIRU) inflation–unemployment trade-off, may have been banished.

In this chapter, we will examine three questions.

1.  Is recent 'Goldilocks' growth really that unusual? Many commentators take the post-1972 performance as some sort of a norm. By comparison, the performance since 1995 certainly does look a lot better. But is that the correct norm to use?
2.  Is the recent growth spurt really due to the existence of a new economy effect? Or, more generally, is it due to favorable supply-side characteristics that have been created over the past two decades? This is the general line of argument adopted by most analysts, and especially by those who argue that US performance has been better than that of most of our OECD competitors precisely because the United States has done more to remove various supply constraints.
3.  Is this growth sustainable? Of course many rely on new economy arguments, comparing IT innovations to earlier productivity-enhancing innovations such as the telegraph or electricity. Thus, we might only be in the very early stages of a long wave of technological innovation. If, however, the Clinton expansion is not really based on IT innovations or other new economy features, is it based on some alternative, sustainable basis – such as greater reliance on 'free markets'?

We conclude that the Goldilocks economy is not really all that unusual.[1] Rather, we seem simply to have returned to a more normal growth rate after a quarter-century of below-normal growth. We will argue that the constraints that kept growth low during the last quarter of the 20th century were the same constraints that have periodically limited growth in the United States, and that have limited growth in other OECD countries – namely demand constraints. Thus, we reject the supply-side arguments that really underlie the new economy view, as well as other arguments that focus on supposed US advantages deriving from greater reliance on free markets. We will argue that neither slow growth between 1973 and 1993, nor rapid growth post-1995 should be attributed to slow or fast productivity growth. Indeed, we see productivity growth as mainly an uninteresting residual that results from the interplay between employment growth and growth of output – both of which are primarily demand-driven. Finally, we will point to disturbing trends that seem to us to threaten US growth. Similar trends are evidenced in many other OECD countries, although to a lesser degree. The real constraints in the coming years in the United States as well as in other OECD nations will be demand constraints, as they usually are. Thus, we argue that the US Goldilocks expansion is not sustainable. This does not mean, however, that Goldilocks growth built on a firmer foundation would not be sustainable.

## IS THE CLINTON EXPANSION REALLY THAT UNUSUAL?

From 1820 through 1973, US real GDP grew at an annual rate of 3.7 percent per year. Over that span of time, the economy went through civil and (two) world wars, as well as (six) depressions (at least one of which could be described as 'great'). Obviously, one can single out shorter periods with higher growth rates, and other periods with low growth. For example, growth in the 1870s was low. Industrial output fell by nearly 15 percent between 1872 and 1876. Still, from 1870 to 1913 the economy grew even faster than its long-term trend – at 4.42 percent per year. This is a period often pointed to as being characterized by rapid technological innovations, and a period with which the IT revolution is frequently compared. As mentioned earlier, the economy grew at a slightly higher pace after 1995 – at about 4.9 percent. If the expansion were to continue for another four decades at that pace, we could still beat the growth rate achieved during the 43-year relatively peaceful post-civil-war period. In that context, the current expansion looks rather puny. And for reasons we will discuss, it takes a real Pollyanna to suppose that growth will continue for 40 more years.

Of course, everyone prefers to compare the current expansion with the dismal post-1973 period, when growth fell by nearly 1.5 percentage points below the long-term trend. It is true that this period was unusually bad – probably worse than any other carefully chosen 25-year period. The question is whether that is the appropriate reference point. The affirmative case relies on poor productivity growth since 1973. It is pointed out that over the long haul – since 1870 – US labor productivity has grown at approximately 2 percent per year. From World War II to 1973, productivity growth actually improved to 2.7 percent per year. However, productivity growth after

1973 collapsed, falling by more than half of its long-term trend to just 0.9 percent per year. Again, the question is the relevant period for comparison – are we stuck with performance such as that achieved between 1973 and 1993, or can we enjoy a return to our long-run trend?

In the late 1980s through mid-1990s, a number of writers made a strong case that the United States would not be able to return to long-term trends. Many emphasized that post-war US growth was unusually strong because of the destruction of Europe and Japan; as these nations caught up, US growth necessarily 'converged' toward the average (Nelson and Wright 1992). One problem with this thesis is that US economic growth was higher for a long time (see below). However, as Nelson and Wright, as well as Madrick, emphasize, the United States for long enjoyed conditions that were most beneficial to mass production techniques, something we discuss in greater detail below. The problem is that we have already achieved the economies of scale that can be attained through mass production, largely because an affluent society quickly becomes satiated in mass production commodities. What we want are specialized goods and services, 'niche' products using 'flexible production' processes. Note that Madrick in particular goes beyond the usual argument that recognizes that we have become a service economy (hence, must expect slower productivity growth because technology usually benefits manufacturing). Thus, while some were arguing five years ago that our low productivity growth rates were due to a transformation from an industrial society to a service economy, Madrick recognized that this transformation has been taking place throughout the century and cannot therefore explain slow growth post-1973. Indeed, many of the 19th century technological innovations came in the service sector: instantaneous communication (the telegraph, and then the telephone), wholesaling and retailing on a mass scale, and tremendously falling transportation costs. Already by the 1880s, an American could approach a merchant who could instantaneously place an order and have goods delivered just about anywhere in about a week (Madrick 1997: 45). (Amazon.com can occasionally beat that speed of service 120 years later.) Nor does Madrick attribute past growth rates solely to high growth of labor productivity, or other 'supply-side' factors alone. He recognizes that part of the reason the United States had such high growth rates was due to high aggregate demand, as we'll discuss in a moment. In other words, he recognizes that past growth required the complementary supply and demand-side elements to ensure a sort of balance between the 'two blades of the scissors'.

Thus, the problem with moving from mass-produced goods to flexibly produced goods is not simply that smaller-scale production is less efficient. Perhaps even more importantly, niche market goods also have higher costs of wholesaling, retailing and marketing associated with them. Designer jeans targeted to carefully selected segments of the population might require only marginally more labor in their production than mass-produced, one-model-fits-all, blue jeans, but, they require much more labor to reach the final consumer and to stay abreast of the latest trends. Flexible production processes are even finding their way into the automobile industry, arguably the most important symbol of mass production, as witnessed by the emergence of various niche market autos (Plymouth's Prowler, Isuzu's Vehicross). These trends appear almost inevitable in an affluent society in which consumers seek personalized products as an expression of individuality. While internet marketing might negate some of the inefficiencies involved in selling such non-mass-produced products, it is difficult to see how huge economies of scale will be achieved that could rival those created for production and distribution of mass-produced commodities.

We do not have time to go into other arguments, but until the new economy hit five years ago, most analysts would have accepted the conclusion that rapid productivity growth was a thing of the past. This was the standard explanation for slow post-1973 growth, and the basis for the pessimistic projections about America's long-term prospects. As little as two years ago, this view was still commonplace, showing up, for example, in the debate about 'speed limits' to US growth. Many were arguing that the United States was growing unsustainably fast, and that the Fed ought to try to slow growth. As we will discuss below, Chairman Greenspan fortunately disagreed, in large part because he accepted the new economy views. However, Alan Blinder (1997) had argued that the economy's sustainable growth path would be in the 2–2.5 percent per year range. As evidence, he used an identity (similar to the one we will use below) that allocates real growth between growth of the labor force and growth of labor productivity. He cited demographic projections that had the labor force growing at about 1.1 percent into the future. He then extrapolated from post-1973 trends to obtain a projection of about 1.1 percent for labor productivity growth. Summing these, he obtained a 'speed limit' of about 2.2 percent for real GDP growth. He went on to argue that trying to push growth rates above this would sooner or later cause inflation because it would lower unemployment below its non-inflationary rate. We cite Blinder's argument because he is a well-known 'Keynesian' economist who was influential within the Clinton administration; thus, the view that low productivity growth was here to stay certainly was not a fringe view.

Before moving on to the second question, it is important to compare the US experience with that of other OECD nations. Our GDP growth rate has long been higher than those of other OECD nations. From 1820 to 1989 the United States grew at 3.7 percent per year, a rate far higher than the growth rates of Germany (2.5 percent), Japan (2.8 percent) or the United

Kingdom (2 percent). Some would respond that this is not really a fair comparison, because the United States benefited from much faster population growth. With a rapidly growing population, it should achieve faster growth simply because it could put more people to work. Thus, a more relevant comparison would be on the basis of per capita GDP growth. On that score, US GDP generally grew more than fast enough to keep pace with population growth: between 1820 and 1989, US per capita real GDP grew at an annual rate of 1.7 percent, compared with rates of 1.6 percent for Germany, 1.9 percent for Japan and 1.3 percent for the United Kingdom. Hence, while US GDP growth rates have been exceptional, our fast growth of population has kept our per capita economic growth in line with that of our major competitors. To some extent, our rapid labor force growth was responsible for our much higher GDP growth, but rapid population growth also forced us to spread these gains across more heads. Another way of looking at this is to argue that the United States *needs* more rapid growth because our population grows faster, a point to which we will return.

There are two other plausible explanations for US exceptionalism. First, US markets were big, fueling introduction of innovations that generated large economies of scale (Madrick 1997; Nelson and Wright 1992; Dertouzos, Lester and Solow 1989). By contrast, small European markets constrained demand and thus the benefits of mass production technologies. Second, US demand was generally higher and growing more rapidly – partly because our workers had higher wages to support higher consumption and partly because of all the new frontier lands that had to be conquered – leading to large-scale production of canals, railroads and other infrastructure. The United States achieved a sort of 'virtuous' circle: frontier demands stimulated production of public and private infrastructure, which increased capacity and lowered transportation and communication costs. Demand created supply and the supply thus created fulfilled demand. However, with the new global economy, and especially with the development of the European Common Market, the United States has lost its advantages – everyone now has access to large, global, markets (see especially Nelson and Wright 1992).[2] Thus, our growth will be more like that of OECD long-term trends, according to the pessimistic outlook. No more US exceptionalism.

In sum, the 1973–93 growth rates were quite low compared with past US growth, as well as compared with more recent 'new economy' growth rates. On the other hand, the high rates of growth of the distant past greatly exceeded those of our European competitors. They might therefore be seen as 'exceptional', with growth post-1973 being less exceptional and more comparable to European growth. Slower growth after 1973 is often attributed to slower growth of labor productivity, which might be explained as resulting from loss of peculiar advantages enjoyed for 150 years by America, as well as from a transformation of production from mass production to flexible production techniques. Unless there really is something 'new' about the new economy, it is unlikely that the United States can return to the high growth rates of the past. The Clinton expansion might not last if it is based on IT innovations that are transitory; thus the pessimism of the early 1990s need not be abandoned.

## WHY HAS US GROWTH IMPROVED?

Even as many analysts were arguing that slow growth was here to stay, history chose to thumb its nose by returning US growth to its own long-term trends. Pundits immediately seized on two features of the US economy, the supposed explosion of IT and the greater US reliance on free markets – especially on freer labor markets – than in other OECD countries. If only our competitors would free up their own markets, they could enjoy our higher growth rates. In this section we will first examine the new economy arguments before turning to the more general argument that recent acceleration of US growth is due to more favorable supply-side conditions that have generated greater growth of labor productivity. We will conclude this section with an alternative view, namely that the Clinton boom has been fueled by favorable demand-side conditions. In the next section, however, we will argue that this demand-side-led growth is unsustainable, although not for the reasons that conventional analysis would highlight.

### The New Economy

As Robert Solow has famously argued, for a long time the evidence of the computer revolution was everywhere but in the productivity numbers – an insight that came to be known as the Solow Paradox. Then, suddenly, growth and productivity boomed. On the surface, it seems implausible that the timing is right – why did our economy go through two decades or more of investment in computers before anything showed up in the statistics? Furthermore, why doesn't Europe show any new economy statistics? Supporters of the new economy view offered an explanation. Paul David (1990) argued that it takes time for the effects of major new innovations to show up – just as it took a couple of decades for the electrical motor to make its mark on the economy. Applying this to the introduction of computers into the economy, one could explain the lag. Furthermore, while it is true that 'computerization' of the economy has been proceeding for

decades, the new economy is based on an *acceleration* of the pace of innovation, and this occurred only in the mid-1990s. This coincided with the
'*acceleration* in the rate of price decline in computer hardware, software,
and telephone services, the corollary of an acceleration of the exponential
growth rate of computer power and telecommunications capability, and the
wildfire speed of development of the Internet' (Gordon 2000: 2).

This might explain the timing for both the United States and for
Europe – with our competitors demonstrably a bit behind us, their own
new economy may be just down the road. As Wim Duisenberg (president
of the European Central Bank) argued recently, 'There is some evidence
– although not uncontroversial itself – of the emergence of a new
economy in the United States. By contrast, it is difficult as yet to find evidence of a new economy in the euro area' (Buckley 2000: 1). He went on
to note that 'The new economy is primarily a supply-side story'.
According to a program adopted at the Lisbon summit of European
Union leaders in March, the European Union was trying to emulate the
US supply-side model to make the area the 'most competitive and
dynamic knowledge-based economy in the world'. Thus, if the European
Union could 'free up' its supply side, it might eventually enjoy its own
new economy. Similarly equating the new economy with removal of con-
straints on the supply side, and echoing Duisenberg, Chairman
Greenspan has argued as follows.

> An intriguing aspect of the recent wave of productivity acceleration is that U.S.
> businesses and workers appear to have benefited more from the recent advances
> in information technology than their counterparts in Europe or Japan. Those
> countries, of course, have also participated in this wave of invention and inno-
> vation, but they appear to have been slower to exploit it. The relatively inflexible
> and, hence, more costly labor markets of these economies appear to be a signifi-
> cant part of the explanation. The elevated rates of return offered by the newer
> technologies in the United States are largely the result of a reduction in labor
> costs per unit of output. The rates of return on investment in the same new tech-
> nologies are correspondingly less in Europe and Japan because businesses there
> face higher costs of displacing workers than we do. Here, labor displacement is
> more readily countenanced both by law and by culture. Parenthetically, because
> our costs of dismissing workers are lower, the potential costs of hiring and the
> risks associated with expanding employment are less. The result of this signifi-
> cantly higher capacity for job dismissal has been, counterintuitively, a dramatic
> decline in the U.S. unemployment rate in recent years (Alan Greenspan, 4
> September 1998, speech titled 'Is there a new economy?').

We will return to an analysis of supposed 'freer' US labor markets in a
moment. First, however, let us examine exactly how the new economy has
boosted productivity growth. According to Greenspan,

[t]he more-rapid pace of IT and other high-tech innovation also has been accompanied by a visible acceleration of the process of 'creative destruction', a shifting of capital from failing technologies into those technologies at the cutting edge as differential rates of return among prospective investments widened. The resulting process of capital reallocation across the economy has been assisted by a significant unbundling of risks in capital markets made possible by the development of innovative financial products, many of which themselves owe their viability to improvements in IT (Alan Greenspan, speech before the New York Association for Business Economics, NY, 13 June 2000).

While on many occasions Greenspan has recognized that all this 'creative destruction' wrought by the new economy has increased worker uncertainty (thus, held down wage hikes), he paradoxically argues that it has reduced uncertainty for business. Firms today have much better and more timely knowledge concerning 'customers' needs and of the location of inventories and materials flowing throughout complex production systems' (Greenspan 2000), which has allowed them to greatly reduce 'redundancies' of inventories and labor. Such developments, he insists, 'emphasize the essence of information technology – the expansion of knowledge and its obverse, the reduction of uncertainty . . . In short, information technology raises output per hour in the total economy principally by reducing hours worked on activities needed to guard productive processes against the unknown and the unanticipated. Narrowing the uncertainties reduces the number of hours required to maintain any given level of production readiness'. He concludes that these gains to productivity are largely permanent, 'driven by irreversible advances in technology and its application'. Greater access to information directly generates higher productivity because firms do not have to devote scarce resources (including labor) to activities designed to merely deal with market uncertainty.

Robert Gordon (2000) has raised doubts about the new economy effects. Using conventional (production function) methodology, he demonstrates that more than all of the productivity boom can really be explained by an 'unsustainable' cyclical effect supplemented by a productivity growth spurt in the durable manufacturing sector, something that some analysts have emphasized since at least the late 1980s (see, for example, Baumol et al. 1989). He explains that it has long been recognized that a cyclical upswing is always associated with rising productivity, as output grows faster than hours worked.[3] Presumably, this is accomplished by using the labor force more efficiently early in the expansion.[4] Thus, his first step is to separate the cyclical effects from the longer-run productivity effects that are supposed to result from the IT revolution. He calculates that productivity growth during the new economy years of 1995–99 was 1.35 percentage points higher than during the 1972–95 period. Of this, he finds that 0.54

percentage points was due to the cyclical effect, leaving 0.81 percentage points that might be attributed to new economy effects. However, all of this is explained by acceleration of productivity growth in the durable goods sector, and most of that is really in the manufacture of computers and closely related equipment.[5] This means that the remaining 88 percent of the economy – that is, the computer-using part of the economy – is not enjoying any productivity gain from using computers. Gordon concludes that

> [t]he 'New Economy' is alive and well, but only within computer manufacturing and the remainder of the manufacturing sector . . . our decomposition of productivity growth leaves less than nothing left over for the 88 percent of the economy outside durable manufacturing; trend MFP [multi-factor productivity] growth there has actually *decelerated*. Not only has there been no spillover from the New Economy in the form of a structural acceleration in MFP growth in the rest of the economy, but there has not even been an acceleration in trend labor productivity growth in response to a massive investment boom in computers and related equipment. Outside of durable manufacturing, the New Economy has been remarkably unfruitful as a creator of productivity growth (Gordon 2000: 16, 45–6).

So much for new economy effects on productivity. Gordon argues that the IT revolution does not come close to the truly revolutionary 'great inventions' that came between 1860 and 1900 and generated rapid productivity growth through the first three-quarters of the 20th century. Among the great inventions, Gordon counts electricity (lights and motors), the internal combustion engine, development of petroleum and its chemical derivatives, information innovations (including the telegraph, telephone, photography, motion pictures) and indoor plumbing. He argues that no current innovation in information technology comes close to the change in cost and speed of communications accomplished by the telegraph in 1840–50. The IT revolution does not measure up against even one of his five clusters of great inventions.

Madrick has recently argued that while the 'computer revolution' really does represent a significant technological transformation, it is not one that will necessarily lead to a sustained increase in productivity growth. Indeed, he concludes that '[t]he new economy is a return to a contemporary version of a crafts economy, where the most valued contribution is the skill of the worker' (Madrick 1999). In some sense, that actually places the new economy in direct opposition to the earlier industrial revolution with which it is often compared, which largely achieved productivity gains by replacing highly skilled crafts workers with semi-skilled industrial workers. Thus, one should not expect a sustained boost to productivity growth arising from IT.

It is still possible that we can obtain some GDP growth out of the new economy because of all the exciting new consumer products being created – even if it doesn't increase productivity much. That is, maybe supply is creating demand, Say's Law style. Most conventional analyses would reject such an argument, however, because they view demand-side-led growth as a purely cyclical phenomenon that eventually runs up against supply constraints. This point was also made by Greenspan, who emphasized that cyclical factors could stretch output 'beyond sustainable capacity for a time, raising measured output per hour', but said that this could not lead to a sustainable increase of productivity (Greenspan 2000). We will return to that subject in a moment. However, there are two further reasons to doubt that demand for the products of the new economy can sustain rapid growth of output. First, as Frank Veneroso (2000) has argued, for the most part, the IT revolution appears to be running out of steam. He suggests that computer hardware sales growth is already past its peak, a contention supported by preliminary profit forecasts for many computer sector firms in early July 2000. Similarly, Gordon (2000: 31) shows that spending on computers as a percentage of nominal spending did not increase at all from 1987 to 1999. Even if one argues that 'real spending' is rising as a share of total spending because one gets far more computer per dollar today, it is hard to see how the IT revolution can fuel demand-side growth if it remains a constant share of total nominal spending. Furthermore, Veneroso shows that even internet 'eyeballs' (visits to websites) may have already peaked. Anyone who will ever want a computer (at least, anyone who can afford one) may already have got one, and with prices falling rapidly replacement sales and upgrades cannot take up the slack in terms of nominal sales. While it might be true that 'real' aggregate sales that take into account substantial quality adjustments are still rising, this is not the relevant factor in fueling aggregate demand growth.

The jury is still out on all that and we will not know for several more decades whether the IT revolution might eventually measure up to past technological revolutions. What is more important is the general supply-side approach that underlies most of the new economy arguments. Similarly, many pundits focus on supposed greater reliance in the United States on free markets – which reduce supply constraints on growth. Most prominently, many argue that freer US labor markets are largely responsible for better US performance throughout the 1990s. In a sense, the new economy arguments are simply a subset of the more general approach that sees productivity growth as the primary determinant of long-term growth trends. Let us turn to that issue.

### More American Exceptionalism: Reliance on Free Markets Relaxes Supply Constraints

Productivity-based approaches to economic growth emphasize institutional and technological improvements that allow a given quantity of inputs to produce a greater quantity of outputs. Productivity can be measured in a variety of ways. Gordon, as discussed above, prefers to use multifactor productivity, which apportions productivity growth among the various factors of production (usually labor and capital, but occasionally including materials, energy, imports or even entrepreneurial factors). This requires specification of a production function, which is not without some controversy. A more straightforward approach is simply to calculate labor productivity by forming a ratio of total output (measured in nominal or inflation-adjusted terms) either to hours of labor worked or, more simply, to number of employees (see Barro's 1998 article on growth accounting). Obviously, these two measures of labor productivity could give different results if, for example, the average number of hours worked by employees were to change substantially through time. In practice, hours worked per employee change fairly slowly so that results do not vary greatly between the two methods. Labor could become more productive for a variety of reasons: better quality of labor (more education, skills, experience), more capital per worker, better capital per worker, more efficient use of labor (fewer hours wasted on the job due to idleness or bureaucratic red tape) and so on. For example, the new economy is supposed to have improved labor productivity as more and faster computers have allowed each worker to accomplish more.

In addition, it is frequently asserted that greater reliance in the United States on free markets that are subject to ever-declining intrusions by government has contributed to growth in two ways. First, environmental, safety and other regulations have been relaxed, allowing firms to operate more efficiently – which raises labor productivity even in existing plants, while stimulating entrepreneurial initiative to invest in new higher-tech plants. Even supply-side tax cuts could play a role in raising labor productivity, because employees would be stimulated to work harder (and earn more) while employers would be stimulated to invest. At the same time, reducing or eliminating government programs that provide a social safety net would also stimulate supply-side-led growth because more people would be encouraged to flow into labor markets (see the Greenspan quote above). Thus, US economic performance would be doubly enhanced – by increasing productivity of the existing labor force, and also by increasing the size of the labor force as impediments to work are eliminated.

A superficial comparison of the United States with most OECD countries certainly seems to verify this view. US employment rates reached an all-time high during the Clinton expansion even as labor productivity growth boomed. The result, of course, is higher GDP growth rates. In contrast, it is claimed that excessive government intervention – particularly in labor markets – throughout other OECD nations keeps their employment rates low (and unemployment high) and saps entrepreneurial initiative, hindering productivity growth. In the remainder of this section, we will examine in detail the relationship between labor productivity, employment rates and economic growth.

Figure 9.1 compares growth of inflation-adjusted GDP per capita for the United States, United Kingdom, Japan, Italy, France, Canada and

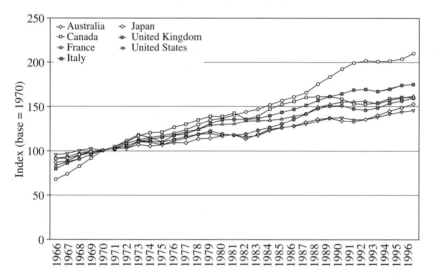

*Note:* Gross domestic product is computed at market prices in 1987 US dollars to create a uniform measure of living standards.

*Source:* World Bank (1998), *World Development Indicators*, CD ROM.

*Figure 9.1 Per capita gross domestic product, 1966–96*

Australia. (We have omitted Germany from our data owing to difficulty surrounding unification of East and West in 1990. However, our analysis reveals that Germany falls squarely in the middle range of European per capita income, employment rates and productivity.) We have used 1970 as the base year, indexing GDP per capita for all countries to 100, which allows us to compare relative growth. Of course, the United States has greater population growth than that of other OECD nations, and if we were to simply plot real GDP growth rather than real per capita GDP growth, the United States would look much better. However, we want to separate growth that can be attributed to greater productivity of the work-force from growth that might be attributable to a growing labor force. For this reason it is more appropriate to compare per capita growth rates. Japan stands out as the unusually successful economy to 1990; its GDP per capita increased by a factor of two. In all of the other countries per capita GDP increased by a factor of one and a half to one and three-quarters. Surprisingly, the United States had the worst performance of the group. In terms of growth of output per head, it certainly does not stand out – in spite of its 'freer' markets – even during the 1990s, although in the last few years there is a bit of an upswing.

On the other hand, US labor market experience does differ markedly from that of most other developed countries. European unemployment rates have remained stubbornly high, often double those of the United States. In addition, our labor force grows much more rapidly for two reasons: our population is growing and the percentage of the population that is in the labor force is also growing. For this reason, it is useful to compare employment rates – the ratio of the number of employed to population.[6]

Figure 9.2 plots the employment rate for the same countries, again using

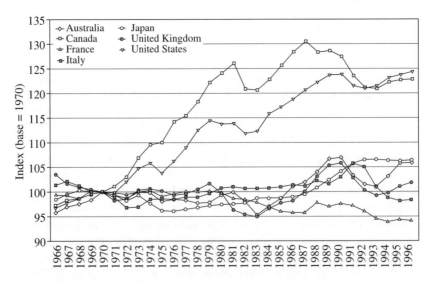

*Source:*    Bureau of Labor Statistics website: http://stats.bls.gov:80/.

*Figure 9.2    The employment rate, 1966–96*

1970 as a base year. By the mid-1990s, the US employment rate had risen by nearly 25 percent over its 1970 level. Growth of the employment rate can occur either because unemployment rates fall or because a larger percentage of the population comes into the labor force (holding unemployment rates constant). Looking to the US case, most of the long-term growth in the employment rate is due to rising labor force participation rates of women; however, since 1990, much of the growth has been driven by falling unemployment rates. Canada, like the United States, also experienced rising labor force participation of women, but high unemployment in recent years has more than compensated, causing the employment rate to fall considerably since its mid-1980s peak. Japan and European countries, however, have had very little change in their employment rates; the rate in France has actually fallen by about 5 percent since 1970. This less favorable experience might be attributed to a number of factors, including older populations, younger retirement ages, more generous social safety nets, various labor market barriers (tax laws, government regulations, union power) that prevent entry, and perhaps cultural norms that limit female participation (for example, in Japan, where married women are expected to leave the labor force).

We conclude, then, that while US per capita GDP growth has not been unusually high, our labor markets have performed much better than have those of our major competitors. This raises a question, however. If we have managed to increase the proportion of our population that contributes to production at a pace that far exceeds that of all our rivals (with the exception of Canada), why haven't we increased output per head more significantly? The answer, of course, lies in lower productivity growth. Per capita GDP growth can be attributed to rising employment rates plus rising output per worker (Box 1). Figure 9.3 compares productivity growth for the same set of countries, again using 1970 as the base year. Japan stands out with productivity that is twice as high by 1990 as it had been in 1970. Italian productivity had increased by a factor of 1.8; most of the other countries increased productivity by between 1.5 and 1.75 times over what it had been in 1970. The United States and Canada lag far behind – US productivity had not even increased by 20 percent by 1996.

On the surface, this seems to be a strange result. The 'freer' US labor markets seem to have contributed to higher employment rates, but did not generate (at least through 1996) the conditions that allow employers to raise productivity much. It is possible that higher participation rates have been produced only by bringing less suitable workers into the labor market, a point to which we will return below. If this is the case, US growth might continue to be supply-constrained, with the constraint having to do with the quality rather than the quantity of labor inputs. However, even if true

---

## BOX 1:   IDENTITY

Start with the following identity:

$$GDP = EMP* \left( \frac{GDP}{EMP} \right) \qquad (1a)$$

where GDP is gross domestic product and EMP is total employment. Without changing the nature of the equation, we can divide both sides of equation (1) by the population (POP) as follows in equation (1b):

$$\frac{GDP}{POP} = \frac{EMP}{POP} * \frac{GDP}{EMP} \qquad (1b)$$

This equation simply says that per capita income, by definition, is equal to the product of the employment rate and productivity. Taking the total derivative, we see that:

$$\Delta \left( \frac{GDP}{POP} \right) = \Delta \left( \frac{EMP}{POP} \right) + \Delta \left( \frac{GDP}{EMP} \right) \qquad (1c)$$

which of course merely says that the growth of output per person (per capita income) is equal to the growth of the employment rate plus the growth of productivity.

---

this makes the case for 'free' labor markets much weaker because one could argue that greater employment is 'purchased' only at the cost of bringing lower-quality workers into the market. Further, it might indicate that a strong case can be made for government programs to try to increase the quality of these workers. In any case, this surely does not present a strong case for freer labor markets if labor productivity suffers so much that there are no net benefits in terms of output per capita – a quite surprising result.

On the other hand, there is nothing terribly magical or surprising about our findings. They are based on identities. If per capita growth rates are roughly the same for the G7 countries while employment rates for Canada and the United States are well above average, then it must be true that productivity growth for these countries is lower. But these kinds of tautologies can be useful in guiding our thinking. First, this suggests that it may be best to think of productivity as a residual. Second, it suggests that we need to think carefully about the role of demand. Third, it suggests that there may be some kind of trade-off between employment rates and productivity.

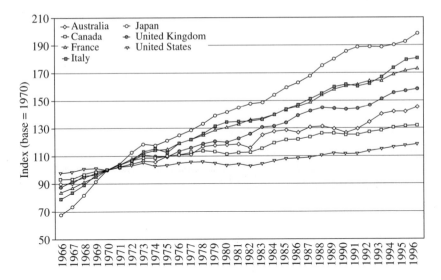

*Source:* IMF (1998), *International Financial Statistics.*

*Figure 9.3 Productivity, 1966–96*

'Choosing' high employment rates implies lower productivity for a given growth rate. Let us take up these points in reverse order.

Buchele and Christiansen (1999) have reached a conclusion similar to ours: there may be a trade-off between economic growth and productivity growth. Comparing the United States and Canada with several European nations, they found that between 1960 and the early 1990s, there appears to be a long-run inverse relationship between employment growth and productivity growth. They attribute this finding to 'the differential effects of labor market institutions' (p. 313), with nations that promote collective bargaining, employment security and social protection having lower employment growth but higher productivity growth than nations that rely to a greater extent on 'free markets'. Furthermore, they find that 'a generalized slowdown in the rate of growth of demand' has 'adversely affected both employment and productivity growth since the 1970s' (p. 313). Thus, low growth of aggregate demand lowers both employment and productivity growth over the long term. As we noted above, many economists recognize a short-run cyclical effect of aggregate demand on productivity growth and employment growth. Booms lead to higher productivity and employment growth while recessions lead to lower productivity and employment growth. However, what we are hypothesizing is a long-run trade-off of

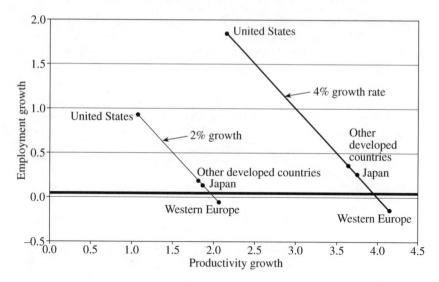

*Note:* GDP is computed in 1986 dollars. Western Europe comprises Austria, England, France, Finland, Germany, Italy, Luxemburg, Netherlands, Norway, Portugal, Spain and Switzerland. Other developed countries comprise Australia, Canada, Israel, New Zealand, South Africa.

*Source:* Alphametrics.

*Figure 9.4    EPT schedule for Western Europe, Japan, other developed countries and the United States, 1970–97 (%)*

employment and productivity growth, given aggregate demand (and hence GDP growth rates).

Figure 9.4 reproduces what Buchele and Christiansen call the employment–productivity trade-off (EPT) schedule for a given growth rate. Notice that the United States is located right in the middle of the two percent growth EPT schedule, suggesting that a given GDP growth rate is about evenly split between productivity and employment growth, as we will show below. The European Union is below the horizontal axis, reflecting slightly negative growth in the employment rate but higher productivity growth. The important thing to note about this figure is that these two regions respond differently to a shock to the growth rate. A positive shock to demand should be evenly split between productivity and employment in the United States but should show up almost exclusively as productivity gains in the European Union. We will argue that this is exactly what has happened in the United States in the last five years and that the demand shock has come from consumer spending. Like Buchele and Christiansen, we believe that higher demand growth has a permanent effect on the rate of growth – maintenance of high growth of demand keeps the EPT schedule out to the right – which is then split between growth of employment or growth of productivity depending on the demographic and institutional characteristics of each individual nation.

It is instructive to plot the data from Figures 9.1 to 9.3 in a different manner. Figures 9.5 through 9.7 show growth of the GDP indexes, divided into the constituent components: growth of employment rates and growth of productivity. These figures show that per capita output growth in

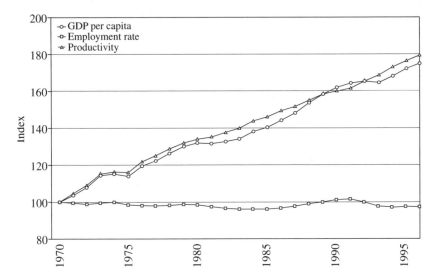

*Notes and sources:*    As for Figure 9.4.

*Figure 9.5    Economic growth: the Western European story, 1970–95*

Western Europe[7] and in Japan is entirely attributable to growth of labor productivity. In contrast, US per capita output growth is just about equally divided between growth of productivity and growth of the employment rate. Cyclical fluctuation of per capita GDP growth in the United States has largely been due to fluctuation of the employment rate; productivity growth has been much smoother. Finally, Figure 9.8 shows the same data for a variety of other developed countries (Australia, Israel, Canada, New Zealand and South Africa); all the long-run growth can be attributed to growth of productivity, but there have been very large short-run swings of the employment rate. Note that each time the employment rate rose, GDP per capita increased sharply.

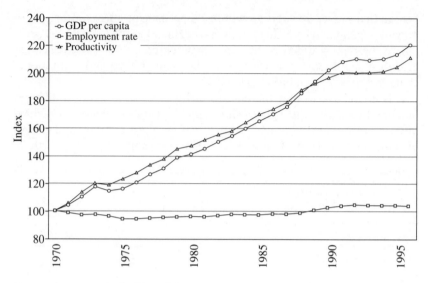

*Notes and sources:*   As for Figure 9.4.

*Figure 9.6     Economic growth: the Japanese story, 1970–95*

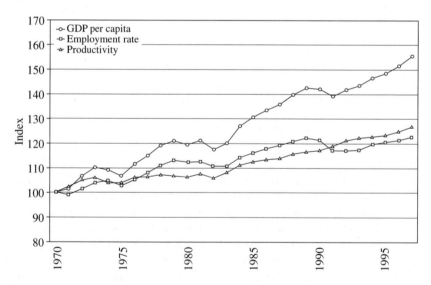

*Notes and sources:*   As for Figure 9.4.

*Figure 9.7     Economic growth: the US story, 1970–95*

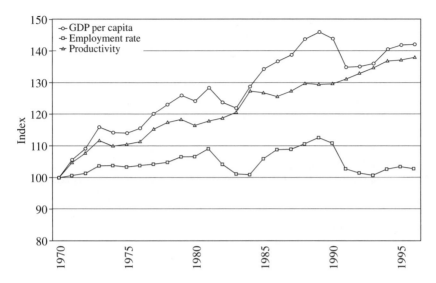

*Notes and sources:* As for Figure 9.4

*Figure 9.8 Economic growth: Other developed countries, 1970–95*

What does it all mean? Before 1990, Japan is the clear economic miracle, increasing its per capita output by two and a half times since 1967 in the face of what would appear to be severe supply constraints. Not only are Japan's non-human resources quite limited, but it also suffers from an aging population and restrictive cultural norms that have prevented any growth in its employment ratio. Further, it has long had strong labor unions as well as informal labor market practices (such as 'life-long employment') that generate great rigidity. Its trade restrictions effectively reduce the opportunity to relieve supply constraints through imports. However, in spite of all this, it has increased relative labor productivity by more than ten times as much as the United States. Note, also, that the first oil price shock did apparently generate a supply constraint, as the rate of economic growth fell and long-term productivity growth suffered a set-back. However, the economy quickly adapted to higher energy prices, and productivity growth resumed. This seems to indicate that whatever supply constraints Japan encountered, it was able to overcome them. A similar story can be told about Western European countries. Even while suffering from 'Eurosclerosis', these countries have managed to generate faster growth of GDP per capita than the United States has, again, with all the growth attributed to growth of productivity. 'Freer' labor markets and more

favorable demographics do appear to generate faster growth of employment rates (and perhaps even lower unemployment rates), but they do not
produce higher rates of growth of per capita output.

One might suppose that higher employment rates are associated with
falling productivity because less able workers are brought into employment.
However, labor productivity and employment rates in the United States are
highly and positively correlated. That there is no necessary relation between
the two, however, is shown by the divergent experiences of France, which
exhibits a strong negative correlation. Looking at Figures 9.5 and 9.8 again,
what we find is that productivity grows steadily for this group of countries,
with deviations from GDP per capita trend growth fully explained by
growth of the employment rate. In other words, high cyclical growth of
GDP draws workers into the labor market, apparently without adversely
affecting productivity.

While it is true that a significant part of US employment growth has been
in the low-productivity portion of the service sector, many analysts have
concluded that there has been a lot of growth in higher-productivity service
sector jobs.[8] Furthermore, as Lester Thurow (1993) has argued, rising
service sector employment relative to manufacturing employment in
Germany has not slowed productivity growth. Indeed, the German service
sector is just about as productive as the manufacturing sector. Thurow
attributes this to a conscious effort by policy-makers to take a 'high road'
approach to employment; setting high minimum wages in the service sector
forces employers to keep productivity high and growing. Even if it were true
that the marginal workers brought into the US labor market had low productivity, this could not explain the very large divergence between productivity growth in the United States and Japan – US employment rates grew
by about 25 percent and productivity grew by less than 20 percent, while
Japanese productivity grew by 190 percent.

There is reason to believe, however, that countries can, to some extent,
'choose' high employment paths or low employment paths. Given the long-
run path of employment, and given long-run growth of aggregate demand,
long-run labor productivity growth is then determined primarily as a 'residual'. In other words, we believe that employment growth can be impacted
by government policy, but given long-run growth of aggregate demand,
productivity growth is largely outside the purview of policy. In a country
like the United States which tends to favor employment growth (by remov-
ing obstacles to participation and to hiring), productivity growth will tend
to be lower than that of countries that do not *unless aggregate demand
growth is commensurately higher*. This does not mean we believe there is no
limit to productivity growth – surely beyond some point, technology and
institutional arrangements would come into play. However, we believe that

those constraints are rarely reached. Obviously, there is no simple way to demonstrate this, but the evidence we have presented certainly is consistent with the view that at the rates of growth of aggregate demand that have existed in most countries since 1970, productivity growth has not been the constraining factor.

The Japanese experience before 1990 might be taken as the practical limit to productivity growth (simply because it has the highest rate of productivity growth of the countries analysed). Japan 'chose' a low employment path – essentially holding the employment ratio constant – with high aggregate demand, which generated rapid growth of productivity. Demand was maintained at a high level through a combination of very large government deficits, high investment demand, and generally a high flow of net exports after 1980 (in large part due to US willingness to run huge trade deficits with Japan). However, toward the end of the 1980s, the government deficit fell rapidly and the budget moved into balance. When the United States 'double-dipped' in the early 1990s recession, and as other Asian countries began to compete effectively with Japan for world markets, foreign demand for Japanese products was hurt. Together, these negative influences lowered aggregate demand and contributed to a deep and prolonged recession, which was worsened by various financial system 'shocks' in Japan and Asia. After 1990, demand growth was insufficient to generate much growth of per capita GDP; this led to low growth of labor productivity.

Of course, since 1995 the United States has enjoyed higher growth of aggregate demand, which has shifted the EPT schedule out to the right (as shown by a shift of the curve in Figure 9.4). As usual, this can be divided between growth of the employment rate and growth of productivity. Thus, the 'new economy' productivity boom has largely resulted from growth of demand that exceeded growth of the employment rate. The final question we will examine in this section concerns the source of demand. We will argue that the United States has been able to enjoy above-average growth in productivity and employment rates because of a strong demand stimulus from consumer spending.

How can we test this hypothesis? A simple way is to follow the method developed by Wynne Godley to look at the evolution of three key financial balances, namely the public, private and foreign sectors. By definition, the private sector surplus equals the government deficit plus the trade surplus (Box 2). Over the course of the Clinton expansion, the government budget moved from a large deficit to a large surplus; in addition, the trade account became increasingly negative. By accounting identity, the private sector balance moved from surplus in the early years of the expansion to large, and growing, deficits by the end of the 1990s. Figure 9.9 shows what the data for this equation look like for the United States. The key thing to note is that (as

---

**BOX 2:   THE PRIVATE SECTOR DEFICIT, THE
                    GOVERNMENT SURPLUS AND THE
                    CURRENT ACCOUNT DEFICIT**

Most economic data reported by the media come from what are called the national accounts. These 'accounts' were devised by economists and put into practice in and around World War II as a way for government to measure what was going on in the 'real' world. These accounts adopt the double-entry book-keeping system used by all accountants everywhere. In other words, for every positive there is a negative and the pluses and minuses must sum to zero. That's why we can say that the private sector deficit exactly equals the government surplus plus the trade deficit. It is true by definition or, in other words, by design. Here's why:

By definition (the '≡' symbol means 'by definition' in mathematics), we can write that :

$$GDP + Y_n - Y_f \equiv GNP \qquad (1)$$

where *GDP* is equal to the output of all persons residing in this country, whether they be citizens or not, $Y_n$ is income earned by all American citizens, whether they live in the United States or not, and $Y_f$ is foreign income, that is, income earned by foreigners residing in the United States.

From this, if we ignore government, we can also write:

$$GNP \equiv Y \equiv C + I + NX \qquad (2)$$

where *GNP* is the output of all nationals living here and abroad, *C* is consumption, *I* is investment and *NX* is net exports, which can be gleaned from the current account of the balance of payments (which, by definition, always sums to zero). This in turn can be written as:

$$NX \equiv Y - C - I \qquad (3)$$

which produces the familiar result that:

$$NX \equiv S - I \qquad (4)$$

---

where $S$ is savings and, again, by definition, is equal to $Y-C$, since we can conceptually imagine all output being explained by either expenditure or savings. By rewriting (2) above we can bring government $G$ and private spending $PX$ (household and business) into the picture.

$$Y \equiv PX + G + NX \tag{5}$$

Without changing the relationship, we can next subtract government taxes to arrive at:

$$[Y - T - PX] \equiv [G - T\} + NX \tag{6}$$

This says that the private sector balance (income minus expenditures and taxes) on the left-hand side of the equation is equal to the government surplus (where $T > G$) and the trade deficit ($NX$ would have a minus sign). This accounting identity, like the one we explored earlier in Box 1, does not necessarily imply a causal relationship in the real world. There is also no a priori reason to link this relationship to overall growth rates, although there are good theoretical reasons to do so, as we argue in the text.

of summer 2000) the private sector balance is at an unprecedentedly low level, running a deficit equal to 5.5 percent of national income. Most of this private sector deficit is attributable to households, who are spending more than their incomes by a record amount. This has been the engine of economic growth – the necessary demand stimulus for this expansion. Government sectors and external trade have been net drains on the expansion.

So what we experienced post-1973 was not a productivity slowdown, but rather an output slowdown that lowered our measured productivity growth. As output increased in the last half of the 1990s, productivity growth boomed – as it must when output growth exceeds growth of the labor force at a sufficiently rapid pace. This was not due to freer markets or the new economy – we simply returned to the usual US case, which is higher aggregate demand growth. At best, our freer markets simply lead to higher employment rates when compared with those of Europe or Japan. The 1973–95 experience was more European-like because demand did not grow fast enough to keep pace with our growing population and raise productivity. This was due to monetary and fiscal policy austerity, low growth of

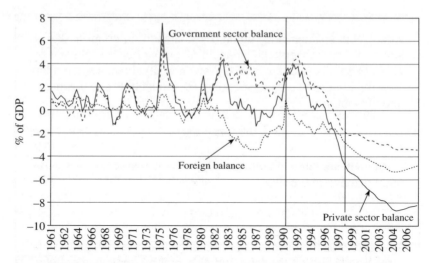

*Note:*   The period between the two vertical bars begins in 1991 Q2 and ends in 1999 Q1, corresponding to the current expansion. Data after 1999 Q1 are projections. Note that a government deficit is recorded as a positive number.

*Source:*   National Income and Product Accounts (NIPA) and Wynne Godley of the Jerome Levy Economics Institute. Projections implied by Congressional Budget Office (CBO) analysis.

*Figure 9.9    The three financial balances as a percentage of GDP, 1961–2006*

wages – indeed, falling real wages – a growing trade deficit and worsening income distribution. All these things worsened demand growth, holding output growth to little over employment growth. This necessarily generated very poor productivity growth. Post-1995, we have had a nice consumption boom led by private sector deficits. Is this sustainable? In the next section we will argue that it is not.

## IS GOLDILOCKS SUSTAINABLE?

As we argued above, the US boom, especially in the post-1995 new economy period, is consumer-led. In fact, it is fueled by unprecedented household borrowing. In order for growth to continue in the context of a government budget surplus and trade deficit, household budgets must continue to deteriorate. Figure 9.9 shows projections (for the year 2000 and beyond) produced by Wynne Godley. He simply took Congressional Budget Office (CBO) projections of growth rates, which have growth falling to just above 2.5 percent and budget surpluses actually growing over time relative to GDP. He then made reasonable projections about what will happen to the US trade account assuming we continue to grow. Our private sector deficits are already far and away larger than ever before, but they must continue to grow – to 8 percent of GDP and more – if the economy is to grow in the presence of a government budget surplus and a trade deficit. This also means that our debt to disposable income ratios must rise. By the first quarter of 2000, the private sector debt to disposable income ratio had already reached 165 percent – easily a record – and this must grow every year that spending grows faster than income, as projected.

There are several reasons to doubt that this can continue. First, the Fed has been raising interest rates in order to slow growth, which increases debt service ratios. Debt service ratios peaked in the United States in the late 1980s at a bit above 14 percent of income; while they are currently just under 14 percent, they will rise as more debt is reset at higher interest rates. Eventually, the private sector will retrench, slowing its growth of indebtedness so that it can service its old debt. Since late spring 2000, we have begun to see a variety of data showing that the economy may have slowed down: retail sales have been down, housing starts are down, employment fell sharply in late spring, although it has rebounded, and even imports were down. Looking to our own history, we see that when the private sector retrenches and reduces its deficit or increases its surplus, economic growth slows. In the current US situation, with a trade imbalance, this is practically true by definition.

We can also look at OECD data to find similar situations. Just as the United States sharply reduced its government deficit in the second half of the 1990s, the other OECD countries have followed suit (Figure 9.10). The United States and Canada have large budget surpluses, and the United Kingdom is hovering around a balanced budget. The other countries have reduced their deficits from 4–8 percent of GDP to a little over 2 percent of GDP – with Japan as the lone exception, but it is obviously in a different situation with its chronic recession. The figure shows a strong cyclical movement, with government deficits expanding during recession and continuing early in the recovery, then narrowing as the expansion peaks and deteriorates into recession. If we look at the private sector balance, using a methodology similar to the one we used earlier to calculate the US private sector balance, we obtain Figure 9.11. Again, we note a strong cyclical movement, with large private surpluses in recession and a movement to smaller surpluses as the expansion proceeds and households and firms become more confident.

Note that the United States, United Kingdom and Canada stand out as having significant private sector deficits at the end of the 1990s. Looking

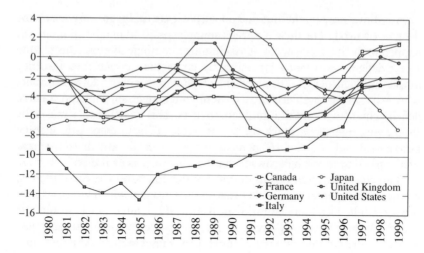

*Source:*   IMF, *International Financial Statistics.*

*Figure 9.10     Budget deficit (negative) as a percentage of GDP, 1980–99*

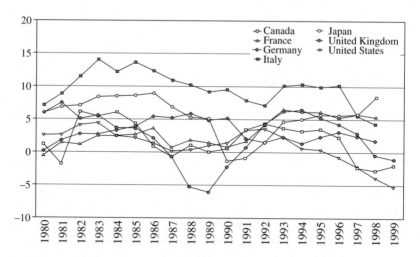

*Note:*   GDP data were converted into US dollars from the national currencies in order to calculate ratios. Conversion was done using the IMF's average annual exchange rate.

*Source:*   IMF, *International Financial Statistics.*

*Figure 9.11     Private sector balance as a percentage of GDP, 1980–99*

back in time, only the United Kingdom had ever achieved a private sector deficit of 5 percent of GDP – at the end of the 1980s. That deficit lasted for a little over three years. As it turned around very sharply, the United Kingdom went into a deep recession that generated a private sector surplus of nearly 7 percent of GDP, unemployment above 10 percent and two years of negative real growth. The government budget reverted from a surplus of nearly 2 percent of GDP to a deficit of 8 percent of GDP in 1993 as the slowdown reduced revenues and increased social spending. Before 1995, one can find a couple of other cases of private sector deficits (Canada in 1981 and again in 1987; Japan in 1990), but they did not exceed much more than 2 percent of GDP and none lasted much more than a year. Thus, the closest experience one can find is that of the United Kingdom at the end of the 1980s. One can imagine the distress it would create in the US Congress if we were to follow a path similar to that of the United Kingdom after 1989 over the next four or five years – with our budget deficit exploding to 8 percent of GDP and unemployment reaching double digits.

In Figure 9.12 we have taken simple averages of the G7 for the private sector balance and for nominal GDP growth. Again we see that these tend to move in opposite directions over the course of a cycle. The position

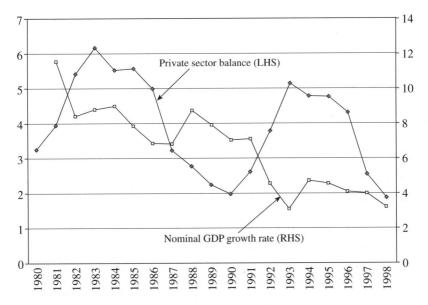

*Source:* IMF, *International Financial Statistics.*

*Figure 9.12   G7 average: Private sector balance as a percentage of GDP and annual growth of nominal GDP, 1980–98*

today looks very much as it did in 1989, with the economies poised for a sharp turn-around of the private sector balance (that is, to move toward rising surpluses) and for a downturn of GDP growth, which is already quite low on average. In large part, the low growth rates as well as the deterioration in private sector balances are due to fiscal retrenchment throughout the G7 (again Japan is the exception, with government deficits that exploded as the recession dragged on). This is in part due to what used to be called 'fiscal drag' – the tendency for budgets to tighten automatically in a cyclical expansion. However, much of the tightening has been discretionary as political moods moved toward 'fiscal responsibility' and as European nations strove to meet Maastricht criteria. Thus, the private sector balance averaged across the G7 is as low as it has been since 1980, while average nominal GDP growth is also equal to its post-1980 low. In other words, in the G7 taken as a whole, substantial fiscal tightening has forced the private sector to take most of the responsibility for sustaining growth by reducing its own surpluses. If and when the private sector retrenches, GDP growth is likely to collapse below its already low levels.[9]

In summary, we think these data are generally consistent with our view that demand is what constrains growth. Given fiscal austerity throughout the G7, economic growth from the mid-1990s has relied on domestic private sector demand as well as foreign demand. Obviously, not everyone can run a trade surplus, so if we include a large enough group of countries, the only possible source of growth is the domestic sector. However, if the public sector is going to run surpluses – as in the United States, United Kingdom and Canada, then growth requires private sector deficits. This is an inherently unsustainable and unstable proposition.

## CONCLUSIONS

What lessons can be learned? We suggest that our analysis leads to the following conclusions.

- Recent US growth has not been extraordinary, even over most of the Clinton expansion. Growth of GDP per capita has been slow through 1996 relative to that of the other major developed economies, although growth did pick up after 1995. While real GDP growth (ignoring population growth) has been somewhat above long-term trends in the past five years, it is not inordinately above the growth rates achieved over four decades during the 'second industrial revolution' at the end of the 19th century – a period frequently compared with our new economy.

- However, we see no reason to attribute new economy growth to any unusual combination of technological innovation or other favorable supply-side characteristics (especially those associated with 'freer markets'). As Gordon has demonstrated, if there are any new economy effects, they are constrained mainly to the computer industry itself.
- The United States has 'chosen' a high employment growth path. It may be true that this is in large part due to 'freer' labor markets, but this has not generated more rapid economic growth.
- Other countries typically have 'chosen' slower employment growth, but still achieved more rapid growth of output per head over the past three decades because productivity growth has long been higher than that achieved in the United States. Again, the past five years represent a deviation from that situation, but this deviation can be explained rather easily by taking note of the US household-led spending boom.
- Apparently, output growth has not been significantly constrained by either the quality or the quantity of inputs. Countries with severe labor constraints (as well as other resource constraints) achieve growth by raising productivity.
- There is no reason to suppose that the United States has come up against supply constraints even during the Clinton expansion. Even if it is true that labor markets are tight, growth of productivity is an alternative to employment growth as a means of expanding output per head.
- As growth appears to be primarily demand-constrained, it is not likely to be increased by policies that would stimulate supply, such as policies to increase national savings (through savings incentives or by reducing government deficits), to increase educational achievement of the labor force, to loosen regulations or to stimulate private initiative. Such policies might affect the contribution to growth made by a rising employment ratio, but these would not increase per capita GDP growth. In other words, policies that would enhance 'human capital' might increase employment but they would perversely lower productivity unless they were supplemented by policies that would stimulate aggregate demand.

We do not want to be accused of simple-minded 'demand-side' economics, however. When we claim that demand has been the major constraint on growth, this is not because we completely dismiss the supply side. Yes, entrepreneurial initiative is important in stimulating and introducing innovations. Yes, a highly educated, trained and motivated workforce can be more productive. Yes, maintaining international competitiveness matters. Yes, adequate and cheap access to natural resources can at times be important – and, conversely, supply shocks (such as a quadrupling of energy prices) can negatively impact growth over even relatively long periods, depending on the strategies adopted to ameliorate effects. And yes, misguided and incompetent policy can impede growth due to supply-side impacts. We do not believe, however, that there is much evidence (outside the well-documented energy price shocks) that these are normally operative in the G7 – either in the short run or in the long run. Thus, we reject the conventional view, which is that demand might matter for the short run, but only supply matters for the long run. Indeed, we would nearly stand this on its head, arguing that supply matters mainly in the short run, over periods that are (by definition) too short for markets and policy to adapt.

Even if one remains unconvinced that post-1970 growth has been largely constrained by demand rather than by supply, the substantial excess capacity and deflationary forces around the world should convince all reasonable observers that the problem today is one of insufficient aggregate – world – demand. In particular, there is no danger that the United States is running up against supply constraints – with countries around the world looking to US markets as the outlet for their excess production. High domestic demand and rapid GDP growth has allowed the United States to reverse its dismal long-term performance in the productivity sphere, to achieve rates of productivity growth similar to those enjoyed by a number of our competitors over the past 30 years. Given our high labor-force growth rates (which are partially due to policies that favor high employment – including both positive policies that make it easier and cheaper to hire US labor, as well as negative policies that make it more difficult for Americans to find alternative sources of income), the United States has to have higher growth of demand in order to achieve European-like productivity growth. Historically, the United States has been able to accomplish just that, partly due to the scale of its markets, partly due to frontier needs, and partly due to higher wages that kept demand high. This allowed US productivity growth rates to match those in Europe, and per capita GDP growth to keep pace even though our population increased more quickly. However, to re-emphasize, the United States can do this only if our aggregate demand growth is higher.

Mark Twain reportedly said that history may not repeat itself but it certainly rhymes. If this is true, Japan's post-1990 experience should serve as a cautionary example. Japan's economic miracle was not ended by the supply constraints that are supposed to limit growth – it has (and had) the highest saving rate in the developed world, its government had achieved a balanced budget by the end of the 1980s (long before this became the norm in G7 nations), its consumers were finally starting to spend, and its many years of exceedingly high investment created ample productive capacity. However, as soon as domestic and foreign demand for its output fell, economic growth collapsed – as did productivity growth. This result is particularly interesting because the United States (and the United Kingdom and Canada) has finally achieved the balanced government budget that many economists have claimed is necessary to remove supply constraints that supposedly limit growth. These surpluses are likely to be fleeting if Japan's experience is anything to go by.

In Figure 9.13, we have superimposed Japan's budget balance from the 1980s over those of the United States and Canada in the 1990s, implicitly assuming that Japan's experience in the 1990s is a fairly good predictor of what might happen in North America during the next ten years.[10] Figure 9.14 performs the same kind of operation but this time looks at output growth rather than the budget balance. Together, these pictures suggest that we may expect, at most, another year or two of surpluses before a recession

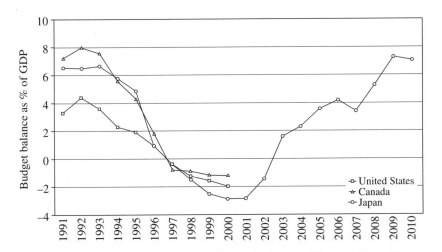

*Note:* Budget surpluses are given a negative sign to reflect their presumed (in Kalecki) negative effect on demand and corporate profits. We have crudely superimposed Japan's experience from 1981 through to 2000 over data from the United States and Canada from 1991 to 2000, implicitly assuming Japan's experience during the 1980s presages events in the United States and Canada.

*Source:* IMF, *International Financial Statistics*; data for 2000 are IMF projections.

*Figure 9.13   Japan's 1981–2000 budget balance as a percentage of GDP superimposed on budget balances in Canada and the United States for 1991–2000*

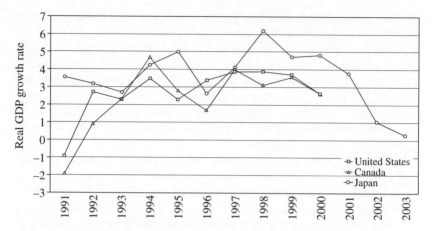

*Note:*  We have crudely superimposed Japan's experience from 1981 through to 1993 over data from the United States and Canada from 1991 to 2000, implicitly assuming Japan's experience during the 1980s presages events in the United States and Canada.

*Source:*  IMF, *International Financial Statistics*; data for 2000 are IMF projections.

*Figure 9.14    Japan's 1981–1993 GDP growth rate superimposed on 1991–2000 economic growth in Canada and the United States*

sets in and social safety net expenditures and last-minute 'pump priming' drive the government into deficit. Unlike Japan, however, saving by the household sector is actually negative in the United States, perhaps due in part to the phenomenal run in the stock market. (Of course, the United States also differs from Japan in that we run trade deficits – which of course means that we can grow in the presence of government surpluses only if the private sector spends in excess of its income.) When the bubble bursts, consumers may reduce purchases. The United States will then face a situation in which firms, households and the government are all retrenching by cutting spending even as the United States runs record trade deficits.[11] Perhaps, at that point, economists will recognize the demand deficiency that we believe has been the real constraint on growth since 1970.

## NOTES

1.  The Goldilocks economy is 'just right' in the sense that it is neither too hot to spur inflation, by which most pundits mean wage inflation, nor too cold to engender high unemployment.
2.  Note that Japan enjoyed favorable treatment in the post-war period, with greater access

to US markets; this may explain at least in part its higher growth rates in the post-war period.

3.  Okun (1983) had long ago recognized that periods of movement toward full employment yield considerably above-average growth rates. This is a point accepted by Greenspan, who distinguishes between short-run cyclical increases and long-run structural increases of productivity. However, he argues that most of the increase since 1995 'appears' to be due to structural effects (Greenspan 2000).

4.  Interestingly, however, the Clinton-era expansion is quite unusual because the productivity growth spurt did not come until after 1995 – three years after it began.

5.  Remarkably, Greenspan cited a study by Oliner and Sichel that also emphasizes that much of the boost to productivity growth has come within the IT sector itself, as 'the companies that produce computers and the embedded semiconductors appear to have achieved major efficiencies in their own operations, which have boosted MFP growth for the economy as a whole' (Greenspan 2000).

6.  Of course, the labor force can increase without necessarily leading to more employment – because the labor force includes the officially unemployed. As we will see below, this distinction is important for the case of Canada. Its labor force as well as its labor force participation rate has been growing as much as in the United States, but higher unemployment since 1985 has actually caused its employment rate to fall off.

7.  As indicated in Figure 9.7, Western Europe includes Austria, England, France, Finland, Germany, Italy, Luxemburg, Netherlands, Norway, Portugal, Spain and Switzerland.

8.  In a previous paper, we showed that the vast majority of jobs created during the Clinton expansion – 10.9 million out of a total of 11.4 million – have gone to those with at least some college education.

9.  We realize of course that inflation has come down considerably across the G7, accounting for some of the slowdown of nominal GDP growth. Still, the average growth rate of under 4 percent is comparatively low.

10. Our projections were obtained by transposing Japan's budget balance for 1981 forward over US and Canadian data for 1991–2000. Note also that this figure reverses the signs on surpluses and deficits to conform with the logic of Kalecki's model, where surpluses are given negative signs because they represent a drain on aggregate profits while deficits are given a positive sign because they add to corporate profits.

11. Granted, the trade deficit is likely to come down in the event of a recession, but it will not happen quickly enough to forestall a downturn.

# REFERENCES

Barro, Robert J. (1998), 'Notes on growth accounting', *National Bureau of Economic Research Working Paper No. 6654.*

Baumol, William J., Sue Anne Batey Blackman and Edward N. Wolff (1989), *Productivity and American Leadership: The Long View*: Cambridge, MA: MIT Press.

Blinder, Alan (1997), 'The speed limit: fact and fan in the growth of debate', *The American Prospect*, 8(3) pp. 57–62.

Blinder, Alan (2000), 'The internet and the new economy', Policy Brief No. 60, Brookings, www.brookings.edu/comm/PolicyBriefs/pb060/pb60.htm, June.

Buchele, Robert and Jens Christiansen (1999), 'Employment and productivity growth in Europe and North America: the impact of labor market institutions', *International Review of Applied Economics*, 13(3): 313–32.

Buckley, Neil (2000), 'Eurozone lags US, says ECB chief', *Financial Times*, 6 July: 1, 14.

David, Paul A. (1990), 'The dynamo and the computer: an historical perspective on the modern productivity paradox', *American Economic Review (Papers and Proceedings)*, 80(2), 355–61.

Dertouzos, Michael L., Richard K. Lester and Robert Solow (1989), *Made in America : Regaining the Productive Edge*, Cambridge, MA: MIT Press.

Gordon, Robert J. (2000), 'Does the "new economy" measure up to the great inventions of the Past?', *Journal of Economic Perspectives*, 14(4), 49–74.

Greenspan, Alan (2000), 'Business data analysis', Speech before the New York Association for Business Economics, New York, 13 June, http://www.bog.frb.fed.us/boarddocs/speeches/2000/default.htm.

Maddison, Angus (1991), *Dynamic Forces in Capitalist Development: A Long Run Comparative View*, New York: Oxford University Press.

Madrick, Jeffrey (1997), *The End of Affluence: The Causes and Consequences of America's Economic Dilemma*, New York: Random House.

Madrick, Jeffrey (1999), 'How new is the new economy?', *New York Review of Books*, September, www.nybooks.com/nyrev/wwwwfeatdisplay.cgi?19990923042f.

Nelson, Richard R. and Gavin Wright (1992), 'The rise and fall of American technological leadership: the postwar era in historical perspective', *Journal of Economic Literature*, 30(4): 1931–64.

Okun, Arthur (1983), 'Potential GNP: its measurement and significance', in Joseph E. Pechman (ed.), *Economics for Policymaking: Selected Essays of Arthur M. Okun*, Cambridge, MA: MIT Press.

Pigeon, Marc-André and L. Randall Wray (1999), 'Did the Clinton Rising Tide Raise All Boats? Job Opportunities for the Less Skilled', *Challenge*, 42(3) 14–33.

Thurow, Lester (1993), 'Productivity', in William F. Christopher and Carl G. Thor (eds) *Handbook for Productivity Measurement and Improvement*, Portland: Productivity Press.

Veneroso, Frank (2000), unpublished manuscript.

# 10. Full employment policies must consider effective demand and structural and technological change: a prime point of Pasinetti's political economy

**Mathew Forstater**

After Keynes and Sraffa, heterodox political economy has taken several different lines of development. Some, especially American post Keynesians such as Davidson, Minsky and their followers, have elaborated Keynes's emphasis on the role of money and finance and the uncertainty of investor expectations, and its implications for aggregate effective demand and the determination of aggregate employment. The relative inattention of the American post Keynesians to issues of structural and technological change and the implications of the theory of value and distribution for the theory of output and employment in the economy as a whole reflects *The General Theory*, where Keynes ignored technology and perhaps himself never 'fully escaped' the marginalist approach to value and distribution.

Other heterodox economists have focused on one or the other of Sraffa's 'negative' and 'positive' contributions. The former regards the critique of the neoclassical (or marginalist) theory of value and distribution, the latter the revival of classical and Marxian approaches to the same topic. Both of these projects have been the focus of neo-Ricardian (or Sraffian) political economists. For the most part, Sraffians have paid relatively little attention to money and uncertainty on the one hand, and technical change on the other, while considerable attention has been paid to effective demand, in particular the attempt to reconcile the principle with Sraffian price theory and extend its application to the long run. A third line of development, in addition to the American post Keynesians and the Sraffians, has been that heterodox political economy that has concerned itself primarily with structural and technological change. Some of this work in fact preceded *The General Theory*, for example the work of the Kiel School, of which Leontief was a participant, as well as that of Schumpeter. Just as the post

Keynesians have paid little attention to technology and the Sraffians have paid little attention to uncertainty, effective demand and money are pushed to the background in much of the work on structural change.

Of course, these are broad-brush claims, and there are exceptions in each case. But even with the exceptions considered, the conclusion is still largely valid: little work has been done that considers at once money, effective demand, and structural and technological change, while thoroughly rejecting the neoclassical theory of value and distribution and replacing it with a logically consistent, revived classical/Marxian approach. If we then add to this Schumpeterian-inspired evolutionary concerns, alternative conceptions of rationality and emphasis on learning, consideration of uneven development and the open economy, and a commitment to social justice in the sphere of economic policy, we will have put forward a tall, tall order indeed.

One name would rise to the fore were such an order placed, however: that of Luigi Pasinetti. For over four decades, Luigi Pasinetti has made seminal contributions to virtually every important debate and discussion concerning economic theory and policy, resulting in a framework that does in fact consider value and distribution, money and effective demand, and structural and technological change in a dynamic, evolutionary context. In this way, Pasinetti has elaborated and synthesized the work and spirit of his teachers and mentors: Kahn, Kaldor, Robinson, Sraffa, Goodwin and Leontief. In doing so, Pasinetti has done more than accomplish a great intellectual achievement. While this he has certainly accomplished, Pasinetti first and foremost has developed a framework for understanding the economic society in which we actually live, one that is characterized by ongoing structural and technical change, deficiencies in aggregate effective demand and persistent unemployment. Such understanding is necessary if policies are to be devised that can eliminate unemployment, reduce poverty and generate the economic security necessary for a more prosperous society.

Considerable attention has been paid lately to Pasinetti's contributions. *Festschriften* and symposia, entries in dictionaries and encyclopedias, and articles by students and colleagues analyzing and developing his contributions may be added to the professor's own writings to form a body of work summarizing Pasinetti's theories and analyses, and it is not the purpose of the present paper to duplicate those efforts. This chapter instead focuses on the importance of the goal of full employment in Pasinetti's political economy, and the prime point of his approach to eliminating unemployment: full employment policies must consider both effective demand and structural and technological change. After defining full employment and considering full employment as a societal goal, the chapter turns to the methodology of full employment analysis. The two broad categories of unemployment at the heart of Pasinetti's analysis are identified, and a full employment policy that can address both the effective demand concern and the structural change concern is proposed.

## DEFINING FULL EMPLOYMENT

The term 'full employment' has come to mean different things to different people, and it should therefore not be taken for granted that it is clear what the term means. The first issue concerns the resources referred to by the term. Does the term refer to full employment of all resources, or only the full employment of labor? While there is obviously *some* relation between the employment of labor and the employment of other resources, full employment will be used here to refer only to labor. Full employment of plant and equipment as well as labor will be referred to as 'full capacity utilization' or 'full employment of resources'. As we will see, it is important to maintain a distinction between the two. First, while Pasinetti often includes both full employment of labor and full capacity utilization as part of his analytical framework and set of policy goals, the two are determined by different (though related) processes. Second, while it will be suggested that full employment of labor may be brought about through economic policy, it is less clear that full (as opposed to high levels of) capacity utilization is an attainable goal (in a capitalist system). Third, we will also see that for a number of reasons, it is not clear that full (again, as distinct from high levels of) capacity utilization is desirable, even if it were possible. It may be that some degree of reserve capacity (which can translate into excess capacity at the industry and economy-wide levels) may perform an important function in a capitalist economy that might be retained even while eliminating unemployment of labor.

The second definitional issue regards the level of employment referred to by the term 'full employment'. Contrary to the intuitive, common-sense meaning of the term, most economists and policy-makers do not equate 'full employment' with 'zero unemployment'. Looked at through the lens of concepts such as the 'natural rate of unemployment' and the 'non-accelerating inflation rate of unemployment' (NAIRU), 'full employment' has come to indicate that level of employment that is associated with price stability, *even if that means millions of individuals ready and willing to work are unemployed*. Such a usage obviously places fighting inflation above combating unemployment in the list of macroeconomic priorities. However, even in many cases where full employment is considered a higher priority than fighting inflation, a trade-off between unemployment and inflation is taken as given. Such an assumption is not made here.

Full employment, for Pasinetti, refers to zero involuntary unemployment. He therefore rejects any notion of a 'natural' rate that includes unemployment:

> If we were to talk at all of a 'natural' level of employment, this could not but be the level of full employment. In the present context, a natural rate of unemployment would make no sense; or, if we like, it couldn't but be equal to zero (Pasinetti 1993: 24).

Thus full employment means that no one who is ready and willing to work for an appropriate wage is without a job. This also means zero involuntary part-time employment. Involuntary part time workers, counted in conventional measures of employment statistics as fully employed, are those who want to be working full-time but can only find part-time employment. There might be included in this definition some very small amount of frictional unemployment, but only *voluntary* frictional unemployment (some individuals may choose to forego employment in order to devote all their time to the job search). Thus we are concerned with true full employment of labor, where every person ready and willing to work full-time has full-time employment, and those ready and willing to work part-time have as many hours of part-time employment as they desire.

## WHY FULL EMPLOYMENT?

Throughout his writings, Pasinetti speaks of 'a permanent, and challenging, task of pursuing the macro-economic goal of adequate global effective demand and full employment' (1993: 59). 'The aim', Pasinetti writes, 'is clear: achieving the full utilization of available labour, i.e. full employment' (1993: 128).

> [A] magnitude of national relevance [is] the physical quantity of labour that is available in the whole economic system. And it is clearly a matter of general concern that it should entirely be employed – i.e., that there should be full employment (Pasinetti 1993: 23).

Pasinetti often points to this emphasis on the goal of full employment as one of the most important contributions of Keynes, a point to which we will have occasion to return:

> But full employment is too important for an economic system as a whole. Keynes was therefore right in advocating, at the institutional level, the inclusion of full employment into the objectives of overall economic policy, in the sense that the

community as a whole takes charge of it as a goal to be pursued with whatever measures of economic policy may be appropriate, whenever the spontaneous forces of interaction between employers and workers fail to bring it about. (Pasinetti 1993: 132).

While it will be our position that Pasinetti does not, contrary to the claims of some authors (see, for example, Shapiro, 1984–85) *assume* full employment, what might be said is that he does assume full employment as a *goal*. This is because, with some exceptions, Pasinetti has not dedicated much space to justifying his placing of full employment as a – perhaps *the* – goal. One of the exceptions was in a 1984–85 issue of the *Journal of Post Keynesian Economics*, the title of which, 'The difficulty, and yet the necessity, of aiming at full employment', serves as a good summary of Pasinetti's position. In that article, Pasinetti states that:

It is the desirability of the full employment path, and the misery and social injustice of unemployment, that makes it a necessity for industrial societies to put the full employment path among the basic aims of economic policy (Pasinetti 1984–85: 248).

There was a time when it could be assumed that full employment was an agreed-upon goal of national governments, central banks and supranational organizations, and Pasinetti often used this as an additional partial justification for his own taking of full employment as a goal of economic policy. In 1974, he could write that

full employment is the situation that matters, and that, indeed, now-a-days forms one of the agreed goals of any economic system (Pasinetti 1974: 119–20).

Halevi (1998: 185–6) has pointed out that 'twenty years later, there is enough evidence to doubt the contemporary validity' of the latter part of that statement, but the fact that the goal of full employment has been abandoned by central banks, national governments and international organizations has not stopped Pasinetti from maintaining it as a most important target, and the arguments for full employment remain as strong, or even stronger, than ever. It might be well to briefly review these arguments.

The first argument for full employment is that the economic and social costs of unemployment – direct and indirect – are staggering. Unemployment causes permanent losses in potential output of goods and services; economic, social, psychological and other problems resulting in crime, ill health (physical and mental), divorce, suicide and so on; deterioration of labor skills and productivity; and more. The argument that full employment is key to social stability may also be included here. Quite

simply, a compelling argument can be made that the benefits of full employment outweigh the costs of its achievement, and that unemployment, rather
than inflation, ought to be viewed as 'Public Enemy Number One'.

The second argument for full employment is based on the idea that, just as
there are human, political and civil rights that may be considered 'inalienable', so too are there economic and social 'rights', of which the right to
employment is one of the most important. This view was expressed by
Franklin Delano Roosevelt in his 1944 State of the Union Address, and may
also be found in a number of UN documents, including the 'Universal
Declaration of Human Rights'. Similar proclamations can be found in many
other countries as well. If individuals are ready, willing and able to work and
have no employment opportunities, it is government's responsibility to guarantee employment. Therefore, even if it were argued or could be shown that
the costs of eliminating unemployment were greater than the monetary benefits, government would still be responsible for guaranteeing full employment.

The third argument is that the promotion and maintenance of full
employment is required in many countries by law. In the United States, this
is through legislation such as the Employment Act of 1946 and the Full
Employment and Balanced Growth Act of 1978 (Humphrey-Hawkins
bill). The former corresponds roughly to the 1944 British White Paper on
Employment Policy. Similar legislation exists in many other industrialized
nations as well. Thus, even if it were argued that the costs are prohibitive
and that employment is not an inalienable right, it may be argued that
under current law many governments are obligated to guarantee full
employment.

The fourth argument is that full employment is an ethical imperative in
a capitalist economy. In a society in which unemployment is systemic,
public inaction constitutes social assignment of workers and their families
to poverty and/or various forms of assistance. Therefore, even if the costs
are prohibitive, employment is not considered an inalienable right, and
current legislation is not interpreted as legally requiring government to take
action to promote and maintain full employment, it would nevertheless be
wrong for government not to promote full employment.

Doubtless there are many other arguments, and these categories overlap
and should be treated as provisional. Clearly, however, the arguments for
full employment – both individually, and taken together – are compelling.
The crucial point is that unemployment is endemic to capitalism. Of
course, even if unemployment were not inherent in capitalism, the arguments for government policies to promote full employment would still be
strong, but the existence of involuntary unemployment provides a strong
justification for the priority of full employment initiatives.

Full employment is the foremost goal in Pasinetti's political economy.

But this goal is not merely a policy *conclusion* of Pasinetti's analytical work, it plays a role in that analytical work itself. This is part of what might be called Pasinetti's 'full employment methodology', to which we shall now turn.

## THE METHOD OF FULL EMPLOYMENT ANALYSIS

There is a methodological issue that should be addressed, and that concerns the place of 'full employment' in economic models or economic theory. Here we must distinguish between: (1) full employment as assumption; (2) full employment as logical or theoretical tendency; and (3) full employment as postulated goal. Models that *assume* full employment are certainly of little value in analyzing unemployment, if they are of any value at all. To assume full employment is, as Keynes remarked, 'to assume our difficulties away' (1936: 34).

Traditional neoclassical theory puts forward a theory of how, under certain conditions, a market economy will tend toward full employment of resources. The price mechanism – perfectly flexible wages, prices and interest rates – constitutes the self-adjusting mechanism that endows the system with an inherent tendency toward full employment of all resources. This is not, strictly speaking, *assuming* the state of full employment, though the conditions under which the self-adjusting mechanism smoothly operates are being assumed. The assumption that all markets are perfectly competitive includes even more than perfectly flexible prices. A trailer load of assumptions are hauled in behind the cab of 'perfect competition': assumptions regarding the knowledge and response time of economic agents, factor mobility, factor substitutability and divisibility, factor homogeneity, the number and size of firms and so on. Nevertheless, there *is* a *theory* – however unrealistic – of how full employment is supposed to be established.

Faced with persistent unemployment, then, there are two possible responses: (1) the theory is wrong; or (2) there are market imperfections and rigidities that prevent the smooth workings of the self-adjusting mechanism. Which view is taken has serious implications for economic and public policy. If the theory is wrong, we can work on formulating alternative theories of employment determination. Such was the approach of Keynes (and the post Keynesians), who demonstrated that even with flexible wages the economy has a tendency toward a state of persistent unemployment due to insufficient aggregate demand. State intervention is thus necessary to promote full employment and economic growth.

Such is also the conclusion of Pasinetti. According to Pasinetti (1993: 131–2), the traditional economic analysis . . . depicting a market for labour, with an overall demand function and an overall supply function for labour, where a flexible wage rate is supposed to act as a price that clears the market and thus always ensures full employment, or rather ensures the absence of involuntary unemployment, does not seem to make sense. To put it in other words, the market-price mechanism, if applied to the labour market, cannot ensure the clearing of such market. It cannot ensure full employment, simply because a labour market does not satisfy the basic conditions of a traditionally intended market, in which there is a market determined price that settles at a point where a downward sloping demand curve crosses an upward sloping supply curve, thus equating demand and supply. A market determined wage simply cannot do that.

The conclusion is clear: neoclassical theory is flawed, and the conclusions it reaches are therefore not justified. In addition, it is not just the neoclassical theory that is flawed; its policy conclusions are not justified elsewhere. Within Pasinetti's own, alternative, framework, as we shall see, unfettered markets do not result in an inherent tendency to full employment. Thus, again invoking the name of Keynes, Pasinetti provides the following response to the question, 'Can the free market institutional system do the job?'

> This is the question Keynes explicitly posited to us. And he gave us his answer . . . [in his scheme the system is] not necessarily one of full employment . . . [and his] scheme also suggests what ought to be done to improve the market results, if not actually achieve full employment. It was a very simple scheme, valid within restrictive conditions (that were, however, relevant for the capitalist economies of the 1930s). It is astonishing how slow we have been – and still are – to learn the lesson that Keynes's simple scheme teaches us (Pasinetti 1997a: 103).

We should note, however, that Pasinetti's rejection of neoclassical theory and its policy conclusions, and his conclusion that free markets do not guarantee full employment, or even a tendency to full employment, do not mean that he sees no role for markets or the price mechanism at all. Rather, since 'the market-price mechanism, when applied to the actual determination of the economic variables, cannot work equally well for all of them', the lesson is that 'it cannot be applied uncritically; it cannot be thought of as the only institutional mechanism to be used for a satisfactory determination of all economic variables' (Pasinetti 1993: 145). Thus, while 'we cannot expect the market-price mechanism to solve for us the macroeconomic problems of . . . ensuring full employment', it may be useful for other purposes. In particular, for Pasinetti, 'it leads the actual commodity prices toward the corresponding costs of production, and induces the producers to look for ever better technical methods' and 'it may be judiciously used to promote an efficient mobility of labour among the production sectors' (1993: 146). We shall have occasion to return to this last point. For now, what is important is that Pasinetti rejects the neoclassical theory and its conclusions, and also does not find support for those conclusions using his alternative analysis, yet he does see some role for markets and the price mechanism elsewhere.

Of course, as noted above, within neoclassical theory there is another explanation for unemployment, with important implications. If it is concluded that unemployment is due to 'imperfections' then the policy implications are that the state should try to eliminate these rigidities – often attributed to government intervention such as regulation or minimum wage laws, or the existence of unions – and promote the conditions for the smooth workings of the price mechanism. Promoters of the neoclassical synthesis ('Bastard Keynesians') were successful for some time in balancing acceptance of neoclassical micro theory with a 'pragmatic' approach to public policy ('fine-tuning' with 'Keynesian' fiscal and monetary policy), but their policy stance did not follow from their underlying theoretical model, and they eventually lost their position of influence within the discipline to supply-siders, monetarists, and adherents of rational expectations and 'new classical' approaches. Pasinetti, a sharp critic of the neoclassical synthesis, has also rejected this view (see, for example, Pasinetti 1974).

Already it appears that we have slipped in the assumption that full employment is an economic goal. Mainstream methodology is not comfortable with such proclamations at the level of *analysis*, however, for it blurs the distinction between 'positive' and 'normative' economics. The third method of full employment analysis listed above, however, takes full employment as a postulated goal as the *analytical* point of departure. In such an 'instrumental' approach (Lowe 1965), the purpose of economic theory is to 'work backward' from the stipulated end state (for example, full employment, price stability, economic growth, more equitable distribution of income) to discover the suitable paths – including policies – by which the goal(s) may be achieved (Forstater 1999a). Such an approach is at once strange and familiar. Strange, because it is so at odds with the traditional approach of beginning with data and then employing the deductive method to explain or predict outcomes, whatever they might be. Familiar, because it has an intuitive, common-sense appeal to it that in fact that is how economic policy is or should be conducted.

This approach is that of both Pasinetti and Lowe. While Lowe made the method the subject of several books and articles (for example, 1965, 1988), in Pasinetti, while its application is present throughout his work (1981, 1993 and *passim*), actual discussion of the method is more infrequent. In the aforementioned article from the *Journal of Post Keynesian Economics*, Pasinetti responded to Shapiro's claim that his model assumes full employment: 'But in fact I do not make any such assumption. I simply state the conditions that full employment *would* require' (1984–85: 247). As Lowe, quoting J.S. Mill in another context, pointed out, such a model, while 'insufficient for prediction' is 'most valuable for guidance' (1965: 243).

Pasinetti asked the question: 'if the full employment path is never to be reached, why then should we keep it as our reference point?' (1984–85: 248). The answer, he suggests, and as we are emphasizing here, regards methodological issues. His answer again invokes the name of John Maynard Keynes.

> It is the really crucial merit of Keynes to have set out to demonstrate that, at any given point of time, the market forces are inadequate to perform the same task [of ensuring an inherent tendency toward] . . . the position of full employment, and I hope to have shown the difficulties that the structural dynamics of technology and demand interpose to the same task through time. But it is equally a great merit of Keynes to have singled out the full employment position, and by implication the full employment path through time, as the natural point of reference for economic policy. The failure of market forces to reach efficient positions does not justify our failure to pursue them by other means (Pasinetti 1984–85: 248).[1]

Another way of posing the problem has been put forward by Halevi.

> Reference to the difference between potential and actual output in aggregate terms can be useful to identify the degree of unused capacity. However, it becomes worthless for the purpose of discussing the condition of accumulation . . . once the system has been brought to operate at full capacity by means of short-run 'Keynesian' policies (Halevi 1983: 347).

In other words, as we will see below, it is necessary to separate out the question of how full employment is *attained* from the question of how it might be *maintained* in the face of ongoing structural and technological change.

While structural and technological change has also to do with the attainment of full employment, even if we have eliminated unemployment, problems still remain. And those problems can never be addressed by reference to the actual state of capitalist economic systems, since they all exhibit unemployment and excess capacity. We therefore need to address the problem by investigating the operational tendencies of full employment systems. To do this, we do not assume the economy is *at* full employment, nor that it exhibits an inherent tendency toward full employment, nor that full employment is necessarily an actual goal of present governments. We investigate the conditions that must be met if full employment is to be attained and maintained, given the operational tendencies of capitalism at and below full employment and full capacity. Such a framework can then guide us in our attempts to formulate and implement effective practical policies.

Lowe referred to this methodological approach of discovering the necessary conditions that must be met to attain a given economic goal or goals as 'instrumentalism,' a term also referred to by Pasinetti. Like Lowe, Pasinetti insisted on the distinction between such a goal or goals and the tools and policies for their attainment. The tools and policies are

> means, and not ends in themselves. Once their instrumental role is properly understood and recognised, it becomes much easier also to operate on them in as detached a way as is possible; to treat them as instruments susceptible to being continually improved and changed, in relation to their suitability (or unsuitability) to ensure tendencies, or near-tendencies, towards agreed ends (Pasinetti 1981: 155).[2]

Students and colleagues of Pasinetti promoting and elaborating his approach have explicitly referred to Lowe's instrumental method as well. Scazzieri, for example, has argued that 'the task of dynamic theory is not to suggest a realistic interpretation of actual processes' (1996: 183). Instead, it

> shifts economic theory away from the theoretical reconstruction of actual processes and turns it into an experiment in instrumental inference, which is, using Adolph Lowe's words, an attempt 'to discover the particular set of causes that are suitable for the realization of some postulated effect' (Scazzieri 1996: 183–4; see also Baranzini and Scazzieri 1990).[3]

In addition to their common methodology, the works of Pasinetti and Lowe, while differing in some important ways, also share a common focus on *structural and technological change*. This focus is different, though complementary (and related), to the post Keynesian focus on aggregate balance, that is, the aggregate demand-constrained nature of capitalism. These two concerns – the effective demand concern and the structural dynamics concern – correspond to two different questions (or sets of questions) and two different theories of unemployment as the normal outcome of unfettered market activity. It is to these questions and theories to which we must now turn.

## ATTAINING AND MAINTAINING FULL EMPLOYMENT

The two analytically separable but related questions concerning unemployment may be posed as follows:

1.  If there is unemployment in the economy, is there a self-adjusting
    mechanism inherent in the market system that will tend to push the
    economy back to the full employment level of output? If not, why not,
    and what policies follow from the analysis? If so, what is the nature of
    that mechanism?
2.  Under what conditions can full employment and full capacity utiliza-
    tion be *maintained* in the face of ongoing structural and technological
    change, such as labor- or capital-displacing technical change, changes
    in the supplies of labor or natural resources, or changes in the compo-
    sition of final demand? Are these conditions likely to be met by the
    market system? If not, what types of policies might be implemented
    that can satisfy the conditions?

As we have seen, and as is well known, neoclassical theory answers 'yes'
to the first question, and the mechanism that assures the tendency to full
employment is the price mechanism, under the condition of perfectly flexible prices (including factor prices) and perfectly competitive markets.
Keynes and the post Keynesians answer 'no' to the same question, based
on an alternative theory of the savings–investment relationship that refutes
Say's Law, and the analysis of capitalism as a monetary production system.
Thus, for Keynes, *involuntary unemployment is normal*, with full employment to be expected 'only by accident or design' (1936: 28). 'Design' refers
first and foremost to demand management policies conducted by the state.

Pasinetti applauds Keynes's contributions. But Pasinetti also warns that
to stop with *The General Theory* would be unwise.

> We cannot expect from Keynesian theories and policies what they cannot give.
> We have gained from them the avoidance of large-scale unemployment and this
> has been a notable achievement. But the resumption of growth is another matter.
> The economic system still has to solve the much deeper problems . . . the struc-
> tural problems of learning the appropriate ways to expand (Pasinetti 1981: 238).

In particular, we need to address the issues that follow from the second
question, as well as the first.

As to the second set of questions concerning the maintenance of full
employment, in the neoclassical view, the same features that provide the
system with the tendency to full employment also endow the system with
an amazing degree of flexibility. Prices (including factor prices) are fully
flexible, and prices correctly convey information that economic agents with
full knowledge instantaneously respond to in pre-determined ways. Factors
of production are perfectly mobile, perfectly divisible, perfectly substitutable, homogeneous. The principle of substitution likewise dominates the
analysis of consumer behavior. There is no historical time, uncertainty or

money. Thus, not only is there an inherent tendency toward full employment and full capacity utilization, but the system in such a state instantaneously and easily adjusts to changes in technology, the supplies of labor and natural resources, and the composition of final demand. The production system, even at full employment of all resources, is fully flexible. As Basu (1995: 64) has remarked, 'in standard neoclassical models, flexibility is unimportant because it is total'. At the same time, the primary source of rigidity in the standard view is government intervention.

Analyses of structural dynamics that reject most or all of the neoclassical assumptions are based on a very different vision of the economic system that is more compatible with the post Keynesian view, and is reflected in their conclusions. Key to these analyses is that economic processes take place in historical time. There are no instantaneous adjustments.

> Instantaneous adjustments are not always possible, particularly in those cases in which it is necessary for each product to use 'specialized' productive resources (such as machinery of a specific type, or workers of a particular skill) (Pasinetti and Scazzieri 1987: 528)

Capital goods are highly specific and in no way necessarily shiftable between different lines of production. Means of production are not highly divisible or substitutable, if at all. There is a significant amount of uncertainty regarding the future, and the past is unchangeable.

Modern economies are inter-industry systems, with complex sectoral interdependencies such as are described in input–output analyses. Even analyses that are not as disaggregated as input–output models highlight the sectoral interdependence and inter-industry linkages and their implications (see, for example, the three sector models in Lowe 1976). There are thus time lags, distortions, bottlenecks and rigidities that reflect the physical and technical nature of the system.

There are two general approaches to the formal analysis of structural change, the 'vertically integrated' approach and the 'horizontally integrated' approach. The former is represented by Pasinetti (1981, 1993), the latter by Lowe (1976). Both of these approaches are non-neoclassical, despite the fact that they analyse systems operating at full employment and full capacity utilization. They do not assume full employment, or an inherent tendency to full employment. Rather, they take full employment as a stipulated goal and then analyze the conditions under which an economy operating at full employment and full capacity utilization might maintain that state in the face of ongoing structural and technological change.

Pasinetti's framework recognizes that the economy is a multi-sectoral industrial system with ongoing technical change, and ongoing changes in final demand. Growth is not proportional – it is highly disproportional and disruptive. This means that the second question – the conditions that have to be met for an economy to maintain full employment and full capacity utilization through time – have to be addressed.

The conditions that must be met for such a modern industrial economy to maintain full employment – even if it could be attained – are neatly reduced by Pasinetti into two conditions: an effective demand condition and a structural change or capital accumulation condition. These two concerns – the effective demand concern and the structural change concern – correspond to two types of unemployment: technological unemployment or Marxian unemployment, and Keynesian unemployment.

We will not reproduce these analyses here; there is a sizable literature on each of these approaches, as well as a number of excellent surveys comparing and contrasting the strengths and weaknesses of vertical and horizontal approaches (see, for example, the papers in Baranzini and Scazzieri 1990; Halevi 1994). In fact, the two approaches may be seen as highly *complementary*. For present purposes, what is important is that both approaches highlight how difficult it would be for a full employment/full capacity system to *maintain* itself, even if it could be *attained*.

For Pasinetti, this means that the macroeconomic condition for the attainment of full employment is 'continually being upset, and thus full employment is continually being disrupted' (1993: 128). Not only is there 'the effective demand condition for keeping full employment through time', there is also 'the capital accumulation conditions for keeping full employment over time' (1981: 86):

> [T]he fulfillment of [the effective demand condition] at any given point in time, no longer automatically entails that it will remain fulfilled through time . . . [E]ven if full employment of the labour force and full capacity utilisation are realised at a given point in time . . . the structural dynamics of the economic system cause that position to change and therefore make it impossible in general to automatically maintain full employment through time (Pasinetti 1981: 87).

The conclusion is clear: the structual dynamics of employment mean that, left to their own devices, capitalist economies will not run at full employment and full capacity. 'This means that it becomes the specific task of institutions – that is, of the way society organises itself' – to ensure full employment (Pasinetti 1997a: 102).

> A confirmation thereby emerges of the necessity of setting up some major coordinating institutions, at the level of the economic system as a whole – a necessity that emerges in the field of fiscal policy and in the field of monetary policy (Pasinetti 1993: 146).

Pasinetti does not propose completely doing away with markets, however. The task, as Keynes pointed out, is finding those spheres where markets are appropriate, and those where public institutions are required, and the way the two relate.

> In fact, one of the great challenges for economists in the near future appears precisely that of finding ways to reconcile and render complementary the automatic stimuli coming from the competitive market-price mechanism with the necessary requirements for overall policies concerning the economic system as a whole (Pasinetti 1993: 146).

A full employment policy must thus address both involuntary unemployment of the Keynesian variety, that is, unemployment due to the inherent demand-constrained tendency of capitalist economies, and 'technological unemployment', here used as something of a catch-all phrase for unemployment due to structural and technological change. Of course, these types of unemployment are related, as technological change can affect the level and not only the composition of aggregate demand. For example, labor-displacing technical change may result in income redistribution between sectors of the population with different saving propensities, which can set off – or exacerbate – an effective demand crisis. In addition, focus on technological and structural change highlights not only issues related to *unemployment*, but issues related to the operation of an economy *at full employment*, when aggregate balance is no longer an issue but sectoral balance very much is. These issues – sectoral proportionalities and imbalances – are key to the bottlenecks and rigidities that are associated with higher employment and capacity utilization rates. System flexibility is fundamentally an issue of economic and technological structure. Until a full employment plan can demonstrate the possibility of flexible and stable full employment, the central banks, national governments and supranational organizations of the world will continue to fulfill Kalecki's (1943) vision of politically enforced unemployment and excess capacity.

## REAL LIFE FLEXIBILITY: UNEMPLOYMENT AND EXCESS CAPACITY

Standard neoclassical theory puts forward an idealized economy where methods of production and factor supplies instantly respond to demand that changes when relative prices change. Structural analysis highlights the impediments to rapid adjustment, the structural disequilibria, the disproportionalities and the physical–technical consistency conditions for system viability (reproduction) that especially confront an economy brought to full employment by, for example, Keynesian demand management. In neoclassical theory there is a trade-off between flexibility and reality; in structural analysis there is a trade-off between flexibility and full employment of resources. The only way to have flexibility in reality seems to be with unemployment and excess capacity. Thus the primary 'real life' factor endowing the system with flexibility seems to confirm the 'central bank' view. Capitalist systems gain flexibility by sacrificing full employment. As Scazzieri, with reference to the Pasinetti model, has pointed out: 'Short run difficulties (unemployment, spare productive capacity, the stagnation of once important industries) have to be considered as the necessary conditions for long-run expansion' (Scazzieri 1983: 73).

Lowe referred to this as the paradox of capacity utilization: 'recurrent, long-lasting stretches of underutilization', while a 'periodic drag on output and income' and thus welfare generally, 'from the viewpoint of growth' have had the 'paradoxical effect' of providing the 'large, pool of idle resources that greatly facilitated the system's adjustment to changes in aggregate demand and technology', that is, 'frictions and bottlenecks that impede inter-sectoral shifts of resources' were avoided. 'Thus growth became a by-product of the cycle and hardly distinguishable from the latter's phase of recovery' (Lowe 1976: 8).

But demand management policies, where successful, by reducing 'the degree of underutilization of resources and the duration of their idleness', can amount to a 'reverse paradox' in which 'the greater the success of this policy of stabilization, the smaller the flexibility of the system, and the greater the difficulties of achieving a smooth expansion path' (Lowe 1976: 9).

Aggregate demand management, which refers to the attempt to push the private sector to full employment and full capacity, will create a system that is fraught with rigidities. Bottlenecks in key industries, such as the machine tools industries, can cause economy-wide disruptions and prevent smooth expansion. Viscous system structure can result in sluggish growth and inflation.

> After Keynes, we have understood that [economic depressions] are due to falls in effective demand and we have learnt how to provide remedies. Demand needs to be stimulated . . . We must note, however, that all these provisions are indeed helpful but only in order to overcome the negative part of the phenomenon: the slump. They will not, by themselves, put the economic system back on a growth path. In other words, Government policy in keeping up demand will help the economic system to avoid setbacks and to stay where it is, but it will not, as such, cause a resumption of economic growth (Pasinetti 1981: 237–8).

> Singling out a 'natural' evolving path upon which full employment may be kept is far more complex, structurally, in any multi-sector production economy

inserted in an international setting, than could be dreamed of from Keynes's simple scheme focusing on the utilization of full-employment productive capacity (Pasinetti 1997: 103).

It is not clear what policies would ensure full capacity utilization. Given the desire for flexibility at the plant or firm level, the system would likely still reproduce some excess capacity even without central bank enforcement policies. (The system would not tend to full capacity utilization just because central banks suddenly stopped promoting slack.) It is not even clear that, despite the potentially negative consequences, true full capacity utilization would even be desirable.

Full employment of labor, however, is both possible and desirable. The problem has been how to maintain the system flexibility and stability that unemployment helps to ensure, without the social and economic costs of unemployment. Lowe (1988), from the perspective of structural analysis, supported what he called 'planned domestic colonization', which is better known as government as the employer of last resort (Wray 1998) or the buffer stock employment model (Mitchell 1998), and we will simply call public service employment. Such a policy approach is consistent with Pasinetti's commitment to true full employment, his analytical concerns with both effective demand and structural and technological change, and his instrumental approach to economic policy.

## FLEXIBLE FULL EMPLOYMENT: THE PUBLIC SERVICE EMPLOYMENT APPROACH

The public service employment approach acknowledges the unlikelihood of attaining or maintaining full employment through indirect means such as stimulating private sector demand, while identifying a number of clear advantages to public employment programs.

> Unlike private investors, public investors are not hampered by uncertainties about future demand, because they themselves determine the purpose that investment and its final output is to serve, for instance the items that make up the infrastructure (Lowe 1988: 107).

In public works there is a degree of variability and flexibility not possible in the private sector, where competitive pressures legislate methods of production, the composition of output and the types of capital equipment and natural resources utilized, and where private decisions governed by narrow economic motives may not be consistent with what is best for society as a whole (Forstater 1999b).

Some of the major obstacles to full employment are rooted in the technological conditions of production. Employing workers available as a result of labor-displacing technical change or increases in the labor supply depends on the prior construction of real capital. But the public sector has the ability to vary the labor intensity of productive activity in ways that the private sector cannot. The public sector may choose a more labor-intensive method of production that would be 'inefficient' for a private firm, but which is quite reasonable from the perspective of social well-being. The public sector may also vary public employment between different tasks, for the purpose of altering overall capital–labor ratios or easing the utilization of certain types of capital equipment or increasing the utilization of yet other types. The spectrum of choices open include activities which approach the level of '*pure services* in the fields of health, education, and general welfare' as well as activities that do not use or make more limited use of precious natural resources and that do not pollute (Lowe 1988: 107).

The public service employment approach can address both the effective demand concern and the structural change concern. This is why it is not surprising that it has been supported by many whose own work is mainly focused on the effective demand concern. When there is unemployment, this is an indication that aggregate demand is too low. Government then hires anyone ready, willing and able to work. This generates income and eliminates unemployment. But unlike the aggregate demand approach, public employment can also address sectoral issues. As demand increases in a sector, the private sector hires out of the public employment pool. Public works can be designed with an eye to sectoral and technological developments. Again, public employees can use those types of capital equipment that are not in short supply; more labor-intensive methods may be used in the public sector to ease capital shortages, because the government can use different criteria – criteria based on larger social and macroeconomic concerns rather than cost minimization or private efficiency criteria (Forstater 1998b).

Pasinetti's observation that the wage mechanism, while incapable of equilibrating a so-called 'labor market', does have the ability to induce labor mobility between sectors, is pertinent here.

[A]ppropriate advantage may be taken of the incentive-generating characteristics of the market-price mechanism in dealing with the problem that always arises inducing labourers to move across sectors. In this case, some market determined wage differentials may perform the function of inducing and favouring the labour mobility required by the structural dynamics that is due to take place (as we have seen earlier) . . . In other words, useful wage negotiations, with due regard to labour requirements and labour availabilities, at the sectoral and even at the individual level, may be allowed to take place to suit intervened sectoral scarcities and redundancies . . . They serve the purpose of giving incentives to the mobility of labour out of declining sectors and into expanding sectors (Pasinetti 1993: 132–3).

The buffer stock aspect of the public service employment approach employs the wage mechanism in just such a way. As demand increases in certain sectors, employers will have to offer workers in the public employment sector a mark-up over the public sector wage–benefits package. As employment declines in other sectors, workers will move out of those sectors and into public employment.

## CONCLUSION: PUBLIC EMPLOYMENT AND THE PRIME POINT OF PASINETTI'S POLITICAL ECONOMY

For four decades, Luigi Pasinetti has demonstrated that full employment policies must consider both effective demand and structural and technological change. He has asked post Keynesians – and heterodox economists of all stripes – to please take all the components of Keynes's description of modern industrial systems as *monetary production* economies seriously. We must consider monetary and financial factors and aggregate proportionality and balance. But we must also consider technological and structural change – including changes in the composition of final demand – and sectoral proportionality and balance as well. As a result of Pasinetti's analysis:

[a] vast programme of research is thereby opening up. But there also emerges a wide programme for action. Not only is there an 'institutional problem' to be solved; there is also a challenge for 'institutional action' to be met (Pasinetti 1993: 147).

Government investment policy enters the scene: not to replace (or 'crowd out') private investments but to complement them because of their insufficiency, if the task to be pursued is that of achieving, and maintaining, full employment (Pasinetti 1997b: 218).

## NOTES

1. Lowe likewise interpreted Keynes in this regard: 'By postulating a state of full employment as the overriding *macro-goal*, Keynes has taken th[e] decisive step, thereby giving to his analytical findings quite a novel meaning. All the obstacles to the attainment of the postulated goal . . . can now be turned into so many reasons for active interference with

the autonomous course of events' (1965: 243). Lowe and Pasinetti also share another view with regard to Keynes's methodology: in certain respects, it has some important features in common with the method of classical political economy, as against neoclassical economics (see Lowe 1954 [1987]; Pasinetti 1974).

2. This distinction between means and ends also has a point of contact with Abba Lerner's 'functional finance'. I have elsewhere (Forstater 1998a) shown the similarities between the method of functional finance and Lowe's instrumentalism.

3. As mentioned in passing, one of Pasinetti's teachers who influenced him in important respects, Wassily Leontief, was for a time a member of the Kiel School. There Lowe served as the director of one of the first institutes for the study of business cycles and Leontief was working on his dissertation (from another university, however). Kiel also served as the other location – in addition to Cambridge – where the reproduction models in the Quesnay-Marx tradition were being revived. It is also worth noting that the Kiel School sought the explanation of cycles in technological and structural change, and believed that cycles were rooted in the same forces that determined secular economic development. Thus, while Pasinetti appears to have worked out his theories and methodology quite independently from Lowe, one can in no way say that the commonalities are purely 'accidental' either.

# REFERENCES

Baranzini, Mauro and Roberto Scazzieri (eds) (1990), *The Economic Theory of Structure and Change*, Cambridge: Cambridge University Press.

Basu, Kaushik, (1995), 'Flexibility in economic theory', in T. Killick (ed.), *The Flexible Economy*, London: Routledge.

Forstater, Mathew (1998a), 'Towards a New Instrumental Macroeconomics', *Working Paper No. 254*, Annandale on Hudson, NY: Jerome Levy Economics Institute.

Forstater, Mathew (1998b), 'Flexible full employment', *Journal of Economic Issues*, 32(2): 557–63.

Forstater, Mathew (1999a), 'Working backwards: instrumental analysis as a policy discovery procedure', *Review of Political Economy*, 11(1): 5–18.

Forstater, Mathew (1999b), 'Public Employment and Economic Flexibility', *Public Policy Brief No. 50*, Annandale on Hudson, NY: Jerome Levy Economics Institute.

Halevi, Joseph (1983), 'Employment and planning', *Social Research*, 50(2).

Halevi, Joseph (1994), 'Structure and growth', *Economie Appliquée*, 47(2).

Halevi, Joseph (1998), 'Structural analysis of development and underdevelopment', in H. Hagemann and H. Kurz (eds), *Political Economics in Retrospect*, Cheltenham, UK: Edward Elgar.

Kalecki, Michal (1943), 'Political aspects of full employment', *Political Quarterly*, 14.

Keynes, John Maynard (1936), *The General Theory of Employment, Interest, and Money*, New York: Harcourt Brace.

Lowe, Adolph (1954 [1987]), 'The classical theory of economic growth', reprinted in A. Oakley (ed.), *Essays in Political Economics: Public Control in a Democratic Society*, Brighton: Wheatsheaf.

Lowe, Adolph (1965), *On Economic Knowledge*, White Plains, NY: M.E. Sharpe.

Lowe, Adolph (1976), *The Path of Economic Growth*, Cambridge: Cambridge University Press.

Lowe, Adolph (1988), *Has Freedom a Future?* New York: Praeger.

Mitchell, William F. (1998), 'The buffer stock employment model', *Journal of Economic Issues*, 32(2): 547–55.

Pasinetti, Luigi L. (1974), *Growth and Income Distribution*, Cambridge: Cambridge University Press.

Pasinetti, Luigi L. (1981), *Structural Change and Economic Growth*, Cambridge: Cambridge University Press.

Pasinetti, Luigi L. (1984–85), 'The difficulty, and yet the necessity, of aiming at full employment', *Journal of Post Keynesian Economics*, 7: 246–8.

Pasinetti, Luigi L. (1993), *Structural Economic Dynamics*, Cambridge: Cambridge University Press.

Pasinetti, Luigi L. (1997a), 'The principle of effective demand', in G. Harcourt and P. Riach (eds), *A 'Second Edition' of the General Theory*, London: Routledge.

Pasinetti, Luigi L. (1997b), 'The marginal efficiency of investment', in G. Harcourt and P. Riach (eds), *A 'Second Edition' of the General Theory*, London: Routledge.

Pasinetti, Luigi L. and Roberto Scazzieri (1987), 'Structural economic dynamics', in J. Eatwell, M. Milgate and P. Newman (eds), *The New Palgrave Dictionary of Economics*, London: Macmillan.

Scazzieri, Roberto (1983), 'Economic dynamics and structural change: a comment on Pasinetti', *Rivisti Internazionale di Scienzi Economiche e Commerciale*, 30.

Scazzieri, Roberto (1996), 'The accumulation of capital and structural economic dynamics', in M. Marcuzzo, L.L. Pasinetti and A. Roncaglia (eds), *The Economics of Joan Robinson*, London: Routledge.

Shapiro, Nina (1984–85), 'Involuntary unemployment in the long run: Pasinetti's formulation of the Keynesian argument – a review article,' *Journal of Post Keynesian Economics*, 7: 235–45.

Wray, L. Randall (1998), *Understanding Modern Money: The Key to Full Employment and Price Stability*, Cheltenham, UK: Edward Elgar.

# 11.   Unemployment and profitability: the case of Spain

## Jesus Felipe*

'*The profits of today are the investments of tomorrow and the investments of tomorrow make the employment of the day after tomorrow*' (Helmut Schmidt, quoted in Malinvaud 1980: 4).

## INTRODUCTION

Unemployment is Spain's foremost economic and social problem. In 1998 there was a reserve army of over 3 million unemployed workers, equivalent to 18.81 percent of the active population. This is close to twice the European rate, and almost four times the US rate. Up to the late 1970s, Spain's unemployment rate was not significantly different from that in other European countries and the United States. But beginning in the early 1980s the rate began soaring at a pace much faster than in other countries, with the result that the average unemployment rate for 1988–92 was more than six times that of 1974–79 (Bean 1994: Table 1). By 1994 it had reached a record 24.16 percent (3.7 million workers). These figures place Spain well on top in the unemployment ranking among the OECD economies.

This chapter explores empirically why unemployment in Spain is so high and persistent. Drawing on arguments from the classical literature, a key variable is introduced in the analysis of unemployment, namely the profitability on invested capital. It seems paradoxical that while this variable is often quoted by businessmen, management specialists or laymen, it has traditionally been neglected by economists (Malinvaud 1982: 11).[1] In a market economy, firms struggle to (at least) maintain their profit rates and competitiveness. To do so they must invest in capital so as to increase labor productivity. The introduction of technical change in the context of capital accumulation raises the capital–output ratio and induces a tendency for the rate of profit to fall. Firms will react by (among other things) reducing employment. In their attempt to re-establish their profit rates, firms will try to increase labor productivity by further increasing the capital–labor ratio,

216

thus engaging in a spiral of ever-increasing capital intensity of the firm, laying off of workers and decreasing profit rates. This process gives rise to a long-run relationship between unemployment and profitability.

There are plenty of theories and explanations of unemployment, and specifically of European unemployment. Bean (1994) and Dent (1997: Table 10.6) are two recent surveys of the literature. Dent notices that 'there is a general lack of consensus between theorists over the issue with certain determining factors prioritised over, or contradicting those emphasised by others' (Dent 1997: 359). Nevertheless, from the mid-1980s some theorists have appealed to different forms of hysteresis in order to explain the persistent high rates of unemployment in Europe. Dolado et al. (1986) and Andrés et al. (1990) provide discussions of unemployment in Spain within the neoclassical framework.

In a series of recent papers, Blanchard (1998, 1999) and Blanchard and Wolfers (1999) argue that in order to understand the evolution of European unemployment, one needs to take into account jointly the shocks which have affected Europe over the last 30 years, and labor market institutions (for example, strong unions, high payroll taxes, minimum wages, generous unemployment insurance, high employment protection). They argue that, up to the mid-1980s, unemployment was mostly the result of the failure of wages to adjust to the slowdown in total factor productivity (TFP) growth. From the mid-1980s onward, on the other hand, the increase in unemployment has been the result of a decrease in labor hoarding, which has led to an increase in firms' profits. This, they argue, will lead over time to capital accumulation and higher employment. On the institutional side, they argue that theory gives an ambiguous assessment of the effects of labor market rigidities on unemployment. Probably, institutions have been such that shocks have had a large and prolonged effect on unemployment; but they are not its original cause. When Blanchard (1999) put his model to work pooling data for 21 OECD countries, it did, overall, a good job. However, the model predicted Spain's unemployment rate very poorly (there was large underprediction).

Real wages in Spain grew above productivity during 1970–76. (This marks the end of the previous political regime; see next section.) And institutions, as argued by Blanchard, cannot be considered the main cause of unemployment. Thus, the most likely explanation for unemployment in Spain is a decrease in labor hoarding for profit reasons. Where the agreement between Blanchard's argument and the one put forward in this chapter ends is in the chain of events. Higher profits *can* lead to capital accumulation but not necessarily to higher employment. As argued above, firms try to increase labor productivity by increasing the capital–labor ratio. This increase in capital leads to a decrease in profit rates.

The rest of the chapter is structured as follows. The next section discusses the historical background of labor relations in Spain. The third section provides a rationale for the relationship between unemployment and profitability. Section 4 proposes a simple model of the unemployment rate. The econometric approach followed is that of Hendry and his associates, which is probably best summarized in Granger (1990), *Journal of Policy Modeling* (1992), Banerjee et al. (1993), and Hendry (1995). Section 5 discusses the results of tests for the order of integration of the series. Section 6 performs systems cointegration analysis. Section 7 derives a conditional equation with constant parameters relating the unemployment rate to the profit rate and capacity utilization. This is followed by a concluding section.[2]

## HISTORICAL BACKGROUND

In order to understand Spain's unemployment problem one must adopt a historical perspective. The developments between the end of the civil war (1936–9) and the death of General Franco in 1975 set it apart from other European countries. In the political sphere, Spain was an isolated country between the end of the civil war and the 1950s. And at the economic level, Spain was virtually closed to foreign competition for many years. Spanish corporatism was based on a peculiar form of coordination among government, the Catholic Church, firms and workers. Labor relations were harmonious because there was an imposed social contract between workers and firms. Trade unions were 'vertical': both workers and employers belonged to the same union so that strikes and class unions were forbidden. The (implicit) agreement was to maintain labor discipline, worker loyalty and high levels of work effort (through propaganda), and to refrain from actions that threatened profitability, management prerogatives and political stability. Firms, on the other hand, agreed to maintain economic growth and job security. Lay-offs were virtually unheard of. For almost 40 years this system was an instrument of wealth creation, social cohesion and, as Kalecki (1971) put it, a solution to capitalism's unemployment problem. Kalecki held that with fascism workers would have jobs, but they would never be allowed to exercise political and economic power.

Modern development of Spain did not begin until the 1960s, approximately one decade after it had begun in other Western European countries (although it was more intense). The significance of this period lies in the mechanization of agriculture. This is the key to understanding the root cause of Spain's unemployment. Since a very large share of the total labor force was employed in agriculture, the introduction of labor-saving technologies destroyed the employment base, and provided the big push for the migrations of the 1960s. During the period 1962–73, the Spanish economy grew at an annual rate of 7 percent. Nonetheless, up to one and a half million workers had to search for better prospects in northern Europe during the mid-1960s and mid-1970s (salaries in northern Europe were approximately twice those in Spain; Roman 1997: 84). Despite this migration, Spain's unemployment rate in 1970 was already 7 percent.

Spain's singular social contract, *an institution*, broke down during the 1970s. On the one hand, the political regime that had sustained it died in 1975; on the other hand, the impact of the oil shocks (a supply shock which increased the real price of a key imported material) and the legalization of class unions became an engine of industrial conflict and strife over the distribution of the national income. (During this period, real wages increased above productivity.) The problem was exacerbated by the return from Europe of a large number of migrants. The result of these events was the interruption of the technical modernization of the Spanish economy. In 1976 the unemployment rate was 9 percent, since Spain was a relatively closed economy and managed to isolate itself and defer, for some time, the impact of the first oil shock. In 1977 the employment survey underwent technical modifications, and the unemployment rate dropped to 3 percent.[3] Since then, however, the increase in unemployment has been Spain's single most important economic problem.

The 1980s proved to be a very painful decade for labor. First, the gradual opening of an economy that had been virtually closed to foreign competition for almost 40 years proved to be a difficult test for most Spanish firms. During the period of autarky, most businesses had not been exposed to demanding international clients and the best practices of overseas competitors. This brought to the surface a key problem, namely the lack of competitive capacity, and with it the lack of people with the necessary skills to compete in the global economy. Second, Spain applied for membership of the European Community. Many Spanish firms, particularly in the industrial sector, were inefficient and had to be downsized, or even closed (as part of the accession treaty).[4] This gave rise to a process of de-industrialization, which exacerbated labor market problems such as worker immobility and skills mismatch, the main causes of structural unemployment. The third blow to the unemployment question was the spread of the personal computer beginning in the second half of the 1980s, which has been used as a substitute for low-skilled clerical workers.

If during the expansion period of the 1960s a large share of investment was aimed at increasing production capacity, from then onward most investments aimed at acquiring new technologies that could substitute labor and reduce the wage bill. Spanish firms entered a period in which firms chose to defend profit margins through the rationalization and modernization of their equipment rather than through the expansion of production and sales, or through the improvement of managerial methods and by competing abroad. The 'new firms', capital intensive and much more efficient, did not contribute to increasing employment. In other words, unemployment in Spain has to do not so much with the evolution of the labor force as with the loss of jobs. The overall result was a quick increase in unemployment. By 1984, almost 19 percent of the active population was unemployed. By 1994 the percentage had reached 24 percent. Since then the rate has declined, but it still hovers around 20 percent (Figure 11.1).[5]

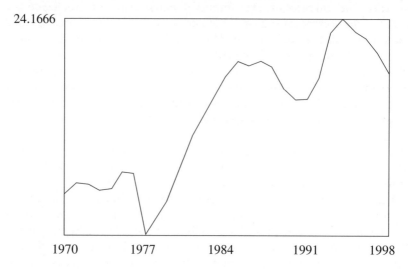

*Figure 11.1    Unemployment rate (%)*

The implications of this situation were recently summarized by Roman as follows:

> If one could only imagine such a situation in the U.S. or the U.K. or any other industrialized country, it would be easy to see why the very extra-ordinary nature of the phenomenon under scrutiny demands the use of equally extraordinary tools of analysis. My view is clear: show me an industrialized country carrying the burden of 25% of unemployment, and I will show you a full-blown depression that cannot be explained away by neoclassical parables (Roman 1997: 6).

There are two important questions to answer in order to understand Spain's unemployment problem. First, is it true that three million people are unemployed? The second question is whether wages in Spain are 'too high' so that the labor market does not clear (classic unemployment). A related question is whether social benefits (for example, minimum wages, employment insurance), layoff costs and payroll taxes are so high that there is a disincentive to hire workers? In other words: is there a problem of rigidity of the labor market and institutions?

The answer to the first question is 'probably yes'. Overall, the figures are correct. On the one hand, Spain has an important underground economy (up to one-third according to some estimates). This could underestimate employment and thus overstate the unemployment figures. It could also be the case that a large number of workers are registered as unemployed but doing odd jobs, or even regular work, which are not legally declared for tax purposes. But on the other side of the equation, there are many discouraged workers who have dropped out of the labor force and are not registered as unemployed.[6] All in all, these are aggregate figures that can be taken as a correct reference guide. Likewise, since the unemployment survey methods are similar to those in other countries, changes in time in the unemployment rate appear to agree with reality.

Answering the second question is more difficult for, in the final analysis, it necessarily involves some value judgment. Unemployment in a classical world is the result of wages being too high to clear the labor market. If wages were perfectly flexible, then in a recession the resultant fall in money wages would induce entrepreneurs to hire more workers (on this see the recent work of Bewley 2000).[7] But the reality is that, in Spain, the average annual rates of increase of the wage rate (2.14 percent) and of labor productivity (2.15 percent) went hand in hand during the period 1970–98. As indicated above, in the case of Spain wages did not grow above labor productivity except during the early period, 1970–76.[8] This coincided with the end of the dictatorship and the creation of unions that demanded increases in salaries with a view to redistributing income. In fact, overall profits declined in 1975 and 1979.[9]

Social benefits in Spain are below those in other European countries having lower unemployment rates (Ferreiro and Serrano 2000). One can even question whether Spain has ever had a true welfare state, given that living standards are still well below those in northern Europe. With respect to the problem of flexibility, one could indeed argue that the Spanish labor market is not the most flexible, but it is certainly far more flexible today than it was two decades ago; yet unemployment was lower. Besides, in recent years the market has become much more flexible, following the standard policy advice.[10] It may surprise many to learn that a recent study by UNICE, the Federation of European Employers, concludes that Spain has the most flexible labor market among the industrialized countries. And the difference is important. Taking the US level of flexibility as 100, while all Western European countries and Japan have indices well below 100 (indicating a lower degree of flexibility), Spain's index is 140.

Likewise, although still at the bottom of the OECD countries, the number of part-time workers (defined as those working less than 30 hours a week) increased from slightly less than 5 percent of the labor force in 1990 to around 7.5 percent in 1998. This compares with around 15 percent for the European Union and the OECD countries. Furthermore, as argued above, at the theoretical level the relationship between unemployment and rigidities is ambiguous (Bean 1994; Blanchard 1999). Workers in Spain are very reluctant to move from one region to another, or to accept lower wages or massive lay-offs in a recession. But flexibility has its own limitations and drawbacks. It is not clear that firms are better off when they can substitute a permanent worker for a temporary one who can be laid off at any time. Cost and labor flexibility arguments have more to do with corporate profits than with employment creation.

It is therefore difficult to believe that the reason (and ultimate cause of) why there are 3 million people (almost 20 percent of the active population) unemployed in Spain is that wages have grown too fast, or that they are too high, or that the labor market is not flexible enough (although it is true that the economic activity of a country and its transformation into job creation are – more or less – encouraged by the degree of flexibility of the economic system). We must look for other causes.

## PROFITABILITY AND UNEMPLOYMENT

Profit is the veritable bottom line of the market system. As firms invest, they add to their aggregate capital stock. With a constant rate of profit, the total amount of profit grows correspondingly. But if profits grow more slowly than the capital stock, then the profit rate falls. A secular decline in the profit rate progressively undermines the incentive to invest and thus slows down the rate of growth of the capital stock itself. These two effects serve to undermine the growth of total profits. Therefore, an initially growing mass of total profits begins to decelerate until at some point it stagnates or even declines. When total profits are stagnant, firms find themselves in a situation where they have invested in additional capital without getting any additional profit. This implies that a proportion of their capital stock is idle. If this situation persists, then investment is cut back, excess capacity becomes widespread and workers are laid off. In the words of Joan Robinson:

> When there is a strong capital-using bias in technical progress, it requires a higher flow of gross investment to maintain a constant long-run level of employment. If sufficient gross investment is not forthcoming, a *reserve army* of long-period unemployed is created again (Robinson 1977: 1333; italics added).

More recently, Zarnowitz has described a similar chain of events:

> If an economic slowdown reduces profit margins and dims the outlook for profits, the likely reaction of business firms will consist first in cutbacks on decisions to invest, then if matters do not improve, in reductions of inventories, output and employment (Zarnowitz 1999: 74).

Figure 11.2 shows the evolution of the profit rate in Spain for the period 1970–98. It displays a clear downward trend from 20 percent in 1970 to around 15 percent in 1998.[11]

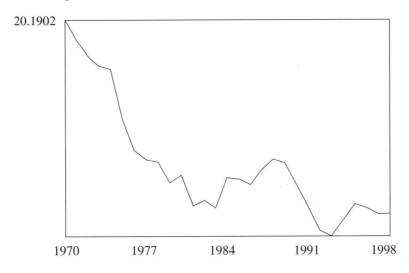

20.1902

| 1970 | 1977 | 1984 | 1991 | 1998 |

*Figure 11.2   Profit rate on invested capital (%)*

Why do profit rates *tend* to fall? From an algebraic point of view, the average gross profit rate is the ratio of overall profits to the stock of capital:

$$r_t = \frac{\Pi_t}{K_t} = \frac{(Q_t - w_t L_t)}{K_t} \tag{1}$$

where $r$ denotes the average profit rate, $\Pi$ denotes overall profits, $Q$ is value-added, $w$ is the average wage rate, $L$ is employment and $K$ is the stock of capital. Equivalently, the profit rate can be written as the ratio of 1 minus the labor share to the capital–output ratio, that is,

$$r_t = \frac{1 - a_t}{K_t/Q_t} = \frac{1 - a_t}{(K_t/L_t)(L_t/Q_t)} \tag{2}$$

where $a_t = w_t \, L_t/Q_t$ is the labor share, and $1 - a_t$ is capital's share. This implies that the profit rate will fall either because the labor share increases or because the capital–output ratio increases. Given that the former tends to be relatively constant – this is true for Spain too (see Figure 11.3) – the most likely reason behind the decline in the profit rate is the increase in the capital–output ratio.[12]

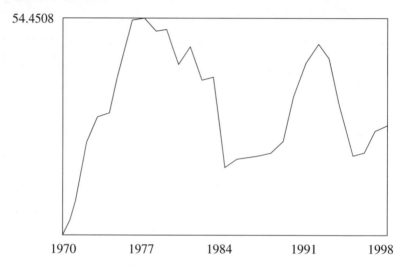

54.4508

1970          1977          1984          1991          1998

*Figure 11.3    Labor share in value added (%)*

Moreover, the latter can be written as the product of the capital–labor ratio times the labor–output ratio (that is, the inverse of labor productivity). Since labor productivity is increasing (that is, the labor requirement per unit of output is decreasing), the reason why the capital–output ratio increases is that the capital–labor ratio increases faster than labor productivity. Indeed, for 1970–98 labor productivity grew at an annual rate of 2.15 percent (3.07 percent, 1.81 percent and 1.17 percent during 1970–80, 1981–90 and 1991–98 respectively), while the capital–labor ratio grew at an annual rate of 3.08 percent (4.49 percent, 1.53 percent and 1.79 percent during 1970–80, 1981–90 and 1991–98 respectively).[13]

The rationale behind the somewhat tautological arguments above is as follows. The essence of a market economy is competition for markets. In the final analysis the crucial variable which determines a firm's survival is the cost of the product. The lower the price for a product of a given quality the better the chances of success. This is why firms are continually worried about the idea of lowering costs, for this is the way to increase their profit rate. The reduction in unit costs is achieved mainly through increases in labor productivity. The drive to raise productivity leads to an ever-increasing mechanization of the production process. However, as more fixed capital per worker is required, machines replace workers (that is, new equipment is labor saving whereas there is an excess supply of labor). But if mechanization (that is, increase in capital intensity) is to be successful in the competition struggle, it must reduce unit costs. Larger-scale plants and equipment require greater amounts of fixed capital per unit of product. This way, higher fixed costs are traded off in return for lower variable costs.

Technical progress implies a substitution of labor for capital (Ricardo 1981). While society at large is made wealthier by the productivity gains achieved through technical progress, this is not true for the particular individual who has lost his/her job. Thus, the important aspect is whether the displaced labor force moves to another sector where new opportunities have been created, for example, agriculture to industry or services (growth-induced employment). Does society *guarantee* these displaced workers a new job? The answer is no. It all depends on a combination of factors such as the elasticity of substitution between inputs; whether unit cost reductions translate into a lower demand for labor; the market conditions confronted by the firm; and the existence of conducive macroeconomic conditions and institutional factors. In the presence of technical change, the labor displaced by mechanization will not be absorbed by accumulation once the falling profitability slows down investment. In the words of Pulido (1995: 347) Spain's unemployment problem is basically 'one of lack of capacity of the system to maintain the necessary level of activity to provide work to those who wish to work'.

Once a new, lower-cost method becomes feasible, the investment picture changes. The first few firms to adopt the new method are in a position to lower their selling prices, undersell their competitors and expand their own shares of the market. All firms now face a round of falling prices, that is, 'first-mover' advantages (Marx 1972; Chandler 1990). Under these new circumstances, the firms with the lowest unit costs will be the ones with the greatest chance of survival. The reason is that price reductions damage the anticipated profit rates of the higher-cost methods more than those of the lower-cost processes.[14]

It is important to emphasize that this process *need not* be generated by rising real wages. It is true, however, that demands for higher wages may accelerate the fall in the rate of profit, as is obvious from the definition of the profit rate above. But this effect is limited because rising real wages are generally constrained by the growth of productivity. No firm can sustain rising unit labor costs for any length of time without risking extinction. In this sense, this analysis does take into account wages. The argument is that wages are part of a firm's profitability *requirement*. Obtaining a rate of return on the capital employed is fundamental to a firm's survival and it is part of its pricing strategy. Scherer, in an analysis of General Motors, described the process as follows:

> GM begins its pricing analysis with an objective of earnings, on the average over the years, a return of approximately 15 per cent after taxes on total invested capital. Since it does not know how many autos will be sold in a forthcoming year, and hence what the average cost per unit (including prorated overhead) will be, it calculates costs on the assumption of standard volume – that is, operation at 80 per cent of conservatively rated capacity. A standard price is next calculated by adding to average cost per unit a standard volume of sufficient profit margin to yield the desired 15 per cent after-tax return on capital (Scherer 1970: 174).[15]

## MODELING UNEMPLOYMENT

Given the previous considerations, this paper proposes a simple model that departs from the standard neoclassical framework. In the latter, the marginal product of labor is the demand-for-labor schedule (the first-order condition that profit-maximizing firms satisfy). However, Davidson (1983) showed that there is no aggregate demand-for-labor schedule with the real wage as the independent variable. Likewise, applying the neoclassical framework at the macro level poses a theoretical problem. As Fisher (1993) showed, aggregate production functions cannot be derived in general. This implies that the optimization condition that the marginal product of labor equals the wage rate is a rather problematic idea at the macroeconomic level.

In the model proposed here, the demand for labor, $L^d$, is a positive function of the stock of capital, $K$, that is, $L^d = L^d(K)$ with $L^d_K > 0$. Thus, the change in labor demand depends on investment ($\Delta K = I$), that is, $\Delta L^d = L^d_t - L^d_{t-1} = f(I)$. The latter, following Kalecki (1954), Steindl (1952), Robinson (1962), Marglin (1984), Bhaduri and Marglin (1990) and Blecker (1989), is a function of the changes in the profit rate ($\Delta r$) and the changes in capacity utilization ($\Delta uticap$), which serves as a proxy for cyclical demand, that is, $\Delta K = I = I(\Delta r, \Delta uticap)$. The expected signs are $I_{\Delta r} > 0$ and $I_{\Delta uticap} > 0$. Desired accumulation depends on profitability because profits are both the returns to investment and the primary source of finance for investment. Capacity utilization influences the decision to invest in the sense that high utilization induces firms to expand capacity more rapidly in order to keep up with anticipated demand whereas low utilization (that is, excess capacity) induces them to cut back on planned investment. In other words, when a portion of the country's factories and equipment are idle, their owners have little incentive to invest in new productive equipment, and thereby expand the underutilized capacity. A high rate of capacity utilization will transform a high profit share into a high profit rate, and will stimulate further investment.

Figure 11.4 shows the rate of capacity utilization in Spain. It has been declining systematically during the 30-year period considered. It has recovered since bottoming in 1993, when it reached a low of 70 percent.[16]

*Figure 11.4   Capacity utilization rate (%)*

Furthermore, one of the main determinants of the output–capital ratio is the level of capacity utilization in the economy. The higher the latter, the higher will be the ratio of output to capital and, for a given capital share, the higher will be the profit rate (equation (2)).[17]

Davidson (1983) also argues against the modern neoclassical derivation of the supply curve of labor where optimizing individuals engage in intertemporal substitution. In fact, Joan Robinson (1942: 2–3) had argued years before in similar terms. Thus, the neoclassical concept of the supply curve of labor, $L^S$, is also dropped. It is taken to be an exogenous variable represented by the labor force and determined by demographic factors, that is, $\Delta L^S = L^S_t - L^S_{t-1} = f(\Delta P)$, where $P$ denotes population. This variable, however, was excluded from the empirical analysis. The reason is that its inclusion always led to very poor results.

The relationships described in the previous paragraphs, especially the investment function, have the advantage of separating demand and supply-side impacts on investment, the former via utilization capacity, and the latter via the profit rate, which shows the cost-reducing effect of a lower wage rate. As pointed out in section 3, wages appear indirectly in this formulation through the profit rate.

The change in unemployment (the difference between the change in the supply of labor and the change in the demand for labor, that is, $\Delta L^S = L^d$) will be the result of the process described in the previous section (that is, firms substitute capital for labor in an attempt to increase productivity with a view to maintaining their profit rates). It appears as the gap or disequilibrium between the employment capacity generated by accumulation and the level of employment allowed by the population of working age.

Given the above considerations, the change in the unemployment rate is a function of the change in profitability and the change in capacity utilization, that is, $\Delta upr = f(\Delta r, \Delta uticap)$ with expected signs $f_{\Delta r} < 0$ and $f_{\Delta uticap} < 0$. A long-run unemployment equation sufficiently general to include these arguments is

$$upr = f(r, uticap) \tag{3}$$

where *upr* denotes the unemployment rate (level), with $f_r < 0$ and $f_{uticap} < 0$. In terms of Blanchard's categorization of shocks versus institutions, the rate of capacity utilization operates as a shock, and it is a source of persistence (Bean 1994: 612–14). On the other hand, the profit rate is both an institution and a shock (it is an institution in the sense discussed in sections 2 and 3).

## UNIT ROOT ANALYSIS

The first step in the modeling process is to test the order of integration of the three series. Results of the augmented Dickey–Fuller (ADF) tests of the series are shown in Table 11.1. They indicate that the three series are well characterized as random walks.

*Table 11.1    Augmented Dickey–Fuller test, 1970–98*

$\Delta y_t = \mu + \beta t + \phi y_{t-1} + \Sigma_{i=1}^k \theta_i \Delta y_{t-i} + \varepsilon_t$

| Series | $k$ | ADF Test |
| --- | --- | --- |
| Profit rate ($r$) | 1 | I(1); RW no drift |
| Utilization capacity (uticap) | 1 | I(1); RW no drift |
| Unemployment rate (upr) | 1 | I(1); RW no drift |
| Unemployment rate, 1978–98 | 2 | I(0); Trend stationary |

*Note:*    Series in natural logarithms. RW stands for 'random walk'.

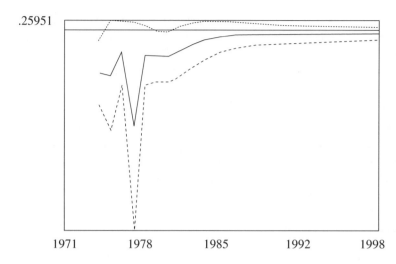

.25951

1971          1978          1985          1992          1998

*Figure 11.5    Recursive OLS estimates of upr( −1) in the ADF regression and two times the standard error*

However, in the case of the unemployment rate, the series might have a structural break in 1977, the year the statistics suffered an important methodological revision and changed (see Figure 11.1). Figure 11.5 shows the recursive estimates of $upr_{t-1}$ in the ADF regression.[18] It seems to provide evidence that there could be a break in 1977. However, for the period 1978–98, the unemployment rate seems to be trend stationary.[19] This would seem to indicate that the unit root in the unemployment rate is induced by the break.

For this reason, the test for the presence of a unit root was also carried out using Perron's (1989, 1993) models and critical values. Although it seems that our case corresponds to Perron's model A, that is, the crash model (one time change in the intercept of the trend function), we also tested the other two models discussed in Perron (1989). Results are shown in Table 11.2. In none of the three cases is the null hypothesis of a unit root to be rejected. The conclusion is that, although the unemployment rate seems to be strongly influenced by the break of the series in 1977, the tests appear to favor the random walk representation.

With the above caveats in mind, a long-run relationship, Engle–Granger cointegration regression, between the three variables was estimated for reference (variables in logarithms):

$$upr = 14.72 - 1.797*r - 4.578*uticap$$
No. observations = 29 (1970–98)    CRDW: 0.42    $R^2 = 0.44$
DF = −1.71 (−4.06)  ADF(1) = −1.94 (−4.07)  ADF(2) = −2.26 (−4.08)

This provides us with some benchmark values for the long-run elasticities. However, note that the cointegrating regression Durbin–Watson (CRDW) and the Dickey–Fuller (DF) and augmented Dickey–Fuller (ADF) tests for the residuals do not reject the null hypothesis of no cointegration (critical values in parentheses).

*Table 11.2    Perron's tests for a unit root, unemployment rate, 1970–98.*

Model A: $\Delta upr_t = \mu + \beta t + \delta DU_t + \gamma D(TB)_t + \phi upr_{t-1} + \Sigma_{i=1}^k \theta_i \Delta upr_{t-i}$

| $\mu$ | $\beta$ | $\delta$ | $\gamma$ | $\phi$ | Critical Values |
|---|---|---|---|---|---|
| $-0.55$ | $-0.003$ | 0.36 | 0.55 | $-0.16$ | $-3.77$: $-3.76$ |
| $(-0.98)$ | $(-0.24)$ | (1.72) | (0.71) | $(-0.76)$ | |

Model B: $\Delta upr_t = \mu + \beta t + \delta DU_t + \gamma DT_t^* + \phi upr_{t-1} + \Sigma_{i=1}^k \theta_i \Delta upr_{t-i}$

| $\mu$ | $\beta$ | $\delta$ | $\gamma$ | $\phi$ | Critical Values |
|---|---|---|---|---|---|
| $-0.20$ | $-0.13$ | 0.73 | 0.13 | $-0.30$ | $-3.72$: $-3.85$ |
| $(-0.43)$ | $(-0.89)$ | (4.44) | (2.88) | $(-2.13)$ | |

Model C: $\Delta upr_t = \mu + \beta t + \delta DU_t + \gamma D(TB)_t + \phi upr_{t-1} + \tau DT_t + \Sigma_{i=1}^k \theta_i \Delta upr_{t-i}$

| $\mu$ | $\beta$ | $\delta$ | $\gamma$ | $\phi$ | $\tau$ | Critical Values |
|---|---|---|---|---|---|---|
| 0.1 | $-0.13$ | 0.61 | 0.74 | 0.13 | $-0.18$ | $-3.99$: $-4.17$ |
| (0.18) | $(-0.96)$ | (3.10) | (1.11) | (2.99) | $(-1.03)$ | |

*Notes:*
$t$-statistics in parentheses; $T=29$ (1970–98); $T_B=8$ (1970–77); $\lambda=0.275$; $k=1$.

Critical values for $\phi$ (0.05 level), for models A and C, are taken from Perron (1989), Tables IV.B and VI.B respectively. For model B they are taken from Perron (1993), Table I. The two values given are for $\lambda=0.2$ and $\lambda=0.3$.

$DU_t=1$ if $t>T_B$, 0 otherwise; $D(TB)_t=1$ $t=T_B+1$, 0 otherwise; $DT_t^*=t-T_B$ if $t>T_B$, 0 otherwise; $DT_t=t$ if $t>T_B$, 0 otherwise.

## SYSTEMS COINTEGRATION ANALYSIS

On the assumption that the variables are integrated of order 1, a vector error correction model (VECM) of the three series was estimated. This could be considered to be our congruent statistical system of unrestricted

*Table 11.3     Johansen's cointegration test, 1970–98*

Eigenvalues: 0.9698; 0.2523; 0.1887

| Maximal Eigenvalue | | | | Trace | | | |
|---|---|---|---|---|---|---|---|
| $H_0$ | $H_1$ | Statistic | CV | $H_0$ | $H_1$ | Statistic | CV |
| $r=0$ | $r=1$ | 91.07 | 21.12 | $r=0$ | $r\geq 1$ | 104.07 | 31.54 |
| $r\leq 1$ | $r=2$ | **7.56** | **14.88** | $r\leq 1$ | $r\geq 2$ | **13.00** | **17.86** |
| $r\leq 2$ | $r=3$ | 5.44 | 8.07 | $r\leq 2$ | $r\geq 3$ | 5.44 | 8.07 |

*Note:*   Order of the VAR = 3. Unrestricted intercepts, no trend. CV is the 95% critical value; *r* in this table refers to the number of unit roots.

*Source:*   Pesaran and Pesaran (1997).

*Table 11.4     Normalized cointegrating vectors ($\beta'$) and adjustment coefficients ($\alpha$)*

| Variable | $\alpha$ (Weighting Matrix) | | | $\beta'$ (Cointegrating Vectors) | | |
|---|---|---|---|---|---|---|
| *upr* | **−0.33496** | −0.24027 | 0.49199 | 1 | 2.2624 | 3.7312 |
| *r* | **−0.00871** | 0.13437 | 0.40975 | −0.0284 | 1 | −3.6696 |
| *uticap* | **−0.00296** | 0.16979 | −0.16733 | 0.01792 | −0.5990 | 1 |

*Source:*   Pesaran and Pesaran (1997).

reduced forms. The VAR includes the three variables under study and a dummy that takes a value of one in 1977 and zero otherwise.[20] Results of the cointegration analysis are reported in Table 11.3.

The results based on both the maximal eigenvalue and the trace statistics seem to indicate the existence of one cointegrating vector. Table 11.4 displays the normalized vectors together with the adjustment coefficients (in bold):

Normalizing the first cointegrating vector with respect to the unemployment rate yields (variables in logarithms):

$$upr = -2.2624*r - 3.7312*uticap$$

This result is consistent with the model outlined (even though the choice of normalization is arbitrary) in the sense that both profit rate and capacity utilization take on negative signs.[21] The elasticities are slightly higher than those obtained through the static long-run regression. It is also important to note that the results in Table 11.4 indicate that the unemployment rate cointegrating vector enters the unemployment equation with a coefficient of $-0.335$, while it does not appear to enter the equations for the profit rate ($r$) or capacity utilization (*uticap*). This is necessary for the latter two variables to be weakly exogenous in a conditional unemployment equation. This is the fundamental concept in modeling (Engle et al. 1983). Weak exogeneity of the current-period regressors is required for estimation and hypothesis testing. A variable is said to be weakly exogenous for the parameters of interest if the latter are only functions of the parameters of the conditional model, and if the parameters of the conditional and marginal models are variation free (that is, there are no cross-restrictions between conditional and marginal models). The results in this section support weak exogeneity, since the unemployment error correction term does not appear to enter the equations for the profit and capacity utilization rates (the weights in the $\alpha$ matrix are zero).

Given these results, it seems that modeling the unemployment rate conditioning on the other two variables is a sensible strategy, assuming that those other variables are weakly exogenous for the parameters of the unemployment rate equation.

## CONDITIONAL MODEL ANALYSIS

To model the dynamics and long run of the unemployment rate jointly, we estimate an autoregressive distributed lag of the three variables. Given that we have 29 years, four lags should suffice to pick up the dynamics in the series, that is, ADL($m=4$, $n=4$; $p=2$), where $m$ is the number of lags on the left-hand side variable (*upr*), $n$ is the number of lags in the right-hand side variables, and $p$ is the number of right-hand side variables ($r$, *uticap*). Thus, in levels (variables in logarithms), the model is

$$upr_t = \alpha_0 + \sum_{i=1}^{4} \alpha_i upr_{t-i} + \sum_{i=0}^{4} \beta_i r_{t-i} + \sum_{i=0}^{4} \gamma_i uticap_{t-i} + \phi DUM77 + \varepsilon_t \quad (4)$$

where $\varepsilon \sim N(0, \sigma^2)$, and DUM77 is a dummy variable that takes on a value of one in 1977, the year the labor statistics underwent changes. Following Bårdsen (1989), equation (4) can be rewritten as ($\Delta$ denotes the growth rate)

$$\Delta upr_t = \alpha_0 + \sum_{i=1}^{3} \alpha_i^* \Delta upr_{t-i} + \sum_{i=0}^{3} \beta_i^* \Delta r_{t-i} + \sum_{i=0}^{3} \gamma_i^* \Delta uticap_{t-i}$$
$$+ \alpha^+ upr_{t-1} + \beta^+ r_{t-1} + \gamma^+ uticap_{t-1} + \phi DUM77 + \varepsilon_t \quad (5)$$

where

$$\alpha^+ = \sum_{i=1}^{4} \alpha_i - 1; \ \beta^+ = \sum_{i=0}^{4} \beta_i; \ \gamma^+ = \sum_{i=0}^{4} \gamma_i \quad (6)$$

The long-run multipliers are given by

$$\theta_r = \frac{\beta^+}{-\alpha^+}; \; \theta_{uticap} = \frac{\gamma^+}{-\alpha^+} \tag{7}$$

Results are displayed in Table 11.5. The model displayed is the one selected after a process of model reduction where the second and third lags in the growth rates have been excluded (except for the unemployment rate). The F-test for the exclusion of the third lag of the three variables $H_0:\alpha_3^* = \beta_3^* = \gamma_3^* = 0$ yields an insignificant F value. On the other hand, the test for the exclusion of the second lag ($H_0:\alpha_2^* = \beta_2^* = \gamma_2^* = 0$) yields a significant value. However, this significance is induced by the (high) significance of the second lag of the change in the unemployment rate; the second lags of the other two variables are highly insignificant. For this reason, it was decided to exclude the latter two while retaining the former. The diagnostic statistics indicate that the regression does not suffer from problems of misspecification or autocorrelation, and the fit is very high.

Given the inconclusive results regarding the order of integration of the series, we undertook the subsequent analysis following the methodology suggested by Pesaran et al. (1999), who have proposed a framework to test whether there exists a long-run relationship among the three variables within the current framework, that is, an ADL $(m, n; p)$ regression, irrespective of whether the variables are I(1) or I(0). The test is simply an F-statistic for the significance of the lagged levels of the variables in the autoregressive distributed lag, for, that is, $H_0$: $\alpha^+ = \beta^+ = \gamma^+ = 0$. However, the asymptotic distribution of this F-test is non-standard. Pesaran et al. (1999) have tabulated the appropriate critical values for different numbers of regressors, and have provided a band of critical values assuming that the variables are I(0) or I(1). The result of the test, shown in Table 11.5, yields $F(3, 15) = 188.57$. In our case, the corresponding band of critical values for a significance level of 0.01 is 5.15 to 6.36 (Pesaran et al. 1999, Table C1.iii). Since our calculated F-test exceeds the upper bound of the band, we reject the null hypothesis of no long-run relationship between the unemployment rate, average profit rate and rate of capacity utilization. If we now consider the significance of the lagged variables in levels in the error correction models explaining the changes in the profit rates ($\Delta r$) and the changes in the utilization capacity ($\Delta uticap$), we cannot reject the null hypothesis that the level variables do not enter these two equations significantly (results available upon request). This is consistent with our findings using Johansen's procedure.

The series of predictive failure tests (testing for whether or not the second period's set of observations falls within the prediction confidence interval formed by using the regression from the first period's observations)

*Table 11.5*   *Change in Spain's unemployment rate ($\Delta$upr); OLS estimates of equation (5), 1970–98*

| Variable | Estimate | $t$-statistic |
|---|---|---|
| Constant | 2.7062 | 1.3745 |
| $\Delta upr_{t-1}$ | 0.0742 | 3.2895 |
| $\Delta upr_{t-2}$ | 0.1173 | 5.3377 |
| $\Delta r_t$ | 0.4868 | 1.9908 |
| $\Delta r_{t-1}$ | 1.1748 | 5.2934 |
| $\Delta uticap_t$ | −1.7825 | −6.5700 |
| $\Delta uticap_{t-1}$ | −0.8820 | −2.7821 |
| DUM77 | −1.1180 | −38.706 |
| $upr_{t-1}$ | −0.3321 | −23.129 |
| $r_{t-1}$ | −0.8087 | −4.4625 |
| $uticap_{t-1}$ | −1.0934 | −2.8368 |

$H_0: \alpha_3^* = \beta_3^* = \gamma_3^* = 0$, $F(3, 9) = 0.90$; $H_0: \alpha_2^* = \beta_2^* = \gamma_2^* = 0$, $F(3, 13) = 8.54$
$R^2 = 0.994$; $DW = 2.44$; $LM (\chi_1^2) = 3.26$; $RESET (\chi_1^2) = 0.438$; $NORM (\chi_2^2) = 0.062$; $HET (\chi_1^2) = 1.027$

LM is the Lagrange multiplier test of residual serial correlation; RESET is Ramsey's test using the square of fitted residuals; NORM is the normality test based on the skewness and kurtosis of the residuals; HET is the heteroscedasticity based on the regression of squared residuals on squared fitted values. Critical values for $\alpha = 0.05$: $\chi_1^2 = 3.84$, $\chi_2^2 = 5.99$.

Cointegration test:
$H_0: \alpha^+ = \beta^+ = \gamma^+ = 0$; $F(3, 15) = 188.57$

Predictive-failure test (Chow's forecast test):
1970–88, $F(10,5) = 0.22$; 1970–93, $F(5, 10) = 0.42$; 1970–94, $F(4, 11) = 0.30$; 1970–95 $F(3, 12) = 0.13$; 1970–96, $F(2, 13) = 0.11$; 1970–97, $F(1, 14) = 0.22$

Chow's test for stability (Chow's breakpoint test) (model estimated without DUM77): 1970–85, $F(10,6) = 0.78$

**Long-run solution ($t$-values in parentheses):**
**$upr = 8.1465 − 2.4349 * r − 3.2919 * uticap$**
**   (1.39)    (−4.34)      (−2.94)**

*Note:*   See Pesaran and Pesaran (1997).

indicates that the specification is correct. And the Chow test for stability indicates that one cannot reject the null hypothesis of equality of the parameters over the two sample periods.

The results indicate that in the short run an increase in profitability leads to an increase in the unemployment rate.[22] On the other hand, an increase in the rate of capacity utilization leads to a decrease in the unemployment rate. The long-run solution yields elasticities consistent with those found with Johansen's procedure. In particular, we note that a 1 percent decline (increase) in the profit rate entails a 2.43 percent increase (decrease) in the unemployment rate; and that a 1 percent decline (increase) in the rate of capacity utilization entails a 3.29 percent increase (decrease) in the unemployment rate.[23]

With this information, the error correction term implied by the long-run solution is:

$$\Delta upr_t = \alpha_0 + \sum_{i=1}^{2} \alpha_i^* \Delta upr_{t-i} + \sum_{i=0}^{1} \beta_i^* \Delta r_{t-i} + \sum_{i=0}^{1} \gamma_i^* \Delta uticap_{t-i} + \phi DUM77$$

$$+ \alpha^+ ECT_{t-1} + \varepsilon_t \tag{8}$$

where $ECT = (upr - \theta_r\, r - \theta_{uticap}\, uticap)$. Results of the re-estimated model are shown in Table 11.6.

The error correction coefficient (ECT), estimated at $-0.332$, is highly significant, has the correct sign, and suggests a moderate speed of convergence to equilibrium. This coefficient is also consistent with our findings using Johansen's procedure. The coefficient indicates that in the short run the unemployment rate increases (decreases) by 33 percent of last year's shortage (excess) of the profit rate and utilization capacity over those in the long run.

Within-sample parameter stability is a desirable property of empirical models. Figure 11.6 shows the recursive OLS estimates of the error correction term $ECT_{t-1}$, and figure 11.7 displays the rolling regression estimates (estimated for 1978–98 without DUM77 with a window size of ten periods) of the same coefficient. Both graphs indicate stability. Finally, the Chow test for stability indicates that one cannot reject the null hypothesis of equality of the parameters over the two sample periods.

## CONCLUSIONS

This paper has explored empirically the relationship between unemployment and profitability in Spain in an attempt at understanding Spain's high and persistent rate of unemployment. The rationale behind this

*Table 11.6    Error correction model of spain's unemployment rate; OLS estimates of equation (8), 1970–98*

| Variable | Estimate | $t$-statistic |
|---|---|---|
| Constant | 2.7062 | 25.986 |
| $\Delta upr_{t-1}$ | 0.0742 | 3.5187 |
| $\Delta upr_{t-2}$ | 0.1173 | 5.7539 |
| $\Delta r_t$ | 0.4868 | 2.3670 |
| $\Delta r_{t-1}$ | 1.1748 | 5.9245 |
| $\Delta uticap_t$ | −1.7825 | −8.9431 |
| $\Delta uticap_{t-1}$ | −0.8820 | −4.1840 |
| DUM77 | −1.1180 | −41.239 |
| $ECT_{t-1}$ | −0.3321 | −25.321 |

$R^2 = 0.994$; $DW = 2.44$; LM $(\chi_1^2) = 2.95$; RESET $(\chi_1^2) = 0.429$; NORM $(\chi_2^2) = 0.062$; HET $(\chi_1^2) = 1.027$
The tests have the same interpretation as in Table 11.5.

Predictive failure test (Chow's forecast test):
1970–88, F(10,7) = 0.216; 1970–93, F(5, 12) = 0.278; 1970–94, F(4, 13) = 0.243; 1970–95 F(3, 14) = 0.133; 1970–96, F(2, 15) = 0.114; 1970–97, F(1, 16) = 0.199

Chow's test for stability (Chow's breakpoint test) (estimated without DUM77):
1970–85, F(8, 10) = 0.08
**ECT = upr + 2.4349 * r + 3.2919 * *uticap***

*Note:*    Note that the estimates of Table 11.6 coincide with those of Table 11.5. This is logical, since we are estimating the same model. The standard errors of the regressions (and therefore *t*-values), however, differ. This is because the standard error of the regression in Table 11.6 is slightly smaller. The reason is that the computer does not correct for the *k* degrees of freedom lost in imposing the long-run elasticities in the ECT term. Bårdsen (1989) provides the formula to correct the standard error of the regression, which leads to the same standard errors of the parameters as in Table 11.5.

relationship is that firms are constantly immersed in a spiral of capital accumulation with a view to increasing productivity, leading to a decrease in the profit rate. In their attempt to stay competitive in the market and in their constant fight with other firms for markets, firms try continually to increase the productivity of labor. This is mostly done through further investment. But the increase in the capital stock entails a secular decrease in the profit rate. When profit rates decrease, firms do not hire and even reduce employment, so that further increases in the capital stock are necessary to increase labor productivity. Thus, in the final analysis, unemployment arises as a consequence of the increase in capital intensity of

*Figure 11.6   Recursive estimates of ECT( −1 ) (equation 8) and two times the standard error*

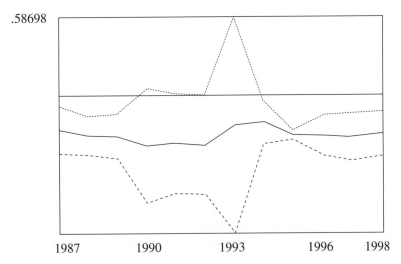

*Figure 11.7   Rolling OLS estimates of ECT( −1 ) (window size = 10)*

production, and during the struggle over the distribution of income; the latter is reflected in the requirement to obtain a pre-determined profit rate on the invested capital. This process is inherent to all firms in a market economy. In the case of Spain, the growing capital intensity of production that began in the 1960s was intended to raise labor productivity and lower total unit costs. However, mechanization raised the capital requirements per unit of output and reduced profitability. The fruits of industrialization were dissipated under the rug of chronic unemployment.

Following Kalecki, the paper posits that the demand for labor is a function of the determinants of investment, namely the profit rate, and the rate of capacity utilization (the supply of labor is exogenous). A conditional model for the unemployment rate has been derived. This model has the property that it contains an error correction term that relates the long-run unemployment rate to the average profit rate of the economy, and the rate of capacity utilization. The long-run elasticities are $-2.43$ and $-3.29$, respectively (over the base values).

From a policy perspective, the model indicates that reducing unemployment in Spain will be a very tough issue; certainly not achievable in the short run. Recent reports (end of 1999) indicate that the unemployment rate has declined to around 15.45 percent of the labor force (2548500 people). There are, however, at least two reasons for a caveat. First, most of the jobs created during the last year were in the construction sector. It is well known that the performance of this sector depends on the business cycle. The second reason is that most of the people who got jobs were offered fixed-term contracts. In fact Spain has one of the highest rates of fixed-term contracts in Europe (33 percent of total employment). Due to this, the cost of laying off a worker is nil, and many of these jobs are the result of bringing to the surface employment in the underground economy. The 'growth model' implemented in Spain during the last few years is not based on technical progress and skilled labor, but on low wages; and current international conditions are responsible for the increase in the rate of capacity utilization and the reduction in interest rates. Given this, it is not clear that when the next recession hits Spain, the unemployment rate will not go back to previous levels.

Since Spain is working at around 80 percent of capacity, there is still some room for an increase in capacity utilization without overheating the economy. However, from a policy perspective there is a critical trade-off that must be considered (Gordon et al. 1994). This trade-off is between the desire to achieve a high rate of capacity utilization to transform a high profit share into a high profit rate, and to stimulate investment; and the desire to maintain a low rate of capacity utilization to sustain high unemployment as a way of maintaining labor discipline (as a mechanism contributing to a high profit share).

# NOTES

\*   I am indebted to Jerry Adams, Willie Belton, Julian Perez, Manuel Roman, Anwar Shaikh and the participants in the Sixth International Post Keynesian Workshop for comments, suggestions and useful discussions. The usual disclaimer applies. I acknowledge partial financial support from the Center for International Business Education and Research (CIBER) at the Georgia Institute of Technology.

1   The connection between profit rate and the rest of the economy via investment is widely acknowledged (ask Bill Gates). However, this variable plays a much more prominent role in classical analyses (Ricardo 1981; Marx 1977, 1981, 1982) than in neoclassical economics.

2   Data were provided by Julian Perez of the Lawrence R. Klein Forecasting and Research Center (Madrid, Spain). All data are from the original sources, that is, national accounts and labor statistics. The stock of capital was computed following perpetual inventory.

3   In 1995 the labor department and the national statistics office began working on another methodological modification. This has not been fully implemented yet, and its impact is still difficult to evaluate. I am thankful to Julian Perez for bringing this point to my attention.

4   It is difficult to quantify the net result in terms of employment of Spain's membership (for example, the positive effect via foreign direct investment). But certainly Spain incurred a severe loss throughout the adhesion process.

5   It may be argued, however, that countries such as Sweden, Japan, Norway, Austria and Switzerland had the same pressure from the crisis, but unemployment did not increase at the same rate. All these countries have gone through extensive restructuring of their industries in the past decade. Their capability to do so without incurring major unemployment lies in the fact that all these countries had a more institutionalized commitment to full employment. This was not the case in Spain, where the main target of macroeconomic policy was inflation.

6   In the 'insider–outsider' terminology (Lindbeck and Snower 1989), we could say that the jobless, especially those who have been unemployed for a long time, are abandoned by the 'insiders' (who have some sort of monopoly power) and fall out of the sphere of regulation; many jobless, for all practical purposes, disappear from the labor market.

7   Bewley (2000) concludes that firms prefer lay-offs to pay cuts because the former harm workers' morale less. The latter hurt everybody, while the former have a transitory impact.

8   In fact the real wage in Spain has remained constant since the mid-1970s. The increase in the overall salary has been due to increases in taxes and social security contributions. I am thankful to Julian Perez for pointing this out.

9   In Spain the reality of unemployment plays a crucial role in keeping wages down, promoting the labor discipline necessary to enforce high levels of work effort, and thus supporting a high profit share.

10   Bean indicates that 'The United Kingdom has probably gone the furthest in enacting such structural policies [flexibility] although so far with rather little beneficial effect on unemployment' (Bean 1994: 615).

11   Some caution must be exerted in drawing the conclusion that the profit rate shows a downward trend. Regression of the profit rate on a time trend indicates a statistically insignificant coefficient (when serial correlation is taken care of). The conclusion remains when the regression controls for capacity utilization. As documented later, the profit rate series is a random walk.

12   By constant I simply mean that there is no visible upward or downward trend (the series contains a unit root). Note Spain's low labor share, around 50 percent, when in other developed countries it is around 70 percent. The labor share in Spain peaked in the period 1976–79, at 0.54 (minimum value of 0.47 in 1970). Even now it is still three percentage points below that maximum. The coefficients of variation of the labor share, capital–labor ratio and labor requirement are 0.034, 0.251 and 0.193 respectively.

13    Regressing the growth rate of labor productivity on the growth rate of the capital–labor ratio for 1970–98 yields a coefficient of 0.65 ($t$-value = 6.61), with an $R^2$ of 0.62. The relationship is also highly significant for 1970–80 and 1991–98, but less so for 1980–90.

14    It can be shown that while more heavily capitalized methods of production may benefit individual firms by lowering their unit costs of production, they nonetheless also tend to lower the average rate of profit for the economy (Shaikh 1987). Therefore, the same factor which fuels competition among firms also produces a slow but steady downward drift in the economy-wide average rate of profit.

15    One could ask whether profit rates fall continuously until they reach zero. The answer is no (Gillman 1958; Marx 1982). The fall in the profit rate must be viewed only as a long-run tendency. Furthermore, the rate of profit being discussed is that for the average of the economy; therefore, it does not mean that profit rates are falling continuously in all firms. Besides, there are counteracting forces that are permanently at play. These forces not only prevent the profit rate from falling, but make it actually rise at times. One such force is the formation of monopolies, and concentration and centralization of capital in general. Large firms displace smaller ones (on efficiency grounds). In the case of Spain this tendency appeared very clearly during the 1980s with mergers of commercial banks and with the establishment of huge retailers. Another mechanism preventing or decelerating the decrease in the profit rate is foreign investment, in particular in developing countries. Spanish companies concentrate their investments in Latin America.

16    The index of capacity utilization that I use is for the industrial sector (provided by Julian Perez). As far as I know there is no such index for the overall economy.

17    It is important to understand this statement the other way around: raising the profit share will not secure a higher profit rate unless it is also accompanied by a high level of capacity utilization.

18    This regression does not include any lagged terms of the dependent variable.

19    In this regression I could not eliminate the autocorrelation. The final regression contained two lags. The time trend was insignificant, while the constant was significant.

20    One could argue that the dummy variable should take a value of zero for the period 1970–76 and unity thereafter. However, as the unemployment statistics are currently being revised, as pointed out above, and as the impact of this revision is not clear, I decided to leave the dummy only for 1977. This is an issue to consider in future work. Likewise, in 1977, government, opposition and unions signed the Moncloa Pact to stabilize the economy.

21    The results including the constant term are worse.

22    This is inconsistent with the theoretical argument.

23    These percentages are over the base rates. Thus, for example, an increase in capacity utilization of 1 percent when capacity utilization is 75 percent implies a rate of capacity utilization of 75.75 percent; and an increase in profitability of 1 percent when the profit rate is 18 percent implies 18.18 percent.

# REFERENCES

Andrés, Javier, Juan J. Dolado, César Molinas, Miguel Sebastián, and Antonio Zabalza (1990), 'The influence of demand and capital constraints on Spanish unemployment', in J. Drèze and C. Bean (eds), *Europe's Unemployment Problem*, Cambridge: MIT Press, 366–408.

Banerjee, Anindya, Juan Dolado, John W. Galbraith and David F. Hendry (1993), *Cointegration, Error Correction, and the Econometric Analysis of Non-Stationary Data*, Oxford University Press.

Bårdsen, Gunnar (1989), 'Estimation of long run coefficients in error correction models', *Oxford Bulletin of Economics and Statistics*, 51(2) 345–50.

Bean, Charles (1994), 'European Unemployment: A Survey', *Journal of Economic Literature*, 32: 573–619.

Bewley, Truman (2000), *Why Wages Don't Fall During a Recession*, Harvard University Press.

Bhaduri, Amit and Stephen Marglin (1990), 'Unemployment as the real wage: the economic basis for contesting political ideologies', *Cambridge Journal of Economics*, 14: 375–93.

Blanchard, Olivier (1998), 'Revisiting European unemployment: unemployment, capital accumulation, and factor prices', MIT, mimeo.

Blanchard, Olivier (1999), 'European unemployment: the role of shocks and institutions', MIT, mimeo.

Blanchard, Olivier and Justin Wolfers (1999), 'The role of shocks and institutions in the rise of European unemployment: the aggregate evidence', MIT, mimeo.

Blecker, Robert (1989), 'International competition, income distribution and economic growth', *Cambridge Journal of Economics*, 13: 395–412.

Chandler, Alfred D. (1990), *Scale and Scope. The Dynamics of Industrial Capitalism*, Cambridge: Belknap Press of Harvard University Press.

Cohen, Daniel (1995), *The Misfortunes of Prosperity*, Cambridge, MA: MIT Press.

Cohen, Daniel (1998), *The Wealth of the World and the Poverty of Nations*. Cambridge, MA: MIT Press.

Davidson, Paul (1983), 'The marginal product curve is not the demand curve for labor and Lucas's labor supply function is not the supply curve for labor in the real world', *Journal of Post Keynesian Economics*, 6(1): 105–17.

Davidson, Paul (1998), 'Post Keynesian employment analysis and the macroeconomics of OECD unemployment', *Economic Journal*, 108, May: 817–31.

Dent, Christopher M (1997), *The European Community: The Global Context*, London and New York: Routledge.

Dolado, Juan J., José L. Malo de Molina and Antonio Zabalza (1986), 'Spanish industrial unemployment: some explanatory factors', *Economica*, Supplement, 53(210): S313–34.

Drèze, J. and C. Bean (1990a), 'Europe's unemployment problem: introduction and synthesis', in J. Drèze and C. Bean (eds), *Europe's Unemployment Problem*, Cambridge: MIT Press, 1–65.

Drèze, J. and C. Bean (1990b), 'European employment: lessons from a multi-country study', *Scandinavian Journal of Economics*, 92(2): 135–65.

Eatwell, J. (ed.) (1996), *Global Unemployment: Loss of Jobs in the 1990s*, New York: M.E. Sharpe.

Engle, R., D. Hendry and J. Richard (1983), 'Exogeneity', *Econometrica*, 51: 277–304.

Fazzari, Steven M. and Tracy L. Mott (1986–87), 'The investment theories of Kalecki and Keynes: an empirical study of firm data, 1970–82, *Journal of Post Keynesian Economics*, 10(2): 171–87.

Ferreiro, Jesus and Felipe Serrano (2000), 'The Spanish third way: between the liberalism of the eighties and the classic social democracy', Paper presented at the Sixth International Post Keynesian Workshop, Knoxville, Tennessee, 23–28 June.

Fisher, F.M (1993), *Aggregation. Aggregate Production Functions and Related Topics*, Cambridge, MA: MIT Press.

Fontela, Emilio (ed.) (1980), *España en la Decada de los Ochenta*, Madrid: Instituto Nacional de Prospectiva, Presidencia del Gobierno.

Gillman, Joseph M. (1958), *The Falling Rate of Profit*, New York: Cameron Associates.

Gordon, David M., Thomas Weisskopf and Samuel Bowles (1994), 'Right-wing economics in the 1980s: the anatomy of failure', in Michael A. Bernstein and David E. Adler (eds), *Understanding American Economic Decline*, Cambridge University Press, 243–75.

Granger, C.W.J. (1990), *Modelling Economic Series*, Oxford University Press.

Hendry, David F. (1995), *Dynamic Econometrics*, Oxford University Press.

*Journal of Policy Modeling* (1992), 'Special Issue: Cointegration, Exogeneity, and Policy Analysis', 14(3–4).

Kaldor, Nicholas (1956), 'Alternative Theories of Distribution', *Review of Economic Studies*, 23: 83–100.

Kalecki, M. (1938), 'The determinants of the distribution of income', *Econometrica*, 6.

Kalecki, M. (1941), 'A theory of long-run distribution of the product of industry', *Oxford Economic Papers*, 5 (old series).

Kalecki, M. (1954), *Theory of Economic Dynamics*, London: George Allen & Unwin.

Kalecki, M. (1971), *Selected Essays on the Dynamics of the Capitalist Economy 1933–1970*, Cambridge: Cambridge University Press.

Lindbeck, Assar and Dennis Snower (1989), *The Insider–Outsider Theory of Unemployment*, Cambridge: MIT Press.

Malinvaud, Edmond (1980), *Profitability and Unemployment*, Cambridge: Cambridge University Press.

Malinvaud, Edmond (1982), Wages and unemployment', *Economic Journal*, 92, March: 1–12.

Marglin, S.A. (1984), *Growth, Distribution and Prices*, Cambridge, MA: Harvard University Press.

Martin, J. (1994), 'The extent of high unemployment in OECD countries', in Federal Reserve Bank (ed.), *Reducing Unemployment: Current Issues and Options*, Kansas City: Federal Reserve Bank of Kansas City.

Marx, Karl (1972), 'Wage labour and capital', in Robert C. Tucker (ed.), *The Marx–Engels Reader*, New York: W.W. Norton & Co. Inc, 167–90.

Marx, Karl (1977), *Capital*, Vol. I, New York: Random House.

Marx, Karl (1981), *Capital*, Vol. II, New York: Random House.

Marx, Karl (1982), *Capital*, Vol. III, New York: Random House.

OECD (1994), *L'Etude de l'OCDE sur L'emploi*, Paris: OECD.

Perron, Pierre (1989), 'The Great Crash, the oil price shock, and the unit root hypothesis', *Econometrica*, 57(6): 1361–401.

Perron, Pierre (1993), 'Erratum', *Econometrica*, 61(1): 248–9.

Pesaran, H.M. and B. Pesaran (1997), *Working with Microfit 4.0: Interactive Econometric Analysis*, Oxford: Oxford University Press.

Pesaran, M.H., Y. Shin and R.J. Smith (1999), 'Bounds testing approaches to the analysis of long-run relationships', unpublished manuscript, Cambridge University.

Pesenti, Antonio (1959), 'The falling rate of profit', *Science and Society*, 23(3): 235–52.

Pollin, Robert (1998), 'The "reserve army of labor" and the "natural rate of unemployment": can Marx, Kalecki, Friedman, and Wall Street all be wrong?', *Review of Radical Political Economics*, 30(3): 1–13.

Pulido San Roman, Antonio (1995), *Economia para Entender: Una Guia de Temas Economicos de Actualidad*, Madrid: Piramide.

Ricardo, David (1981), *On the Principles of Political Economy and Taxation*, New York: Cambridge University Press.

Robinson, Joan (1942), *An Essay on Marxian Economics*, London: Macmillan.

Robinson, Joan (1962), *Essays in the Theory of Economic Growth*, London: Macmillan.

Robinson, Joan (1977), 'What are the questions?', *Journal of Economic Literature*, XV(4): 1318–39.

Roman, Manuel (1997), *Growth and Stagnation of the Spanish Economy*, Aldershot: Avebury, Ashgate Publishing Ltd.

Scherer, F.M. (1970), *Industrial Market Structure and Economic Performance*, Chicago, IL: Rand McNally.

Shaikh, Anwar (1987), 'Organic composition of capital', in John Eatwell, Murray Milgate and Peter Newman (eds), *The New Palgrave: A Dictionary of Economic Theory and Doctrine*, London: Macmillan.

Shaikh, Anwar (1993), 'The falling rate of profit as the cause of long waves: theory and empirical evidence', in A. Kleinknecht, E. Mandel and I. Wallerstein (eds), *New Findings in Long Wave Research.* New York: St. Martin's Press.

Steindl, J. (1952), *Maturity and Stagnation in American Capitalism*, Oxford: Blackwell.

Zarnowitz, Victor (1999), 'Theory and history behind business cycles: are the 1990s the onset of a golden age?', *Journal of Economic Perspectives*, 13(2): 69–90.

# 12. VAT reduction for consumption-oriented, labor-intensive services in the European Union: a stimulus to employment? The case of Germany

**Hubert Hieke**

## INTRODUCTION

Moonlighting and illegal employment have caused severe strains on the German economy. Some economists estimate that annual untaxed total revenue accumulated from these activities amounts to more than DM500 billion or 250 billion euros (Kornhardt 1998; Schneider and Ernste 2000). At the same time, the German economy has been facing persistent high levels of unemployment, and labor-intensive, consumption-oriented sectors in particular have been confronted with an increasing tax burden and labor costs, including those of fringe benefits. Studies suggest that relative prices for services that are good substitutes for those offered by the underground economy have risen considerably, and that demand for a wide range of products offered by the formal sector has consequently declined (Haase and Alefs 1997).

Although partial measures, such as a value-added tax (VAT) reduction for labor-intensive services, are usually considered inefficient and rather inappropriate in stimulating overall employment, a VAT reduction might reduce the gap between prices charged to consumers by the formal sector relative to those charged for similar services by the underground economy. If this was the case, employment in the formal sector might increase due to substitution effects between the two competing sectors.

The current debate about the impact of a possible VAT reduction on specific labor-intensive goods and services that are primarily demanded by private consumers has been controversial, particularly because the potential net effects on tax revenue and employment are hard to quantify, and no reliable data exist on either issue. For example, the net impact on tax revenue clearly depends on the demand and employment stimulus in the formal sector resulting from substitution, as well as the multiplier effects of a partial VAT reduction. Whether the stimulus will be sufficient to compensate for the initial decline in VAT revenues has been one of the main controversies surrounding the proposal, particularly in Germany.

Previous experience with VAT changes provides mixed evidence. Several EU countries, such as Belgium and the Netherlands, have recently introduced a VAT reduction for specific services in small-scale, labor-intensive industries, but Germany has been very hesitant to advocate or introduce such a policy.

The German crafts, consisting primarily of small and medium-sized enterprises,[1] employ approximately 6 million workers – almost one-sixth of the German labor force – and are clearly one of the main potential beneficiaries of a VAT reduction. In the following, an attempt is made to assess which sectors of the crafts would benefit from such a proposal, based on clearly identified benchmarks with respect to labor intensity and consumer orientation. No attempt is made, however, to quantify the potential effects on actual employment or revenues that may result from a VAT reduction. Rather, we try to outline the range of branches within the German crafts that appear to fulfill alternative criteria for a potential partial VAT reduction. In the following, we present some preliminary empirical results on that issue, based on data from the Handwerkszaehlung (1995). Two alternative proposals are considered. The first relates to a suggestion by Kornhardt (1998) and is similar to proposals made by the EU Commission. The second relates to a proposal by Haase and Alefs (1997).

According to Haase and Alefs (1997), there are two requirements for a reduced VAT rate. First, labor intensity, measured in terms of gross labor cost, must be at least 35 percent of total sales revenue. Second, at least 50 percent of total revenue must originate from sales to private consumers.

Another suggestion that has had some popularity among advocates of a partial VAT reduction is by Kornhardt (1998). He lists sectors of the German crafts that appear to be both labor-intensive and particularly threatened by moonlighting and illegal employment. His proposal is close to that of the EU Commission.

Unlike Kornhardt (1998) and Haase and Alefs (1997), we do not assume that it is feasible to apply a reduced VAT rate based on whether or not a particular single sale is made to a private consumer. Neither do we consider the issue from the perspective of individual firms. We assume that in practice it is almost impossible to identify labor-intensive production based on a particular sale of a product of a firm. Rather, we take the perspective that if a preferential VAT is introduced, is politically feasible, and is not leading to excessive legal distortions or considerable additional bureaucracy, the tax reduction must apply to all firms within the branch of the German crafts.

We also address the issue of whether technology-intensive sectors of the crafts would benefit from a VAT reduction. This issue is important, because R&D-intensive companies are widely seen as the main source of the future prosperity and international competitiveness of the German economy. The impact of a partial tax reduction on the relative performance of technology-intensive companies should, therefore, not be neglected.

## LABOR INTENSITY AND PRIVATE CONSUMPTION

According to the first proposal mentioned above (Haase and Alefs 1997), labor intensity and private consumption are the criteria for a VAT reduction. Which branches of the German crafts would benefit from such a proposal?

Our results demonstrate that, based on the highest available level of sectoral disaggregation of the data, only nine branches comprising 63000 firms and 289000 employees are significantly labor-intensive as well as providing the majority of their services to private consumers.[2] Of these, hairdressers are the primary craft that would benefit from a VAT reduction. Although no data are available on illegal services competing with the formal sector in this branch, it is generally believed that legal employment and the revenues of hairdressers are, in fact, considerably affected by moonlighting. On the other hand, it must be stressed that the German crafts would, overall, benefit hardly at all from a VAT reduction based on these two criteria.

## A MODIFIED EU PROPOSAL

If Kornhardt's (1998) suggestion is considered, and the branches are defined according to the classification established by the German Craft Association, the findings indicate that approximately 50 percent of the crafts, employing 3 million workers, would potentially benefit from a VAT reduction. However, only one branch fulfills the two criteria of labor intensity and private consumption. This branch again primarily consists of hairdressers, a finding already derived from the assumptions in the previous section of this paper. The range of potentially benefiting companies is negligible, but it is not surprising that the Association of German Hairdressers has been lobbying heavily for preferential tax treatment.

# ADJUSTMENTS OF LABOR INTENSITY

Almost all companies belonging to the German crafts are managed by their owners. Furthermore, often nobody except the owner and his/her relatives are actively employed in the business. According to our assessment, this necessarily results in a considerable bias with respect to official statistics on labor intensity, because the labor costs (including fringe benefits) of owners actively engaged in running their companies are not accounted for in the official statistics.

In order to adjust for this bias, a hypothetical annual wage of DM100000 per company is added to the official absolute values on labor costs. As a result of this adjustment, many branches, according to the classification of the Association of German Crafts, now seem to be labor-intensive (that is, labor intensity is above 35 percent) as well as sufficiently oriented to private consumption (that is, private consumption is above 50 percent).

According to this procedure, branches comprising approximately 172000 firms now potentially benefit from a VAT reduction. These businesses employ about 1.2 million workers and earn revenues in the range of DM110 billion. In essence, under this more realistic assessment, a considerable and essential number of branches of the German crafts would conform to the two criteria of labor intensity and private consumption.

# SMALL–MEDIUM ENTERPRISES IN TECHNOLOGY-INTENSIVE INDUSTRIES

The technological competitiveness of the German economy has been a major issue in recent years. It is widely claimed that Germany's international competitiveness and prosperity are critically dependent on technologically advanced economic sectors. Consequently, many economists and political advisors observe these particular sectors closely and often suggest a more active government role, including subsidies. The question arises as to what extent the current proposals for a VAT reduction would supplement such efforts directly or at least indirectly.

The most comprehensive and widely acknowledged definition of technology intensity has been established in annual reports to the federal government of Germany (BMBF, 1999).[3] Two levels of sectors are distinguished: high technology (HT) and leading technology (LT). HT comprises sectors where average expenditure on R&D is between 3.5 and 8.5 percent of total revenue; LT comprises sectors where the share of R&D expenditure is above 8.5 percent.

One-quarter of all firms and employees of the crafts belong to manufacturing sectors. Of these, the number of firms operating in technology-intensive sectors is considerable, with employment of roughly 400000. On the other hand, within the technology-intensive sector, the relative share of firms operating in the LT sector is negligible. Similarly, only 6 percent of employees within the technology-intensive branches of the German crafts are employed in LT sectors.

Private domestic consumption is the most important revenue source of the crafts, although, as already indicated, most sectors do not achieve the required VAT preference rate of 50 percent. Exports, on the other hand, generally play a relatively minor role for the German crafts as a whole. Within the manufacturing sector, exports, although still relatively modest, increase significantly, whereas sales proceeds derived from sales to other companies rise from 41.5 to 55.6 percent. In the technology-intensive sectors, however, the demand structure is even more surprising, considering the relatively small average firm size of the crafts. More than 70 percent of output in the technology-intensive sector is sold to other companies, and exports now make up a significant share of total revenue (11.5 percent). This is in sharp contrast to the findings for the German crafts, as well as manufacturing crafts as a whole. Given the fact that only 7 percent of sales proceeds are derived from sales to private consumers, the technology-intensive sector on average clearly does not reach the benchmark for VAT preference.[4]

Not a single branch within the technology-intensive crafts derives 50 percent of its revenue from private consumers. Private consumption based on the highest level of disaggregation ranges from 36.6 to 0.6 percent. Consequently, none of these branches would fall in the category suggested as having the minimum requirement for a preferential VAT reduction. The VAT proposal therefore clearly benefits primarily those branches of the small–medium enterprise sector that are not necessarily considered as internationally oriented, competitive sectors of the German economy.

Another interesting aspect in this context is the fact that Germany has lost considerable employment in both LT and HT sectors in recent years, and that the renewed increase in (the shares of) R&D expenditure has not stopped this trend. These changes are reflected rather in major productivity improvements. This trend is also currently occurring in small–medium enterprise. A VAT reduction for consumer-oriented companies would obviously not improve the situation.

# CONCLUSION

The actual employment and multiplier effects of an introduction of a partial VAT reduction is beyond the scope of this chapter, although it is certainly one of the most important issues in the current debate. No reliable data, however, exist on the subject. This means that any quantitative suggestions would be rather hypothetical, and we consequently do not take them into consideration.[5] Nevertheless, our analysis has provided clear indications about the range of sectors that may potentially benefit, in the formal sector of the German crafts, from a partial VAT reduction when alternative plans are considered.

Without denying the structural economic problems of the German economy, it seems that suggestions for a partial VAT reduction, irrespective of any potential employment effects, are a desperate attempt to find ways to increase employment in the formal sector of the German economy. The primary cause of high unemployment and illegal employment is, however, the prolonged and inappropriate macroeconomic policy which led to insufficient domestic demand and a reliance on export-led growth. Rather than an alteration in these policies to stimulate economic growth and domestic demand, some economists and political advisors have suggested a partial VAT tax reduction. Depending on which proposal were to be implemented, a VAT reduction might benefit some smaller companies, primarily those belonging to the German crafts.

But many of the workers engaged in the underground economy have been forced into early retirement due to slow economic growth and a lack of employment opportunities in the formal economy. Whether these individuals will have a high incentive to participate in and re-enter the regular workforce is questionable. It is equally debatable whether demand for goods and services will increase sufficiently in branches of the German crafts that comply with the criteria set by Kornhardt (1998) or Haase and Alefs (1997) to increase employment of those individuals still officially registered as unemployed. Furthermore, many of the labor-intensive, consumption-oriented services are offered in sectors where demand from individuals with above-average wealth and income is relatively high. Pursuing a partial VAT reduction might, consequently, result in an indirect subsidy for these consumers. This suggestion somewhat resembles similar claims that a reduction in fringe benefits or real wages in certain economic sectors would necessarily stimulate employment in Germany significantly.

# NOTES

1  Average employment per company is 10.8 people.
2  These findings as well as all of the following empirical results are available in detail from the author upon request.
3  NIW (Hannover), DIW (Berlin), ISI (Karlsruhe), SV (Bonn), ZEW (Mannheim).
4  Data on labor intensity are not available, but based on our findings this aspect does not need to be considered.
5  Kornhardt (1998) suggests an increase in employment due to substitution effects in the range of at least 122 000. This value appears highly questionable.

# REFERENCES

BMBF, 'Zur technologischen Leistungsfähigkeit Deutschlands', Bonn, January 1999.
Haase K. and R. Alefs (1997), *Umsatzsteuerermäßigung*, Deutsches Handwerksinstitut, München: Deutsches Handwerkinstitut.
Handwerkszählung (1995), Statistisches Bundesamt, Produzierendes Gewerbe, Fachserie 4.
Kornhardt U. (1998), 'Gesplitteter Mehrwertsteuersatz für arbeitsintensive Dienst-bzw.' Handwerksleistungen, Seminar für Handwerkswesen an der Universität Göttingen, 16 September.
Schneider F. and D.H. Ernste (2000), Shadow Economies: Size, Causes, and Consequences', *Journal of Economic Literature*, 38, March, pp. 77–114.

# Index